# THE CRY OF A WATCHMAN
## A LIGHT IN THE DARKNESS

By

*Laura Lea Sisney*

To Marsha + Paul,

With Blessings!

Laura Lea Linney

Romans 15:4

Dear M & P,
I hope this devotional is as inspiring for you as it has been for me.
Merry Christmas!
I love you both very much..
Nikki
XO
XO

2014

# INTRODUCTION

*(Ezekiel 33:7 "Son of man, I have made you a watchman for the house of Israel; so hear the word I speak and give them warning from me.)*

**T**he prophets of old warned people that if they did not listen and obey the voice of God, they would fail in whatever they did. They were called watchmen, and their voices are still heard today if we will allow our hearts to listen and to hear.

In a world of chaos and doubt about our future—brought on by our disobedience to God—there are many who just don't know where to turn. They seem to think that there is nowhere to hide from the doom and gloom that seem to face them each day. For those of you who seem to have no hope for the future, I have good news.

*(John 1:1 In the beginning was the Word, and the Word was with God, and the Word was God. He was with God in the beginning. Through him all things were made; without him nothing was made that has been made. In him was life, and that life was the light of men. The light shines in the darkness, but the darkness has not understood it.)* In this world of darkness, we need to run to the light.

For every problem we face, there is an answer in God's Word. And therein lays the hope for our future. But there is a mystery in discerning His Word—to find the hope that is promised to us: And that mystery is revealed in *(Colossians 1:27 To them God has chosen to make known among the Gentiles the glorious riches of this mystery, which is Christ in you, the hope of glory.)*

In this world we will always face problems, but when our time on this earth is over, we who have that hope will receive eternal life in Heaven. There will be no more worry and no more tears and no more fears. Our security and hope for the future is found in our Lord Jesus Christ.

I pray that as you read this book, it will inspire you to read God's word: And that it will open your eyes, your heart, and your soul to receive the peace that He has to offer. I implore you to read His Word, believe it and receive it. It is your hope for the future: The hope of glory.

# January 1

# A NEW RESOLUTION

*(1 Corinthians 2:1-3 When I came to you, I did not come with eloquence or human wisdom as I proclaimed to you the testimony about God: For I resolved to know nothing while I was with you except Jesus Christ and him crucified. I came to you in weakness with great fear and trembling.)*

We are beginning yet another new year. Many people make New Year's resolutions to change something about their life—something that will improve them in one way or another. The problem is, if they don't enlist the aid of Christ, they more than likely will fail.

I am venturing into new territory this year and I know that without God at the helm, I will surely fail. I will be giving my testimony to many people and in and of myself I am terrified because I am weak. But like Paul, I am resolved to know nothing when I speak except Jesus Christ and Him crucified. I want to be a witness for Christ, and I need Him to give me the words that will penetrate the hearts of those who will be listening.

*(Psalms 32:8 I will instruct you and teach you in the way you should go: I will counsel you and watch over you.)* What wonderful knowledge and encouragement we find in His word. How can we fail if we resolve to allow God to direct our path?

My resolution this year is to allow God to be in control of everything I do. I pray that God will help me each day of this New Year and those following, to live the life that He has called me to. I am confident with His help, I will succeed.

## January 2

# MOVING ON TO GREENER PASTURES

*(Ruth 1:1-2 In the days when the judges ruled, there was a famine in the land, and a man from Bethlehem in Judah, together with his wife and two sons, went to live for a while in the country of Moab. The man's name was Elimelech, his wife's name Naomi, and the names of his two sons were Mahlon and Kilion. They were Ephrathites from Bethlehem, Judah. And they went to Moab and lived there.)*

Nowhere does it point out that Elimelech sought God's wisdom for the decision that he made to move his family. And why in the world would he take them to a land that was their enemy: A land that worshipped foreign gods?

It is a dangerous thing to run away from a place where God is worshipped as the one true God to a place that does not even recognize Him. If you are familiar with the book of Ruth, you know that not only Elimelech died but also his two sons after only ten years in Moab. I wonder if they had stayed where they were, would they have lived longer?

It makes me wonder also, how many times we run when times get tough, thinking that we would be much better off. There is a saying; 'grass always looks greener on the other side of the fence.' That is usually not the case. How many times have you heard about people divorcing because they think they would be better off with someone else, only to realize that they had made a bad mistake? Or how many, I wonder, have left jobs thinking that they could do better and found themselves in a far worse spot? These kinds of wrong decisions could go on and on. One thing is for sure; if we are not seeking the Lord's direction, we will surely make the wrong move.

# January 3

# SETTING AN EXAMPLE

*(Ruth 1:16-17 But Ruth replied, "Don't urge me to leave you or to turn back from you. Where you go I will go, and where you stay I will stay. Your people will be my people and your God my God.)*

Do you imagine when Naomi's sons took Moabite women for their wives that she must have been heart broken? I know I would be. After all, she was a woman who worshipped the only true God: And these daughters-in-law were raised to worship other gods. It can't have been easy for her. Don't you know that she prayed that God would give her the grace to accept them? I feel certain that she did and that He answered her prayers. Evidence shows that she treated them with love. It also shows that she must have set a very good example to have gained their love and respect.

Ruth not only respected Naomi for the kind woman that she was, but she was greatly influenced by her God. So much so that she did not want to stay home, she wanted to go with Naomi to the country where the true God was worshipped. She had no idea as to what she would be facing, but because of the love that God had given her toward Naomi, and her determination to serve Him, she went willingly.

What an encouragement for us to set a good example to those around us who may not know Jesus as their Lord and Savior. *(Titus 2:7 In everything set them an example by doing what is good. In your teaching show integrity, seriousness and soundness of speech that cannot be condemned so that those who oppose you may be ashamed because they have nothing bad to say about us.)* I want to be like Ruth, don't you?

# January 4

# NEVER ENDING WAR

*(Matthew 24:4-8 Jesus answered: 'Watch out that no one deceives you. For many will come in my name, claiming, 'I am the Messiah,' and will deceive many. You will hear of wars and rumors of wars, but see to it that you are not alarmed. Such things must happen, but the end is still to come. Nation will rise against nation, and kingdom against kingdom. There will be famines and earthquakes in various places. All these are the beginning of birth pains.)*

A friend of mine was telling me that he had been listening to an old Billy Graham message the other night and one of his statements was, (quote "The world is weary of war". end quote). It has never been truer than it is today: Every time we turn the TV on, we here of more conflict in one place or another. Think about all of the times that America has been engaged in conflict since it was discovered. It is staggering: And it is true with every other nations as well.

Ever since Adam and Eve's sin there has been war between people. Peace never has lasted for long. It is true that no one knows the day or the hour when Christ will return to take His people home, but we can know the season, and it seems to me that we are in that season.

I believe that from now on we will constantly be at war, but the one thing that Christians have in common is the fact that we can have peace in the midst of it all. We may be weary but we are not defeated. We know what our future is so we can withstand the battles that come our way.

The spiritual battles that we fight are the ones that we should be most concerned about. God's word tells us this: *(For our struggle is not against flesh and blood, but against the rulers, against the authorities, against the powers of this dark world and against the spiritual forces of evil in the heavenly realms. Therefore put on the full armor of God, so that when the day of evil comes, you may be able to stand your ground, and after you have done everything, to stand. Ephesians 6:12-13)*

## January 5

# GOD'S WORKMANSHIP

*(Philippians 1:3-6 I thank my God every time I remember you, In all my prayers for all of you, I always pray with joy because of your partnership in the gospel from the first day until now, being confident of this, that he who began a good work in you will carry it on to completion until the day of Christ Jesus.)*

Do you ever get upset with yourself for something you have said or done; and wonder if you will ever learn? I sure do. One of my friends who had spouted off one day over an email he read that he was not in agreement with; was later ashamed of his reaction and apologized for his remarks. My reply to him was, "We are all under construction." From the first day that we became a child of God, He began a work in us. He is always busy building and rebuilding our character.

If we have truly accepted Jesus as our Lord and Savior, I believe we will have a desire to learn more about Him. We will have a desire to seek His knowledge to determine how we should live; and He will give us wisdom to live our life to honor Him. His Holy Spirit will remind us when we get off on the wrong track. His grace will always lead us back to His center.

I am so glad that God is not through shaping me in to the person that He wants me to be. Aren't you? Sometimes He has to soften us like clay and reshape us. But isn't it wonderful that His Holy Spirit speaks to our heart and says, "You know you really shouldn't have said that" or "You really shouldn't have done that". He loves us enough to point out our flaws, weaknesses, and mistakes. But he doesn't throw us away; he just keeps on shaping us.

We are not perfect, we are human; however we should strive for perfection. God's Word says: *(Not that I have already obtained all this, or have already been made perfect, but I press on to take hold of that for which Christ Jesus took hold of me).* If you are thinking that you have stumbled, don't be discouraged; be glad that the Holy Spirit has shown you, and take heart—God isn't finished with you yet.

# January 6

# AN UNGODLY LEADER

*(Psalms 2:1-2 Why do the nations conspire and the peoples plot in vain? The kings of the earth take their stand and the rulers gather together against the Lord and against his Anointed One.)*

Do you ever wonder why people will forsake God to follow another leader? I ask myself that question almost daily as I see Christians turn their back on the Lord's commands to vote for someone who is blatantly against them. Do you have any idea why?

I don't know the reason. But if we study the bible and read about the Kings that have led their people astray in the past, surely we can get a glimpse of the destruction that comes to them because they have forsaken God to please their demand for change.

Remember how Germany was led astray by a madman who claimed to be the savior that would lead them out of their depression. He was a man who hated the Jewish race and murdered over 6 million of them with the aid of the ignorant people who fell for his promises.

Hitler was not the only one in this modern age that brought destruction to his people. There are many out there today who are using their own agenda to convince the people of their country to vote for them. There are many who do not give God a thought at all when they are seeking power. In fact they go out of their way to serve themselves instead of God. And unfortunately many people listen and believe their lies and fall for them.

We need to consult God every time we go to vote. And we need to read their bios in order to see where they stand when it comes to God's word. If it is not synonymous with the word, we need to back away from that candidate. It is a frightening thing to elect someone who does not put God's authority over his.

# January 7

# KEEPING ON

*(Philippians 1:23-24 I am torn between the two: I desire to depart and be with Christ, which is better by far; but it is more necessary for you that I remain in the body.)*

Of all people, Paul certainly had cause to say that his desire would be to depart this world to be with Christ. After all, this innocent man was in prison only because he had taught the truth of Christ. But he was a man who had suffered persecution many times in the past, and it had not stopped him from continuing in his ministry. His focus was on one thing—and that was Christ. He was an encourager to others. Even while imprisoned he encouraged them through his letters. And he realized that it was his mission in life to remain in this world continuing the work that God had called him to do

There are those today who are ridiculed, imprisoned, tortured, and some even put to death because of their determination to spread the word of God to a lost and dying world. They are very much aware of the dangers that they face in their pursuit to turn others hearts toward God. And they are still willing to risk their lives.

Sometimes we Christians become discouraged about our life, our ministry, our world, our personal problems, etc. And there are times when we even think we would like to go on to be with the Lord. But is that a right attitude? I don't think so, although I can honestly say that I have been there before. We should not dwell on the negative things in this life, but rather on the mission that God has set before us. I doubt that any person reading this has suffered what Paul did.

After pondering this Scripture, and realizing that God has a purpose for my life, I have come to the realization that I want to remain in this world until God is finished with me. He did not call me to witness and encourage others for no reason. And He didn't you either. We must not let evil forces discourage us, but remain strong and faithful as long as we live. If and when we give in to the temptation to quit, we will no longer be effective Christians. We must keep on keeping on until God calls us home. And I want it to be in His timing, not mine. Don't you agree?

## January 8

# TEACHING A CHILD

*(Proverbs 22:6 Train a child in the way he should go, and when he is old he will not turn from it.)*

A friend of mine was telling me that she has a habit of raising her voice with her children. She was recently put in her place by her 5 year old son. He was telling her that his sister hollers a lot. When she asked him why he thought she did that, he said, "Because you holler". When she inquired of him how he thought the situation should be handled, she got a very surprising answer. She was sure he was going to say that his sister needed to mind better, but instead he replied "You need to stop hollering mom, because she does everything you do". Wow what a shocker—more like a bolt of lightning.

Isn't it amazing how little children can be wiser than a parent at times. When we think that we are teaching our children the right way and then hear one of them pointing out just one of our flaws, it is enlightening, to say the least. Our children are watching everything that we say and everything that we do. Do we model the role that we want them to play as they mature into adults? I doubt that any of us are model parents all of the time. But we are responsible for teaching our children the things that will bring honor to their name. Even to the tone of our voice. We must be careful with what we say, and what we do. Children usually emulate their parents! Now that is a humbling thought. If we took the time to think before we acted or spoke, it would make a huge difference.

I am reminded of the phrase 'what would Jesus do' (WWJD) that was used so much a few years ago. It was a good thing to consider. We parents should live our life as if we were considering that phrase. Wouldn't it be a wonderful thing if we set an example that would glorify God in everything we do and say? Our Father set an example for us—let's set that same example for our children.

# January 9

# A HOLY REVIVAL

*(2 Chronicles 31:1 When all this had ended, the Israelites who were there went out to the towns of Judah, smashed the sacred stones and cut down the Asherah poles. They destroyed the high places and the altars throughout Judah and Benjamin and in Ephraim and Manasseh.)*

The other day I wrote a devotional on how the assembly of Israelites had praised God for two weeks joyfully. The Scripture this morning is the result of that. Those two weeks had inspired them to tear down the high places and altars.

I believe when people are filled with the Holy Spirit as a result of worship, it inspires them to tear down those walls ('altars and high places') that have been a hindrance to their worship time. We may not realize it, but there are things in our lives that get in the way of our joyful praise to the Lord. We allow them to control the time that should be spent in praise and worship.

It concerns me that the world has allowed things to come between God's people and their Sabbath worship. Sports have become a huge stumbling block for some people. Even our children are being drawn away from church because they have games or practice on Sunday. Adults sometimes stay home to watch a game rather than going to church.

This is wrong. I can remember a time when the 'blue law' was in effect that did not allow stores to be open on the Sabbath. When we caved in to the people who wanted to open their doors to shop on the Sabbath, it brought about a change in many other ways: And I might add, it was not a good change.

We need a Spirit filled Holy revival in our churches today where the Holy Spirit is allowed to penetrate the hearts of the people. We need to be inspired to tear down those walls that keep us from worshipping joyfully. We need a heart changing experience to get back to the basics of Worship just like the Israelites did.

# January 10

# THE NEW JERUSALEM

*(Isaiah 65:18-19 But be glad and rejoice forever in what I will create, for I will create Jerusalem to be a delight and its people a joy. I will rejoice over Jerusalem and take delight in my people; the sound of weeping and of crying will be heard in it no more.)*

We live in a world that is full of all kinds of evil and strife: Not only because of nations warring against nations; but many families feud amongst themselves. This causes pain and distress for everyone. It is difficult to be joyful in this world with its constant battles. Even the strongest and most grounded Christians fight these battles. The evil one is free to roam about seeking someone he can discourage and destroy.

One day it will not be this way. Those who have put their faith and trust in the Lord—those who have given their hearts to Jesus will one day walk the streets of this renewed earth 'The New Jerusalem' in joy and peace. There will be no more weeping and crying. This is not a dream; it is a promise from God to His people.

We are so used to being stressed out over everything that goes on in this evil world; it is hard to imagine the wonderful state of mind that we will have in the New Jerusalem. I don't know about you, but I cannot wait for that day. Just think about it—God says that in that day He will take delight in us. Wow! What a wonderful day that will be.

# January 11

# SOAR LIKE AN EAGLE

*(Isaiah 40:31 But those who hope in the LORD will renew their strength. They will soar on wings like eagles; they will run and not grow weary, they will walk and not be faint.)*

Have you ever watched an eagle soar? It is a beautiful sight to see. Their wings are stretched out to the fullest and they glide across the sky with amazing freedom.

In speaking with different people in the last few weeks, so many have said that the struggles they are having are almost more than they can bear. I have had many prayer requests from those who are faltering in their struggles, asking for strength to carry on.

They struggle with one thing or another; such as addiction, relationships, financial problems, spiritual problems, health problems, emotional problems: And the list goes on and on. If we allow these struggles to take hold of our lives, they will destroy our peace and joy—because we are not leaning on the Lord to give us the strength that we need.

I think we have all gone through those desperate times at some point in our life. I know I have, haven't you? But when we have the Lord on our side, even in the worst of circumstances we can overcome them. We are never defeated. Look at what God's word tells us—when we put our hope in the LORD, He will renew our strength. And we will soar on wings like eagles. We will not be faint.

If you are going through struggles right now and are wondering if you can go on under your circumstances; Rejoice in the fact that when you put your faith in God, you can soar like an eagle. Let go of your struggle and put your hope in the Lord. Picture yourself with wings like an eagle flying above all of the problems that surround you. You can have peace and joy and strength even in the face of adversity.

# January 12

# THE SIN OF COMPLACENCY

*(Zephaniah 1:12-13 At that time I will search Jerusalem with lamps and punish those who are complacent, who are like wine left on its dregs, who think, 'The Lord will do nothing either good or bad.' Their wealth will be plundered their houses demolished. They will build houses but not live in them; they will plant vineyards but not drink the wine.)*

We live in a world of people today that care nothing at all about what goes on around them. They look out only for themselves and as long as they are doing alright (or at least they think they are), they do not concern themselves with other people or the circumstances around them.

It is especially true where spiritual things are concerned. There are many people who will tell you that they don't care about spiritual matters. Even Christians seem to be oblivious to the need to witness for the Lord. They get so wrapped up in themselves and their pursuit of happiness, that they forget there are those in need of the Savior.

God's word has much to say about the complacent person: And I might add it is not soothing words to salve our conscience. They are stinging words warning us to step out of our complacency.

Webster's dictionary describes complacency this way:

1. *Self-satisfaction especially when accompanied by unawareness of actual dangers or deficiencies*
2. *An instance of usually unaware or uninformed self-satisfaction*

*(Revelation 3:16-17 So, because you are lukewarm—neither hot nor cold—I am about to spit you out of my mouth. You say, 'I am rich; I have acquired wealth and do not need a thing.' But you do not realize that you are wretched, pitiful, poor, blind and naked.)*

Complacency is a sin: Make no mistake about it. And we will have to answer for it. We must step out of our complacent attitudes before it's too late. How can we be a witness in this world if we are complacent?

# January 13

# GROUNDED IN TRUTH

*(Ezra 9:1a After these things had been done, the leaders came to me and said, "The people of Israel, including the priests and the Levites, have not kept themselves separate for the neighboring peoples with their detestable practices.)*

The above Scripture is written about the exiles who had returned from captivity. Wouldn't you think that they would not do anything to dishonor God? They did not keep themselves separate from the people around them and their detestable practices. They knew what was right and ignored it.

As I was reading this, I was reminded of some acquaintances that had been raised in an evangelical church, and had been taught the ways of the Lord. But when they were in their thirties they fell into the hands of a religion that is far from being evangelical. It is a religion that was founded by taking one or two Scriptures from God's Word and twisting it to their liking.

I have been puzzled ever since, as to why they would forsake the ways of God that were taught to them from an early age, and align themselves with a group that have based their ways on lies and the distortion of the Holy inspired Word of God. I think it is a very dangerous thing to become involved with those around us who misconstrue the word of God and try to engage others in their belief and practices. Even those Christians, who have known the way, can be led astray by those who are ignorant of the truth.

We can't just think we are grounded in God's Word—we must know that we are. These people who are so blinded can sometimes be convincing to those who are weak in their knowledge of God. They go around knocking on doors to try and convince people that their way is the right way. Let's be sure that we have been grounded in the word of God; so that we can stand firm in our convictions.

# January 14

# CONTENTMENT AT HOME

*(John 14:6 Jesus answered, "I am the way and the truth and the life. No one comes to the Father except through me.")*

I was reading something the other day that a minister had said and it was so enlightening I would like to share it with you. He said when someone makes the statement that they need to find themselves; it almost always means that they are about ready to do something stupid.

Although he did not mention it, I suddenly thought of the parable of the 'prodigal son'. I am sure that you are all familiar with this passage of scripture in Luke 15:11-32. It is about the young man who wanted his inheritance so he could leave to do what he thought would make him happy. And we know what happened to him. He squandered all that he had and found himself in the lap of poverty until he came to his senses and returned home.

There are many people just like this prodigal son, that think there must be a better way to live than what they are living. So they make the decision that they are going to find their own way: A way to the happiness that they dream of. They mistakenly believe that they surely deserve it.

Many times marriages break up because one of the mates has decided that they just are not happy in their circumstances: So without considering the heartache that will ensue for the other members of the family—they take off and leave in pursuit of happiness.

There are many children that leave the protection of their parents' home to 'find themselves'. They usually find themselves in a position just like the prodigal son did—in a state of poverty and with an empty life that is going nowhere but down.

I am convinced that none of us will ever find true happiness until we find our way to Jesus. When we go our own way to pursue happiness, I can assure you that the happiness that you are looking for will elude you. Only through Christ can we achieve what will satisfy our hunger for happiness.

*(Matthew 16:24 Then Jesus said to his disciples, "Whoever wants to be my disciple must deny themselves and take up their cross and follow me. For whoever wants to save their life will lose it, but whoever loses their life for me will find it.)* One commentary says (Let him, deny himself - That is, let him surrender to God his will, his affections, his body, and his soul. Let him not seek his own happiness as the supreme object; but be willing to renounce all, and lay down his life also, if required.)

# January 15

# PRAYING WITH FAITH FROM THE HEART

*(Hebrews 11:36 Some faced jeers and flogging, while still others were chained and put in prison. They were stoned, they were sawed in two; they were put to death by the sword. They went about in sheepskins and goatskins, destitute, persecuted and mistreated—the world was not worthy of them.)*

I got an email from a friend last week asking me to pray for those who had been imprisoned in Tehran for their choice to worship God as Christians. I quickly said a prayer and then forgot about it. Can you identify? As I opened my bible yesterday morning, I was lead to Hebrews 11: A chapter that most Christians are very familiar with as being the faith chapter. However, yesterday was quite different as I read this book on faith that I thought I was so familiar with. I read about the faith of Abel, Enoch, Noah, Abraham, Isaac, Jacob, Joseph, Moses, Joshua, and many heroes of faith: And then suddenly I read about the faith of some others that I hadn't noticed so much before. As I read verse 36, I was suddenly stopped by the Lord's voice.

God spoke to my heart: "Laura," he said, "You are sitting in a comfortable, warm home, in a country where you are free to worship me. How would you respond if you were in the position that those who are imprisoned and sometimes tortured because of their faith in me?" As I sat there trying to take it all in. I thought to myself that if someone had a gun to my head and asked me to deny Christ; I felt confident that I would gladly take the bullet. But then the thought came to me; 'what would you do if you were being tortured or your children or grandchildren were being tortured because of me'? What would I do then? Would I still stand up for Christ? Suddenly I began to cry and pray for those people who were being held in prison, some maybe being tortured. God opened my eyes and my heart with compassion for them that I have never had before.

I have had these last 24 hours to ponder on all of this. I have prayed for these people and have asked the Lord to give them strength to stand. But along with that prayer for them, I have prayed that God would give me strength to stand for Him no matter what comes my way.

I encourage you to go back and read slowly this wonderful chapter on faith. Take it all in and consider the position that you would take under their circumstances. I dare say that you will be disturbed at the pictures that will come to your mind. It will stir you on to fervently pray for those who are being persecuted in any way.

# January 16

# COMFORTING OTHERS

*(2 Corinthians 1:3-4 Praise be to the God and Father of our Lord Jesus Christ, the Father of compassion and the God of all comfort, who comforts us in all our troubles, so that we can comfort those in any trouble with the comfort we ourselves have received from God)*

I absolutely love this particular Scripture. It does not matter what we go through God is there to comfort us. He never leaves us, nor does He forsake us. He gives us strength to go on. And after we have been comforted, and we come through the fire, we will be able to help those who are going through the same trials.

God did not promise that we would not face trials. When we read His Word, we can see how His people suffered many trials. God uses them for good. We can learn and grow through our trials. They equip us to help others who need encouragement.

So when we grasp the fact that we can gain understanding and compassion for others as a result of our trials. When we come through our trials in victory, we will be able to share our story of how we were not defeated. We can truly say that our compassionate God comforted us and He brought us through the fire. People are much more willing to accept the help of someone who has suffered the same battle.

It makes it worth it all—doesn't it? When God can take our experiences, whether good or bad, and share it with the world to help others, we can give thanks and praise to God.

Instead of feeling sorry for ourselves when we go through trials—let's allow God to comfort us and pray that He will use it ultimately for His glory, and to help others. Only those who have experienced the pain can identify with others.

# January 17

# WALKING IN FAITH

*(Deuteronomy 31:6 Be strong and courageous. Do not be afraid or terrified because of them, for the Lord your God goes with you; he will never leave you; nor forsake you.)*

When my granddaughter, Tahlia, was about 10 months old; every one in her immediate family tried to coax her to walk. We would hold out our arms and say to her, "Come see me", thinking that she would have the confidence and courage to take those steps that we so anxiously awaited. But she would look at us and then sit down, as if she was not a bit interested. And then one day while we were visiting at my sister's house—suddenly Tahlia took off across the floor as if she had been walking for some time. It was almost as if an invisible hand took hold of hers to give her confidence to walk without faltering. Needless to say we were thrilled and amazed at her sudden tenacity.

Isn't that a picture of how we react sometimes when God is trying to coax us to step out in faith to do something that he has asked us to do? We might ignore His voice for a while and then suddenly we develop the courage to step out with confidence.

I think the reason we hesitate is because we are seeing our own weaknesses. But God would never ask us to do something that He would not equip us to do. We must learn to trust God and not look at our inabilities. God will supply all that we need to carry out His request. It is Him that we need to put our trust in. We will never step out for the Lord if we continue to look at our own weaknesses. It is when we see God's magnificent grace and put our faith and trust in Him that we will gain the confidence to step out to do that which He has called us to do.

I am so glad that God does not see us as weak individuals. He sees us as vessels that He can and will use, if we avail ourselves and put our faith and trust in Him. Let's be courageous and step out in faith, because we know that He will never leave us helpless.

# January 18

# FIGHTING FOR FAMILY

*(Nehemiah 4:14b "Don't be afraid of them. Remember the Lord, who is great and awesome, and fight for your brothers, your sons and your daughters, your wives and your homes.)*

There are circumstances in our life that causes us to fear the enemies that surround us. Whether we realize it or not we all have enemies.

Webster's Dictionary defines enemy this way: (one that is antagonistic to another; especially: one seeking to injure, overthrow, or confound an opponent.) There are acquaintances who do not wish good fortune for us. In fact they are the ones who would like to drag us down to a level of sin. We might even define them as a friend: But you can be assured that if they drag you down, they are definitely not your friend.

We all have a common enemy and he is out to reduce us to being so fearful that we lose hope that our circumstances will ever change. If he can't entangle us in sin, then he goes after our family: Our children, our spouses and sometimes even our parents. It is devastating when that happens. Since we have no control over others, we cannot change their circumstances. But we know that God can change any heart and he can turn any life around.

We of course can't put our faith in people, but we can certainly put our faith in God. In fact the only way that we or anyone else can be victorious in conquering sin is through Jesus Christ.

We can take heart in *(Jeremiah 31:16 This is what the Lord says: "Restrain your voice from weeping and your eyes from tears, for your work will be rewarded," declares the Lord, "They will return from the land of the enemy. So there is hope for your future." declares the Lord. "Your children will return to their own land.)*

If you or anyone in your family are frightened because of the enemy—turn to the one who can help you through the battle—fight for yourself and your loved ones. God hears and answers our prayers. When we allow Jesus to fight for us, we have already won the victory.

# January 19

# RUN TO THE LIGHT

*(2 Samuel 22:29-30 You are my lamp, O Lord; the Lord turns my darkness into light. With your help I can advance against a troop; with my God I can scale a wall.)*

Once again the evil one has tried to discourage me from doing something that God has asked me to do. I started to fear my inabilities to carry out what God has put on my heart: And out of nowhere, just at this time, I read the following statement 'Raymond Edman (former president of Wheatland College) once said, "Never doubt in the dark what God told you in the light."' I knew right away that it was just for me. God had put this right in front of me. It was His way of telling me that I did not have to fear because it was Him who called me and equipped me. I cannot tell you how relieved I was. Not just because of what I read, but because I realized that God loved me so much that He would confirm His call on my life in such a clear and concise way.

I also knew that I needed to write a devotional about this wonderful experience and I prayed that God would bring me to the Scripture that would enlighten me and others. I was extremely in awe when He led me to 2 Samuel 22:29-30, the Scripture above. God hears and answers our prayers. He knew that I needed encouragement and confirmation through His word. His word lights our path. *(Psalms 119:105 God's word is a lamp to my feet and a light for my path.)*

Make no mistake, when we are ready to step out in faith and do what God has called and equipped us to do—the evil one will try and undermine our confidence. I have talked to many people who say it happens to them almost every time God has called them to do something. We need to remember that God calls us to the light but Satan would like for us to live in darkness. Don't doubt what God has given you in the light. Let's step out in the confidence that God wants us to have as a result of our faith and trust in Him and His call to us.

# January 20

# I CAN'T DO WHAT?

*(Nehemiah 1:4 When I heard these things, I sat down and wept. For some days I mourned and fasted and prayed before the God of heaven.)*

It is reported that those who survived the exile were back in the province but were in great trouble and disgrace. The walls of Jerusalem were broken down, and its gates had been burned with fire. (Ref. Jeremiah1:3)

Nehemiah was hurt and devastated over the conditions around them. But Nehemiah was a praying man. It is recorded 11 times in this wonderful book that he prayed. And so the first thing he did was to pray.

When Nehemiah began leading the task of rebuilding the walls surrounding Jerusalem, he was pressed on every side by opposition and ridicule. The task seemed impossible. But in record time (52 days) the task was completed. There is not a doubt in my mind that the reason the task was successful was because of the prayers that were poured out to God by Nehemiah.

Is there some task that you face that seems impossible? *Nothing is impossible with God. (Ref. Luke 1:37).* Don't ever give up thinking that there is no hope of success. You may feel weak and helpless for the task ahead of you, but we are reminded in *(Philippians 4:13 that we can do all things through Christ who gives us strength.)*

There is power in prayer; if we could only grasp on to that knowledge; we would gain confidence to do the tasks ahead. We must remember that and take everything to the Lord in prayer. We may be surrounded by ridicule and opposition: But when God is on our side there is nothing impossible.

# January 21

# SHOWERS OF BLESSINGS

*(Deuteronomy 7:12-13a If you pay attention to these laws and are careful to follow them, then the Lord your God will keep his covenant of love with you, as he swore to your forefathers. He will love you and bless you.)*

Do you ever go through dry spells spiritually? I sure do, but God is always near to remind me that His mercy drops are falling everyday. And then there are days that I seem to be standing right in the downpour of blessings. This is one of those days.

Nothing that you might think special has happened—but it is. God blessed me with several emails from my Christian brothers and sisters that blessed my heart: And then there was a simple phone conversation with one of my dear Christian sisters that thrilled my soul. We were simply talking about how God has blessed us with so many things. We seemed to have so much to share about it. When I got off of the phone, I felt like I was walking on a cloud. God felt so near and His spirit so present that I almost felt like I could reach out and touch Him.

Blessings are a gift from God, they don't have to be anything tangible or earth shaking; just a thought, and a word from someone can be a blessing. However, if we don't recognize them, we just might miss them. Even in the storms of life, God can and still does shower us with blessings. Let's look for His blessings. He has promised His people that He will bless us. God keeps His covenants.

There shall be showers of blessing:
This is the promise of love;
There shall be seasons refreshing,
Sent from the Savior above.

# January 22

# NOT EGOTISTICAL—JUST CALLED

*(1 Corinthians 15:10. "But whatever I am now, it is all because God poured out His special favor on me—and not without results. For I have worked harder than any of the other apostles; yet it was not I but God who was working through me by His grace.)*

I have a friend who said one time that he could not stand Paul—yes the same Paul who wrote the above Scripture. When I asked him why in the world he would say that, he told me this: "Because he was so egotistical." I was flabbergasted. When I read this Scripture I think of my friend: How sad it is that people would make a judgment call on such a godly man.

Paul was not an egotistical man. He was always quick to say that the work he did was ordained by God. He would not have been effective in his ministry if he had struck out on his own. Think back to who Paul was before he met the Lord. He was a persecutor of Christ and his followers until he was confronted by God on the Damascus road. (Ref. Acts 9). He was blinded but Scripture tells us that something like scales fell from his eyes and he was filled with the Holy Spirit. From then on God gave him specific instructions on what he wanted him to do.

From that time on, he sought God's wisdom and favor, and followed through on his commitment to Christ. There are people today who serve God because of His call on their lives. They work diligently to proclaim the word of God. There are always those who would describe them as egotistical, and would say—that they think they are better than others—and that works will not get them to heaven. It is true that we cannot work our way into heaven, but when we are called by God we should be ready to respond to His call.

There is a huge difference in doing work that God has not called you to do, and doing the work that God has called you to do. An egotistical man or woman is one who strikes out on his own without the help of the Holy Spirit—their efforts will surely fail. Those who give their lives to the Lord because of His call may suffer persecution, but they will be steadfast in their walk, their work, and their love for the Lord because of God's blessing on them.

# January 23

# FACING OUR SINS OF OMISSION

*(James 4:17 Anyone, then, who knows the good he ought to do and doesn't do it, sins.)*

There are sins of commission and sins of omission. Which is worse? That is a question we must ask ourselves. James was writing to the Christian in this book of the bible. The above verse is pretty simple and plain. If we Christians fail to do the good things that we ought to do—it is sin.

It does not matter who we are, how much or how little we have, what our title is or where we live. What matters is whose we are. If we are Christian people, then we should be using whatever God has given us in whatever way that He asks us to. God has blessed all of us with all we have. How are we using it?

These are pertinent questions that we should all ask ourselves. If you have money, are you keeping it all for yourself or are you using it to help others. God has given everyone some kind of talent. How do you use yours? Are you using it in the way that God wants you to: Are you using it at all? Do you live to satisfy your own selfish desires, or do you look to the needs of those around you? Do we boast and brag about what we have? God's word says all such boasting is evil. The only boasting we should ever do is when we boast in the Lord.

We Christians should always consider God and His will in all things. We should never make our own plans without consulting God. Have you gone your own way and made your own plans? How is it working for you? Anytime I have gone my own way without consulting God, it never turns out well: And I know why; it is because I have sinned by not consulting Him.

Isn't it interesting that we can see the sins of commission all around us, but we never seem to see the sins of omission in our own life. Do you remember what Jesus said? *("If any one of you is without sin, let him be the first to throw a stone at her." John 8:7b).*

Let's be honest—are we doing the good that we ought to do? If we aren't; we are sinners.

# January 24

# UNGODLY INFLUENCE

*(Deuteronomy 11:16 Be careful, or you will be enticed to turn away and worship other gods and bow down to them).*

We live in a world where many people ignore God and His word. We are in the world but God warns us not to be like the world. *(Romans 12:2 Do not conform any longer to the pattern of this world, but be transformed by the renewing of your mind. Then you will be able to test and approve what God's will is—his good, pleasing and perfect will.)* Why do you think that God warns us about that? I believe that He knows that in our human weakness, we can be led astray by those who are not people of God.

*(Titus 2:11-12a For the grace of God that brings salvation has appeared to all men. It teaches us to say "No" to ungodliness and worldly passions and to live self-controlled, upright and godly lives in this present age.)* Unfortunately Christians can be caught up in doing things that some of their non-Christian friends do. I heard a wise minister say, "When you hang out with the wrong people at the wrong place at the wrong time, then it is only a matter of time until you do the wrong thing."

We cannot ignore those around us who are not Christians. But we must be on our guard. We are to witness to those around us who do not know the Lord. We cannot and must not allow them to bring us down to their level. Ask yourself this question: Do I act differently when I am around my non-Christian friends than I do when I am with Christians? Do I give in to the influence of those who are not serving God? Do I compromise my walk with the Lord when I am around them? If the answer to any of those questions is yes, you had better separate yourself from them.

Make no mistake—sometimes sin is fun—but be assured that if you are making the wrong choice to follow those in their sin—you will one day regret it. If you have a difficult time with self-control, do this: LET GOD HAVE THE CONTROL.

# January 25

# WILLING TO DIE

*(Esther 4:16b When this is done, I will go to the king, even though it is against the law. And if I perish, I perish)*

Queen Esther was well aware of the fact that entering the presence of the king without an invitation could mean her death; but she was willing to go in spite of it. The Israelites were threatened with annihilation and she was more concerned about them than she was her own life.

When people are called to be missionaries in other countries, they are aware of the dangers that they could encounter, but they have a calling and are willing to take the chance. Many people have been saved because those brave souls have given up their comforts of home to go into enemy territory and spread the news of Jesus Christ to the world.

It is disturbing, to say the least, when we hear stories like the one that occurred on April 26, 2007. It is the story of three Christians who were killed in Turkey. One of them was a former Islam who turned to Jesus Christ. They were horribly tortured for three hours prior to being killed. They lived daily knowing that they might at any time be tortured and/or killed and were still willing to carry out their mission

We may ask what good came out of such a horrific incident. Even through their death they left an undeniable testimony to those left behind. The testimony that their wives gave and the forgiveness that they extended to those who were responsible for their husband's deaths, is in itself a testimony to the world of the love that Christians exhibit, even to their enemies.

I wonder how many of us would stand firm in our faith if we were being tortured. I would like to believe that I would be able to withstand the torture, don't you? We probably will never be put to the test as the ones in the story above were, so we will never know the answer to that. I feel certain that the only way anyone can stand that kind of torture is because of the strength that would come from the Father.

We must remember to pray for those missionaries who risk their lives to go in to enemy territory to witness for the Lord. I admire those who have been called to this kind of ministry and have said yes to God. They are exceptional people of God. Surely God chooses them because He knows that they have what it takes to meet the extreme challenges.

# January 26

# BEWARE OF PRIDE

*(Proverbs 16:18 Pride goes before destruction, a haughty spirit before a fall.)*

There is no better picture of the dangers of a prideful person than the one described in *(Esther 5:11-13 Haman boasted to them about his vast wealth, his many sons, and all the ways the king had honored him and how he had elevated him above the other nobles and officials. "And that's not all," Haman added. "I'm the only person Queen Esther invited to accompany the king to the banquet she gave. And she has invited me along with the king tomorrow. But all this gives me no satisfaction as long as I see that Jew Mordecai sitting at the king's gate.")*

I don't know about you, but I am totally turned off by people who want to brag all the time about themselves or what they have, the people they know, etc. Haman was one of those people. He wanted to go on and on about himself, what he had, and the influential people that he knew. But when you hear the rest of his story, you see that his pride got him nowhere, in fact it was ultimately his downfall.

Haman was a hateful man full of self-pride; looking out always and only for himself. He was willing to annihilate the entire Israelite community because he had developed such a hatred for Mordecai because Mordecai was not willing to bow down before him. His plot to kill him by hanging backfired on Haman and he ended up on the gallows that he had built for Mordecai. *(Esther 7:8c-10 As soon as the word left the king's mouth, they covered Haman's face. Then Harbona, one of the eunuchs attending the king, said, "A gallows seventy-five feet high stands by Haman's house. He had it made for Mordecai, who spoke up to help the king." The king said, "Hang him on it!" So they hanged Haman on the gallows he had prepared for Mordecai. Then the king's fury subsided.)*

We should never boast about what we have, or who we know, or how successful we have been. What difference does it make when our final day on this earth is over? What we have done and what we have acquired will not matter if we haven't laid up treasures in Heaven. Self-pride is very destructive. The only thing that we should ever boast about is our Lord and Savior.

## January 27

# THE REST OF THE STORY

*(Job 10:3 Does it please you to oppress me, to spurn the work of your hands, while you smile on the plans of the wicked?)*

Job was a Godly man. He gave God praise for everything that He had given him in life. He did not let his wealth forget who he was and to whom he belonged. As we all know Job lost everything he had in life. He was devastated and questioned God about it all. If anyone had reason to question, it certainly was Job.

I wonder why when we have negative things happen in our life; so many times we seem to blame God. Satan had approached God about Job and God did give him reign. But it was Satan who tested Job's dedication to God. God being omnipotent knew that he would never destroy Job's love for Him and His faith in Him no matter what happened.

I used to love listening to Paul Harvey. The true stories he told were always so riveting and I would listen with anticipation to the ending. It was always a good ending. He would say, "And now you know the rest of the story."

Even though Job questioned God, he stood faithful to God through all of the pain in His life. Even when he was condemned by others who tried to convince him that he was the cause of it all, he stood faithful.

(Job 42:12-13 The LORD blessed the latter part of Job's life more than the former part. He had fourteen thousand sheep, six thousand camels, a thousand yoke of oxen and a thousand donkeys. And he also had seven sons and three daughters.) Yes, he lost it all but now we know the rest of the story.

It is encouraging to realize that God will stand by us even in the worst of times. He will see us through every hurt and pain in life. God does not cause these things to happen, but He does allow them. I will not try to tell you that I understand it all—but I do believe that the rest of our story will have a good ending if we are faithful Christians

# January 28

# UNCONTOLLED ANGER

*(Psalms 37:8 Refrain from anger and turn from wrath; do not fret—it leads only to evil.)*

Anger is one of the most destructive things in relationships. It is amazing how many people are in anger management counseling these days. Many marriages fail because one or the other person in that marriage cannot control their temper. Many suffer from mental and often times even physical abuse because of it. Many children in our world today are abused because someone loses their temper. No matter what the circumstances are, somebody suffers as a result of uncontrolled anger. As the scripture tells us, it leads to evil; there is no doubt about that.

We all suffer from anger once in a while. It is not a sin to feel anger, there is a righteous anger. There are several Scriptures in the bible that speaks of this type of anger. If you have a concordance bible take the time to look at those Scriptures that speak of the differences between selfish anger and righteous anger.

Some anger is justified, but when it becomes selfish anger it is sin. *(Proverbs 29:11 A fool gives full vent to his spirit, but a wise man quietly holds it back.) (Ephesians 4:26-27 Be angry and do not sin; do not let the sun go down on your anger, and give no opportunity to the devil.)*

There is absolutely no excuse for uncontrolled anger. Make no mistake about it—it is blatant sin. If we don't manage to get it under control, somebody is going to be hurt. We can get all of the counseling there is, but if we don't let God have control of that anger, it will probably not do much good.

Do you have a difficult time with controlling your anger? Do you hurt people by your inability to get a grip on your temper? If the answer to either or both of these questions is yes, you have a problem: and it is called sin. Only God can help you with that. Turn your anger over to Him and allow Him to break those chains that have you in bondage.

# January 29

# A GENTLE WITNESS

*(1 Peter 3:15…in your hearts set apart Christ as Lord. Always be prepared to give an answer to everyone who asks you to give the reason for the hope that you have. But do this with gentleness and respect.)*

I received an email from a friend, and she was telling me of a conversation that her little 5 year old girl had with a friend who was constantly unkind to her. She said that she had told the girl that she was going to go to the devil because she did not have Jesus in her heart. Her mother said that she was thankful that her little girl recognized what it takes to get to Heaven, but that she had to have a talk with her about her attitude.

After reading the account of what happened, I started thinking about how we Christians witness to those that have not prepared themselves for Heaven. Do we come across as an abrasive 'holier than thou' person? There is a right way and a wrong way to be a witness for Jesus. We must have a tender heart, a sweet spirit, and a gentle attitude; or we might turn others away. I can remember the days before I was a Christian that there were some people who offended me very much when they tried to witness to me with the wrong attitude. And then there were those who were gentle and respectful: They were the ones who touched my heart and gave me a desire to become like them.

The story of this little girl has caused me to ponder about the way I witness to others. How about you?

# January 30

# OBVIOUS OR OBLIVIOUS

*(John 1:1 In the beginning was the Word, and the Word was with God, and the Word was God.)*

One day as I was driving through Wyoming, I suddenly saw a red light flashing in my rear view mirror. I thought surely he was not after me; I had done nothing wrong, but knowing the rules of the road, I pulled to the right. And horror of horrors, the patrolman pulled in right behind me. I nervously rolled down my window to inquire about why he had stopped me. He said, "You were going 70 in a 55 mile an hour zone." I was astounded and said that I was unaware of that fact: To which he informed me that it was posted: But I had been oblivious to the sign.

As I was remembering this, I thought about how many times we are oblivious to the obvious. Many times people are killed because they have failed to see obvious stop signs.

Isn't it funny that two little letters can make such a difference in the meaning of a word.

Webster's dictionary defines these two words this way:

Obvious: easily discovered, seen, or understood.

Oblivious: lacking active conscious knowledge or awareness.

God's word is a love letter to us, and it is an instructional book as to how we should live our lives. Without the knowledge that we attain from it, we will surely die. How many people have bibles in their homes, sometimes in obvious places, yet they walk right by them oblivious to the fact that they are there.

Most of the time when we are oblivious to warning signs, it is because we are too much in a hurry to go about our business; or we have our minds on other things. We can get by with it sometimes, but many times it can mean life or death to us.

Even if we do read His Word, are we oblivious to what it teaches us? Every Word in the bible is obvious if we are searching for the truth. If we are not; it can become oblivious to us. When we ignore God's Word, we are ignoring God Himself. The above Scripture says in the beginning was the Word and the Word was God.

# January 31

# A LOVING WORD

*(Job 19:1-3 Then Job replied: How long will you torment me and crush me with words? Ten times now you have reproached me; shamelessly you attack me.)*

Job had lost everything he had in the world, including his family: And as if he was not suffering enough, his so called friend was talking incessantly about his faults. He is suggesting that surely he had done something to cause the entire calamity in his life. With friends like that; who needs enemies?

I actually get upset when I read how Job's friends went on and on about his situation: As if they knew exactly why he was in the situation that he found himself in. Hadn't he experienced enough pain without their condemnation?

Nobody in this world can determine what only God knows. When our friends and loved ones find themselves in great pain, we are supposed to surround them with our loving presence; not our disparaging empty words. It is a terrible thing to add hurt to a person who is already heart broken.

Our place as friends is not to put blame on their circumstances, but to stand beside them supporting them with love. All we need to do is to be there for them, offering what comfort we can give. They do not need empty words of our so called 'wisdom'. They just need a loving arm placed about them and a prayer for peace and direction.

Some people are so audacious that they think they have the answer to every problem. Wouldn't that be nice? The truth of the matter is we do not have the answers. The best advice to those who are hurting is to simply tell them that we love them, and that we do not have the answers but we know the one who does.

# February 1

# SHARING WHAT GOD HAS GIVEN

*(1 Timothy 6:17-19 Command those who are rich in this present world not to be arrogant nor to put their hope in wealth, which is so uncertain, but to put their hope in God, who richly provides us with everything for our enjoyment. Command them to do good, to be rich in good deeds, and to be generous and willing to share. In this way they will lay up treasure for themselves as a firm foundation for the coming age, so that they may take hold of the life that is truly life.)*

There are some people in this world who have been given the ability to make money—lots of money. I wonder how many of them realize that it is by the grace of God that they have been given their fortune. I doubt that there are many, however, there are those who use theirs for the purpose of furthering the gospel. I know a man personally who seems to fit the above scripture well.

He is one of those who have been blessed with the gift of making lots and lots of money. He has just recently sold his Lamborghini (yes I said Lamborghini). Many of us cannot even comprehend having that kind of money: And if we did, I wonder what we would do with it? This particular man I'm talking about knew just what he was going to do with the money that he redeemed from the sale of his car. God had told him to sell the car and give it away to further His gospel. He didn't hesitate to do it. This is just one example of how this man uses the money that God has given him. He is constantly helping out to the benefit of those serving the Lord. God has given him a wife who not only encourages him to give, she herself is a giver. *(Psalms 49:20 A man who has riches without understanding is like the beasts that perish.)*

Wouldn't it be wonderful if all of those people who are rich would gladly give generously to the Lord? *(Deuteronomy 15:10 Give generously to him and do so without a grudging heart; then because of this the Lord your God will bless you in all your work and in everything you put your hand to.)*

Few of us have the kind of money that this man has, but if we give generously as God directs out of what we do have, God will surely bless the giver in one way or another. We should never give grudgingly, but with a happy heart. My mother was always saying, "You can't out give God." My parents didn't have much, but they were always more than generous with what they had.

# February 2

# FOOLISH OR WISE

*(Psalms 14:12 The fool says in his heart, "There is no God." They are corrupt, their deeds are vile; there is no one who does good. The Lord looks down from heaven on the sons of men to see if there are any who understand, any who seek God.)*

Have you ever noticed that a lot of atheists and agnostics are people who are wealthy and/or famous? They are influential to the worldly people who do not put their faith in God and His Word. They would like you to believe that they have all of the answers. They are prideful because they have made a name for themselves: And because they have the money to do it, they buy people off. I am thinking of one individual (a man who proudly says there is no God) that has a big influence on those who lead our country. He is an extremely wealthy man and uses his wealth to further his cause. But the above word says those kinds of men and women are fools.

Now I am not condemning those who have made money honestly and use it to help others. In fact without those kinds of people our country could not survive. It is because of them that jobs are created and it is through their taxes that those who do not or cannot work are supported. I am talking about the foolish people who use their wealth to influence others to attain power.

It is a frightening thing to see our country and our homes being destroyed by those kinds of influences in our society. We must not let those people turn our hearts away from God. We must not be fools. We must seek our wisdom from God. *(Psalms 111:10 The fear of the Lord is the beginning of wisdom; all who follow his precepts have good understanding. To him belongs eternal praise.)*

Those who do not seek God's will and His wisdom are total fools; they do not realize what they are doing to themselves and to those who are influenced by their money and false beliefs. It is the people who seek God's wisdom who will gain truth and understanding:

Are you a fool or are you one of the wise ones who put your faith and trust in the knowledge that God gives you? Your very life depends on the answer to the question.

# February 3

# ARE YOU STUPID?

*(Proverbs 12:1 Whoever loves discipline loves knowledge, but he who hates correction is stupid)*

Do any of your children argue with you when you try to tell them things that they don't really want to hear? From the time they learn to talk, it seems as though they want to do their own thing. They don't want to listen to the warnings that we give them. They think that they should be able to learn things on their own. Sometimes we have to discipline them to teach them that they must listen to wisdom. We discipline them because we love them.

I know I was that way with my parents. I turned a deaf ear to them when they would try to give me good, sound advice, unless of course it was something I wanted to hear. There were many times that I would do stupid things that I had been warned against, and it led to trouble. They would have to discipline me for doing the wrong thing. I did not like the disciplinary measures at the time; however, looking back on it, I realize that it was for my own good. Without the disciplinary actions that my parents took, I most likely would have been a mess.

When we begin to rebel against God, he sometimes has to discipline us to bring us to our senses. It is for our own good. I don't know about you, but I do not want to be labeled as a stupid person. The truth of the matter is—It is a smart thing to listen to Godly council and to be thankful for the disciplinary measures that God takes with us. We learn and grow through them. We discipline those we love, and there is no greater love than our Father has for us.

## February 4

# WASHED AS WHITE AS SNOW

*(Isaiah 1:18 "Come now, let us reason together says the Lord. Though your sins are like scarlet, they shall be as white as snow; though they are red as crimson they shall be like wool.)*

February seems to be the month that most people are just weary of winter. We who live in areas that don't have green grass and leaves on the trees and some kind of flower growing year around, see the land as a little bleak and ugly at this time of year. Yesterday however was quite different. It started snowing in mid-morning and by 10:00 last night we had about 18" of snow.

When I got up this morning and opened the blinds, I was almost blinded with the blanket of white spread across everything in sight. It was one of the most beautiful sights I had ever seen. I was wishing that I had a camera to take snapshots of the beauty of it all, but unfortunately mine was broken so I will have to commit the sight to memory. The day before, the ground looked ugly and barren and suddenly it was a beautiful sight to behold.

As I stood there taking the beauty of it all in, I thought to myself, 'That's what Jesus blood did for me. His blood washed away all of the ugly black sin in my life and clothed me with a robe of white." What a beautiful picture that is. I don't think I will ever see a snow like this again without it reminding me of what Jesus did for me on the Cross. Come let us reason together—why would we not want to choose to serve the one who will wash us whiter than snow?

# February 5

## GOD'S GRACE

*(John 1:16-17) From the fullness of his grace we have all received one blessing after another. For the law was given through Moses: grace and truth came through Jesus Christ.)*

Last night in the evening service at church, one of the songs we sang was about God's grace. That song has been ringing in my ears ever since; and I cannot stop thinking about the grace of God. How can we possibly explain the grace of God? There are simply not enough words to describe it. I believe the reason we can't explain it is because we are humans; therefore, we are limited to the full understanding of the kind of grace that God shows to us.

His grace of course was shown to us when He gave His life for our sins. But it does not stop there; it is shown to us every day in one way or another. His grace holds us fast when we might fall: His grace forgives us when we mess up: His grace shows us unimaginable things by giving us the ability to do things we could never do without it. His grace gives us peace in the midst of trials: His grace is sufficient in all things. And the list goes on: But the bottom line is Jesus; and the fact is, His grace is everlasting.

That song we sang says 'Grace, grace, God's grace; grace that will pardon and cleanse within. Grace, grace God's grace, grace that is greater than all our sin.' Yes it is true—God's grace is truly amazing.

# February 6

# TRUSTING IN GOD

*(Psalm 20:6-8 Now I know that the Lord saves his anointed; he answers him from his holy heaven with the saving power of his right hand. Some trust in chariots and some in horses, but we trust in the name of the Lord our God. They are brought to their knees and fall, but we rise up and stand firm).*

I was very excited when the team that I am a part of entered the church where we would be doing our very first women's conference. We had put much prayer into the preparation. I personally had thought that I was prepared for everything. I felt confident that everything would go alright. I was to sing two songs along with giving my testimony.

When we got to the church, I immediately went to the man who would be running the sound system. I gave him the two cd's that I would be using and told him that we did not have to practice because I would warm up when we sang praise songs. I told him which tracs to use and I thought that would be sufficient. I trusted that he knew what he was doing. I went back to the room where our team was meeting to pray. As we finished praying, something just told me that I needed to go back and practice. I retraced my steps to the sound guy and asked him if it would be ok and he said yes. When I began practicing, I knew immediately something was terribly wrong. When I asked him if he had it on Trac 2, he said no that he had it on trac 3. He changed it to the correct one and everything went without a hitch.

God has been trying to teach me to trust in Him for all things. He gave me a good lesson that day. I was not putting my complete trust in Him, I trusted in the sound guy and in my decision not to practice. If God had not nudged me to practice, it would have been a disaster.

Why do we put our trust in ourselves, or in other people instead of the Lord? We may think we are in control and we take things in to our own hands; but if we don't seek God's wisdom and allow Him to be in full control, we can, and often do, make big mistakes. God alone knows everything we need to be successful in what He calls us to do. Let's not put ourselves at the head where God should be. We need to allow God to be in control of all things. After all, we can do nothing without Him, but through Him we can do all things. If we put our trust in Him he will raise us up and we will stand firm; but if we don't put our trust in Him, we will surely fall.

# February 7

# SEARCHING FOR WISDOM

*(Job 38:36 Who endowed the heart with wisdom or gave understanding to the mind?)*

I have been praying that God would reveal Himself to a friend of mine for some time. I received an e-mail from her a few days ago telling me that she has spent a month in the hospital. She related to me that she had been totally confused her entire life about who God is or even if He exists. She said that she has been reading the bible while in the hospital and that everything was beginning to make sense to her.

Can you relate to her story? I certainly can. For years I would try and read the bible, but it did not make any sense to me, so I would become discouraged and put it aside. And it would be a long time before I would try again. It was during a crisis in my life that God began to speak to me. That was when I heard His voice and I gave my heart to Him. And at once the truth of His Word began to make sense in my mind.

God's Word does not make sense to us because we are trying to use our own carnal minds to understand it. It is His Holy Spirit penetrating our hearts and minds that suddenly opens our eyes to His truth. Without His Holy Spirit we will never understand His Word.

God reminds Job of that very fact and He will remind us during those times that we are asking questions. We may not understand why God does certain things or why He allows things to happen to us: But we can be assured that His Word is true. And we can know that He will see us through every hurdle, every obstacle and every pain in our lives. We can trust in Him no matter what happens to us. He will restore our peace as we seek to understand His Word.

## February 8

# PRAYING WITH EXPECTATION

*(Psalms 3:3 In the morning, O Lord, you hear my voice; in the morning I lay my request before you and wait in expectation.)*

Do we arise in the morning and kneel before the Father in prayer. And if we do how many of us wait before Him with expectation for what He wants to say to us. Or do we arise each day with an insincere rhetoric prayer out of habit; and quickly go about our day, not giving it another thought. It is something to contemplate.

When we pray with a contrite and sincere heart, we can expect and should anticipate an answer to our prayers. Sometimes it takes a while to receive the answer: But no matter how long it takes, we must patiently wait on Him and not take things into our own hands.

He does answer some prayers immediately, such as when we ask Him to lead us each day in the paths of righteousness. There is no question that He will if we are sincere in our request. Even when we have struggles, and most of us do, we can depend on God's protection and direction through them.

There are many mornings when I have prayed for something specifically and I will open His Word and it is amazing how many times, the answer is there, right in front of me. Other times it takes a while before He answers. There are prayers that I have prayed for a long time and I have not gotten an answer; but I believe and I am expecting that in time my prayers will be answered.

We become stronger in our walk with the Lord when we come to Him in prayer with faith that He hears and answers in His time and according to His will, it is then that we can wait with expectation. There is a song that says; 'Strength will rise as we wait upon the Lord.'

Let's have faith and wait upon the Lord.

## February 9

# WOVEN BY THE MASTER

*(Psalms 139:13 For you created my inmost being; you knit me together in my mother's womb.)*

I once heard a speaker who used a woven canvas to demonstrate her life. It was beautiful. She told how her life had not always been perfect and that she had faced much heartache. But God had always been by her side. She pointed out that those times were used to help weave the completed canvas.

I believe that we could all tell the same story that she told except for different details. I do not think that there is anyone who has not gone through life free from sorrow. The one thing that Christians have that makes their canvas lovely is Jesus.

God takes every thread of our life and weaves them in to something beautiful. He uses even the tragedies that have occurred to weave them in the final lovely canvas. When He created us in our mother's womb, it was only the beginning of the picture that He had in mind for those who love Him.

If you are going through difficult times, just remember that Jesus will use those to complete the work that He is doing in your life story. At the end of your day on this earth, the canvas that He has woven in your life story will be beautiful.

# February 10

# WHY QUESTION?

*(Habakkuk 1:2-5 How long, O Lord, must I call for help, but you do not listen? Or cry out to you, "Violence!" but you do not save? Why do you make me look at injustice? Why do you tolerate wrong? Destruction and violence are before me; there is strife, and conflict abounds. Therefore the law is paralyzed, and justice never prevails. The wicked hem in the righteous, so that justice is perverted. "Look at the nations and watch—and be utterly amazed. For I am going to do something in your days that you would not believe, even if you were told.")*

I don't know anyone who is not questioning what in the world is going on, do you? Every day I encounter someone who engages me in the conversation about the activities that are happening, not only in our country, but the entire world. Things are happening all around the world that are, to say the least, downright puzzling. We see evil all around us, not only in our country, but also in our own towns, and sometimes even in our own homes.

We, like Habakkuk, would like to have some answers as to why all of these things are happening—or would we? I wonder if we really want to know what is happening. Would we be able to handle it? We don't have to understand everything. What if we were to learn that it is because of our sins that all this is happening? Whether we like to think about it or not, I think we have all been guilty of bringing about the changes that are destroying the world.

When I was reading the book of Habakkuk this morning, I could not help but relate it to what is going on in our world today. Read it for yourself—I think you just might see the similarities.

But one thing that stood out to me was right in the middle of God's answer to Habakkuk in chapter 2 verse 4 *(the righteous will live by his faith.)* No matter what goes on around us, we Christians can put our faith in Christ. He is the only one that we can put our faith in. He knows what He is doing; therefore we need not question Him we just need to trust Him. *(The Sovereign Lord is my strength; he makes my feet like the feet of a deer, he enables me to go on the heights. Habakkuk 3:19)*

# February 11

# SEEKING FOR ANSWERS

*(Daniel 2:2 So the king summoned the magicians, enchanters, sorcerers and astrologers to tell him what he had dreamed.)*

Nebuchadnezar had a disturbing dream and went in search of answers to his dream. He went to the magicians, enchanters, sorcerers and astrologers to tell him what it meant? Naturally they could not tell him. How could they when they did not put their faith in the only one who could interpret it for them? How foolish he was to think that they could. He was finally able to find someone who could interpret his dream. And that was a man who trusted the only true God—Daniel. It is so easy for us to see the fallacy in Nebuchadnezzar's thinking.

Things are not all that different today. We do not have to look far in our world to know that there are many people hurting in one way or another. They are searching for answers to their problems. Unfortunately the majority of them are looking in all of the wrong places and to all of the wrong people. There are some today who actually consult astrologers for answers. If people are looking to anyone other than the Lord for an answer to their problems, they are searching in vain. Unless they are children of the King, they are not going to receive any helpful answers. God is the only one who can give us wisdom and understanding in any situation. That is not to say that if we are Christians we will not have problems. Of course we will, but the difference is we have someone to turn to; and we no with certainty that He will hear and answer our call for help. It may not be exactly as we would want it: But rest assured it will be the one we need.

Daniel was able to interpret Nebuchadnezzar's dream because he was a child of God: And God is the one who revealed it to him. If you are looking for answers, be sure you are consulting the right people—those who know the one who has the answer—or better yet, go directly to The One who has the answer.

# February 12

# CONFIDENTLY YOURS

*(Psalms 27:3 Though an army besiege me, my heart will not fear; though war breaks out against me, even then will I be confident,)*

So many times we live like scared rabbits; we run into our holes hoping that we can hide ourselves from the danger that surrounds us. I must admit, I was like that at one time. I did not face my fears with confidence. In fact I didn't face them at all. I just hoped that they would go away. Can you identify?

Or are you one of those people who are self- confident, thinking that you can handle anything? You think nothing will come into your life that you won't be able to control. Well I am here to tell you; if you have not faced things before now that you haven't been able to handle—I can guarantee you—you will.

How many people do you know who are in chains of some kind? Whether it is alcohol, drugs, illicit sex, un-forgiveness, anger, un-repentance, jealousy, worry, or anything else—I can tell you that they will not be able to overcome them without help.

If we rely on our own self-confidence, we will fail. There are just some things that we will never be able to control. But if we put our confidence in God, we are already conquerors. We will be able to face any force that might come our way. *(Romans 8:37 No, in all these things we are more than conquerors through him who loved us)*. It is God's grace that gives us the ability to conquer anything. His grace is sufficient in all things.

I don't know about you, but I will put my confidence in God.
William Cowper wrote:

Man's wisdom is to seek
His strength in God alone
Even an angel would be weak
Who trusted in his own.

# February 13

# ORCHESTRATED LOVE

*Matthew 5:43-44 "You have heard that it was said, 'Love your neighbor and hate your enemy.' But I tell you: Love your enemies and pray for those who persecute you, that you may be sons of your Father in heaven.)*

While preparing to do 'small talk' at our church, I decided to incorporate Valentine's Day since it was the next day. My first thought was to talk about how we are always excited to send Valentines to family and special friends. But because I had done that last year, I did not want to be redundant. After praying about it God led me to this scripture.

The more I thought about it the more I decided that it should be done for 'big talk': hence——this devotional. It is easy to show love to those who love you back, but what about those who aren't quite so lovable? Do we go out of our way to show them kindness? Jesus was not talking to little kids when He said these words; He was talking to His disciples.

We Christians are supposed to be His disciples, yet sometimes we tell our children one thing and then do another. Our children hear and emulate what we do more than what we say. Do we show the love of Christ to everyone around us? Or by our actions are we sending two different messages to our children. Are we displaying love to our neighbor and hate to our enemies? Let's think about it and be honest with ourselves and then make it a habit to love our enemies and pray for those who persecute us. Only Jesus can orchestrate that kind of love in our hearts.

## February 14

# A LOVE THAT ENDURES

*John 15:13 (Greater love has no one than this, that he lay down his life for his friends.)*

This is Valentine's Day—that day when loved ones acknowledge their affection for others with cards, flowers, candy, and in many other ways. I can remember when I was a young girl, looking forward to those coveted valentine's that I would get at school. I think I enjoyed giving them as much, if not more, than receiving them. I can still remember those sweet little cards as if it was yesterday; and the excitement I had in the giving and receiving them. I would bring them home and spread them out and enjoy them for days.

I wonder how many times people have given gifts of love on Valentine's Day that came with a declaration of eternal love, but somewhere along the line, that love seemed to disappear. How many marriages have come apart at the seams because one or the other in that marriage decided that they just did not love the other one any longer? It is sad to say that statistics show that the rate of divorce in first marriages in America alone is 45% to 50%: In second marriages, 60% to 67%: And third marriages 70% to 73%. What kind of love is that? Love is a choice, we can choose to love someone forever, or we can choose to walk away from that love.

There is a love however, that assuredly lasts for a lifetime. That is God's love for us: A love so amazing that He died on the Cross for our sins. His love is eternal. He would never walk away from us. But it is our choice as to whether or not we will accept that love. He does not force himself on us. There is no other love like His. His love is unconditional. He requires nothing in return. He just asks that we accept the love that He offers us.

Have you accepted God's perfect love? If you have, I am certain that you are having a Happy Valentine's Day as you bask in the glory of His love.

# February 15

# GOD'S CONTINUED COUNCEL

*(Psalms 16:7-8 I will praise the Lord, who counsels me; even at night my heart instructs me. I have set the Lord always before me. Because he is at my right hand, I will not be shaken.)*

Wow! I can certainly identify with the Scripture above. So many times God speaks to my heart in the middle of the night. When I feel the urging of His Holy Spirit, I will arise and write what He is telling me to write. Doesn't it make you feel special, just to think that God loves us so much that He would talk to each of us, even in the still of the night? He never slumbers. He watches over us and He councils us every hour of every day. I love the thought that He is with me at all times, don't you?

God is not a figment of our imagination. He exists; His Holy Spirit has taken up residence in our hearts. He walks beside us always. That is the reason that we will not be shaken. *(Deuteronomy 31:8 The LORD himself goes before you and will be with you; he will never leave you nor forsake you. Do not be afraid; do not be discouraged.)*

There are times when I doubt what God has called me to do. That is when I momentarily take my eyes off of Him and look at my inabilities. But He always reminds me that because I have set Him before me, I will not be shaken. It is then that I remember that I can do all things through Christ, because He gives me the strength to do them. (Ref. Philippians 4:13)

It is a fact that God is always at our right hand. All we have to do is reach out and take hold of Him. No matter what comes our way, no matter how our circumstances threaten to destroy us—He is always there to protect us and deliver us from the evil that surrounds us. I don't know about you, but I have discovered the truth of this many times. God walks right beside us; whether it is on the mountain top or in the valleys. He is there beside us every hour to council us.

What an amazing God!

## February 16

# THE DEFEATED ENEMY

*(Psalms 25:1-2 To you, O Lord, I lift up my soul; in you I trust, O my God. Do not let me be put to shame nor let my enemies triumph over me. No one whose hope is in you will ever be put to shame, but they will be put to shame who are treacherous without excuse.)*

This Scripture is so encouraging to those who are going through the pain of suffering caused by those who threaten to destroy our name and our peace: Those who attack us in one way or another without cause. We need to realize that they are our enemies, driven by Satan, the enemy who invades the spirit of those who listen to his lies. It is because of his influence in their lives that they continue to attack. But we can put our faith and trust in the Lord, with the knowledge that He will never allow us be put to shame.

What a Savior! When we give our hearts to the Lord, He doesn't just tell us to go our own way to fight our own battles:—He walks with us in every situation and every trial, and every threat that comes our way. We will be triumphant in all things, because our hope is in Him. We need not fear the attacks of our enemies—we have already won the battle through our loving Father, and our Savior, Jesus Christ. It is the ones who are treacherous and without excuse who will be put to shame. Their evil lies and hurtful ways will one day be revealed.

If you are suffering because of the mouths of those who seek to destroy you. Remember the verse above and hang on to it. God will never allow you to be put to shame. He is greatly offended by those who attack His children. If you are a parent you can understand this, can't you?

Are you one of those who attack God's people? It is a sin; and if you ignore what God's word says about that, be aware of the fact that one day you will be brought to shame, because your sin will be revealed. *(Numbers 32:23 "But if you fail to do this, you will be sinning against the LORD; and you may be sure that your sin will find you out.)*

# February 17

# VICTORY IN JESUS

*(Psalms 25:14 The Lord confides in those who fear him; he makes his covenant known to them.)*

Life is a challenge to say the least. I don't know anyone who does not face some kind of problem somewhere along the way, most of the time on a daily basis. They may not be major challenges, and then again they may be. Some people have a way of handling the situations in their life with grace, while others rant and rave about their situations.

Many people who are having difficulties in their life ask the question, "Why me Lord." Now that may seem like an audacious thing to ask God, but I don't think so. It may be the catalyst that will send them to the place of knowledge—God's Word. If they are truly seeking answers from the Lord, if they are looking into His word, God will remind them of His covenant. God's word says *(The fear of the Lord is the beginning of wisdom. Proverbs 9:10) We* will find peace in His word.

It is the person who says "Poor pitiful me"; the one that does not go to God's Word for the answer to their problems; those who do not fear the Lord, who come up lacking answers. They will never find peace in their self-pity. It is only through the strength that God gives us and the truth of the covenant that He made with us; that we will be able to function through the trials of life with grace.

God allows things in our life for a reason. We do not understand why trials come our way. But we can find peace through them as we seek God's Word and remember His covenant. He may not answer the 'why me' question directly, but we will find through His Word that we will find peace (Psalms 29:11)—we will find comfort (Psalms 119:50—He will never forsake us (Deuteronomy 31:6) and that we can trust Him for all things for He is our refuge. (Psalms 62:8). At the end of the battles we will find victory in Jesus (1 Corinthians 15:57)

What an amazing God: What an amazing Jesus: What an amazing Holy Spirit. The Holy Trinity: The answer for all of our struggles in this life. We can truly praise Him in all things.

# February 18

# HONOR THE FATHER

*(Exodus 20:12 "Honor your father and your mother, so that you may live long in the land the Lord your God is giving you.)*

When it was discovered that our five year old granddaughter had allergies to all milk products, eggs, and gluten, we felt so sorry for her. Unfortunately most of her favorite things had to be taken away from her. She absolutely loved cottage cheese, yogurt, eggs and ice cream. But I was amazed at the way she handled the situation. Her mom and dad told her that she was definitely not to eat any of these things. Somehow she knew that it would be injurious to her health and she never argued with them about it. As young as she was, she realized that she must honor her parents.

How many times has our Father warned us about partaking in things that would be harmful to us? Yet, we go ahead dishonoring our Father by doing what we want to do. We don't submit to His will. We want to satisfy our own desires regardless of the fact that it may be injurious to our health, both physical and spiritual. Shame on us, we could and should take a lesson from this little girl. She had no choice in the matter, so she obeyed without fighting. As adults we have a choice to either honor our Father or choose to ignore His warnings and do what we desire. Can any of you identify with this? Do we dishonor God in any way by doing things that we know are harmful to us?

## February 19

# GRAY MATTER

*(Psalm 111:10 The fear of the Lord is the beginning of wisdom; all who follow his precepts have good understanding. To him belongs eternal praise.)*

The entire chapter of Psalm 111 praises God for His wonderful works. I believe that His most amazing work was His creation of man. He has formed everything in us with a precise purpose. The brain is made up in segments, each one performing its own purpose. The definition of *Gray Matter is* the ability to learn and understand or to deal with problems- she's got the *gray matter* to figure that equation out.

We talk about the gray areas in God's Word—those areas that aren't spelled out in black and white. But are there really gray areas? I wonder if we don't create those in our own mind. God's word emphatically tells us—*("This is the covenant I will make with the house of Israel after that time", declares the Lord. "I will put my law in their minds and write it on their hearts. I will be their God, and they will be my people." Jeremiah 31:33)*

God has given us a brain to think with and He has written the law on our hearts. That means we should have no problem with figuring out right from wrong. I believe that each of us know in our own heart what our sins are. If we are doubtful as to whether or not we should or shouldn't do a certain thing—we better not do it. If our conscience says no, we had better heed the warning. What one person can do is not necessarily ok for another and vice-versa. God has given us the ability to figure that out for ourselves. We should never allow others to say whether we can and cannot do a certain thing. Let's be honest with ourselves and with God. That gray area in our minds will become black or white when we let God have His way in our life.

We must listen to our conscience. We then won't have to wonder whether it is right or wrong. God will tell us in our spirit and we will then discern what He desires of each one of us. Don't fall in to the trap that because someone else can do a certain thing-you can. That is not true. We must follow our heart and listen to God's direction.

## February 20

# ARE YOU IN AN ASH HEAP?

*(1 Samuel 2:8 He raises the poor from the dust and lifts the needy from the ash heap; he seats them with princes and has them inherit a throne of honor)*

I just finished reading a story about a man who had been addicted to alcohol and drugs. One day after several years of being in bondage, he realized that contrary to the belief that the only thing that he thought made him happy was the thing that made him miserable. He wanted to quit in the worst way. He had no support from his family because they also were suffering from the same thing. He found himself in an ash heap and He needed help to get out. He talked to a counselor who pointed him to God. And he soon found out that He was the one that he had needed all along.

There are so many in this world today that suffers from some kind of addiction. I cannot believe that they really want to be enslaved to those things. But they are trying to fill a void that only God can fill. We could never find happiness in a habit. The only thing that bad habits lead to is destruction.

There is a saying—'misery loves company'. I think that those who are entangled in sin, like to bring others along with them. And because of one thing or another some people find solace in that kind of destructive sick friendship.

I believe that people are lured in to habits because of loneliness, anger, frustration, rejection, and peer pressure, among many other things. They need to know that their habits will not cure any of those ills. They need to know that their lives are not hopeless. And they need to know that they can find immediate help in Jesus Christ. They need to know that God will lift them out of the ash heap. They need to know that they can be seated in the position of honor.

If you are in bondage by a bad habit—replace it with God's love. He is the one in whom you will find the happiness and contentment that you are craving. Nothing or nobody else can take His place. Our peace and contentment are found in a personal relationship with Christ.

## February 21

# EXPLOITING OUR TALENT

*(Ephesians 4:7-8 But to each one of us grace has been given as Christ apportioned it. This is why it says: "When he ascended on high, he led captives in his train and gave gifts to his people.)*

The entire world was saddened and shocked by the death of a well-known singer. She was one of the most talented singers the world had ever known. It was a talent given to her by God. But her life ended suddenly at the age of 48.

I don't know a lot about her; but I did read that she was a girl that had been brought up in church, but had strayed away. After she became famous in the worldly arena as a performing singing artist, she also became addicted to alcohol and drugs. She was in and out of treatment centers, trying to fight the horrible addiction.

As I write this, I do not know what the autopsy report will say was the cause of her death, however, I feel sure that no matter what it says, it will be somehow related to her self-abusive past. Which leads me to ponder the scenario of how different her life could have been had she stayed in church and used her talent in the Lord's service.

It is extremely sad to see someone who has a God given talent to throw their life away in the pursuit of fame and fortune. How many times have we read about those who have made their name famous in the world, but have become slaves to habits that ultimately destroy them?

I don't know about you, but I am always blessed by beautiful voices singing the praises of God. I think those people have a special ministry, and they speak to many hearts through the talent that God has given them.

God gives different talents to each individual to help and encourage others. *(It was he who gave some to be apostles, some to be prophets, some to be evangelists, and some to be pastors and teachers, to prepare God's people for works of service, so that the body of Christ may be built up until we reach unity in the faith and in the knowledge of the son of God and become mature, attaining to the whole measure of the fullness of Christ. Ephesians 4:11-12)*

Are we using our God given talents to further our own name and agenda? Or are we using them in His service so that the body of Christ may be built up, and so His grace and glory can be seen and praised? We should not exploit the talent that God has given us.

# February 22

# FORGIVING AN ENEMY

*(Psalms 55:12-14 If an enemy were insulting me, I could endure it; if a foe were rising against me, I could hide from him. But it is you, a man like myself, my companion, my close friend, with whom I once enjoyed sweet fellowship as we walked with the throng at the house of God.)*

David describes the pain of the realization that a friend had turned against him. He had experienced this pain more than once. I am not certain which time he was referring to in this particular passage of scripture. It could have been referring to either Saul or Absalom. But what is important to note is the pain that he experienced each time if happened.

I am considering the pain that he must have experienced when he found out that Saul was trying to kill him. David had loved Saul as one of his greatest friends. He had been loyal to him in all things. I have no doubt that he thought the same love and respect was returned to him by Saul. But because of Saul's jealousy, he became David's worst enemy: Such an enemy that he was determined to kill him. And David was devastated because of it.

It is one thing to be hurt by an enemy, we expect it, but when we suffer the pain of one that we have shared our love and lives with, it hurts beyond measure. The Scripture says that David and Saul had walked together at the house of God. There have been many times when friends in their own church family, have suddenly turned on their sister of brother with no reason or excuse.

Have you ever had someone that you loved and served in ways that were far and beyond the call of a friend, only to have them mysteriously turn on you? I have, and let me tell you it hurts. Jesus knows that pain: He suffered more than any of us could ever imagine. Judas Iscariot, one of His own disciples sold him out for thirty pieces of silver. And yet He went to The Cross for the sins of the world.

Charles Spurgeon wrote: 'If our enemies proudly boast over us we nerve our souls for resistance, but when those who pretended to love us leer at us with contempt, whither shall we go? Our blessed Lord had to endure at its worst the deceit and faithlessness of a favored disciple; let us not marvel when we are called to tread the road which is marked by his pierced feet.'

We cannot and should not allow the pain of past hurt, keep us from loving and serving others. Christ has set an example of how we are to love others, even our enemies. *(Luke 6:27 "But I tell you who hear me: Love your enemies, do good to those who hate you.)* I believe that it is only through Christ that we can overcome the pain and hurt of others. Only through Him will we have the power to forgive them and move on; and continue in the love that He has called us to.

# February 23

# DANGER—BE ON GUARD

*(1 John 4:1 Dear friends, do not believe every spirit, but test the spirits to see whether they are from God, because many false prophets have gone out into the world.)*

There is something going on in the Spiritual world that we really need to be aware of. It is called the Emergent Church. Let me tell you that the emergent church can submerge your church if you don't arm yourself with the truth of God's Word.

I have had the pleasure of helping a friend whom has never been to church, in her pursuit of finding the truth of who God is and what He stands for. She has become increasingly excited about the things that she is discovering. However, the other day when I was talking to her she said that she had heard a guy speaking that she was very impressed with. She told me that she had just spent over $300 for some of his books and DVD's. She told me his name and asked if I was familiar with him. I told her no, but as she spoke I felt the Holy Spirit urging me to check this guy out: When I googled him, I got sick to my stomach. I realized that he was a part of the emergent church.

This particular guy had been raised in an evangelical church where his father pastored. He himself had pastored an evangelical church of his own until he started listening to the lies that were being told by those false prophets who have claimed that the 'old time religion' just wasn't good enough anymore. And that we needed to modernize our belief system. They are promoting the belief that God does not send anyone to hell, that a homosexual lifestyle is fine; abortion should be a choice, and pretty much that anything is ok—because God is love and will accept anything and anybody.

This is a blatant lie and a satanic attack on the original church of God that was established in Spirit and truth. All of these ministers promoting this so called church are false prophets—they are wolves in sheep's clothing

Satan would love for us to believe that we can live anyway we want to and still go to heaven: But the bible tells us that there is only one way to the Father, and that way is through His Son Jesus. He taught about the hereafter and that only those who know the truth and accept it will go to Heaven. It also talks about Hell. But these people have turned the truth into lies. Many are falling for these lies. If we aren't alert, we could fall in to the trap that Satan has for us.

I am encouraging you to educate yourself on the dangers of the 'emergent church' so that you will be able to withstand the lies that are being told. Check out these lies in God's Word. *(2 Timothy 2:15 Do your best to present yourself to God as one approved, a workman who does not need to be ashamed and who correctly handles the word of truth.)*

# February 24

# MORE PRECIOUS THAN GOLD

*(Psalms 119:72 The law from your mouth is more precious to me than thousands of pieces of silver and gold.)*

The first 42 years of my life I dreamed of having material things that only money could buy. I was impressed by those who had been successful and I envied the lap of luxury that they enjoyed. I don't think that I am the only one who can tell this story, if the truth be told. It is human nature to desire those things that we think will make us happy. Do you agree?

It was the very day that I found the Lord when I suddenly discovered that there are much more important things to concern ourselves with other than our selfish desires. As I started unfolding God's Word, He started showing me things that I had never understood before. The longer I walked in the magnificence of His light, the more I began to realize that the only thing that can make us truly happy is our personal relationship with Jesus.

I can read the scripture above and say for certain that it is very true in my life. God and His word is more important to me than anything that money can buy. His word supplies everything I need and all that I desire. When I look back and see the fallacy of my misguided desires, I am saddened. I wasted so much of my life in the pursuit of happiness in the things that could never fulfill that empty space.

What about you? Are you searching for things that you believe will make you happy? It is ok to want to have things in this life. But if you are thinking that those things will make you happy—you are very wrong. They may make your life a little nicer and a little easier but they will never supply the happiness that you desire. Look to the one who will fulfill that role—look to Jesus.

# February 25

# GODLY COUNSEL

*(Job 38:1-2 Then the Lord answered Job out of the storm. He said: "Who is this that darkens my counsel with words without knowledge? Brace yourself like a man; I will question you, and you shall answer me.")*

There are so many people that I know today who are going through many kinds of struggles. Not just daily aggravations, but great trials in their life. Their homes and their marriages are in jeopardy. They need help in determining what to do. Most of them are too weak to make a decision and so they look to others for wisdom. And of course there are those who want to offer their advice, which is a very dangerous thing, if they are not grounded in The Word.

Our wisdom comes from the Lord. He is the only one who can advise us to make the right decisions. It saddens me to see those who are being counseled by un-Godly men and women. Without the knowledge of the Lord, one can't possibly find the right path

If you are going through severe trials and feel that you need some counseling, ask God to lead you to the right counselor. God uses others to help us find our way, but it is a dangerous thing to be counseled by the wrong person. It could mean disaster for you if you choose the wrong counselor. *(The tongue of the wise commends knowledge, but the mouth of the fool gushes folly. Proverbs 15:3)*

## February 26

# FORGOTTEN FAVOR

*Judges 6:1, 2, 6, 7, 8, 9, 10 Again the Israelites did evil in the eyes of the LORD, and for seven years he gave them into the hands of the Midianites. Because the power of Midian was so oppressive, the Israelites prepared shelters for themselves in mountain clefts, caves and strongholds. Midian so impoverished the Israelites that they cried out to the LORD for help. When the Israelites cried to the LORD because of Midian, he sent them a prophet, who said, "This is what the LORD, the God of Israel, says: I brought you up out of Egypt, out of the land of slavery. I snatched you from the power of Egypt and from the hand of all your oppressors. I drove them from before you and gave you their land. I said to you, 'I am the LORD your God; do not worship the gods of the Amorites, in whose land you live.' But you have not listened to me."*

The Israelites had once again forgotten about God's favor on them. Because of their evil the Lord had given them into the hands of the Midianites. And they were in the same bondage that they had been in before God led them out of Egypt. We know that this isn't the first time that they had fallen in to the hands of their enemies because of their sin.

Isn't it easy to see the sin that the Israelites committed again and again? When we think about all that God had delivered them through as He led them out of Egypt; and all of the times that He had come to their rescue from that period up until the time we are reading in the above Scripture, we are inclined to be rather disgusted that once again they had fallen in to worshipping other gods and now are again crying out to God for His mercy.

But are we any different. How many times do we forget where we have been and the bondage that we were in before God delivered us? How often are we tempted to become entangled in the same trap? It is dangerous to turn our backs on God's favor. When we forget what all He has done for us, sin can easily overtake us once again. So let's remember God's favor on our lives and determine to be strong in Him and not allow ourselves to be led in to bondage again by the evil one.

# February 27

# MY SAVIOR—MY FRIEND

*(John 15:15 "I no longer call you servants, because a servant does not know his master's business. Instead, I have called you friends, for everything that I learned from my Father I have made known to you.")*

One of the saddest times in my life was when we moved from Kansas City to Clinton. I did not know anyone and I found out that most people that are born and raised in a small town have already established their friendships, and are not usually eager to embrace a stranger. I want to be quick to say that I don't think they intentionally want to exclude strangers, they just do not understand the loneliness that one can experience when they move from a familiar place to a strange one. For 2 years, I cried because of the exclusion that I felt.

I must tell you that at the time I did not know Christ as my personal Savior, and I suffered from a terrible inferiority complex. So because of my shyness, I did not know how to reach out to others. As a matter of fact, I have been told since that time that others thought I was stuck-up.

But God placed a couple in our lives that made all of the difference in the world. He was the pastor of a local church and he came by to tell us that he wanted to be our friend. It was because of the love that he and his wife showed us that we would attend his church at times. It was during that time that I found Christ. God used that precious couple as a huge influence and encouragement to accept Jesus as my personal Savior. Suddenly, I had many friends. Not only were they friends, but sisters and brothers in Christ

Today I realize that I had a friend all along, I just did not know Him: Not by His choice but by mine. He had wanted to be my friend from the time I heard His name, but I would not accept that extended invitation. What a difference Jesus makes in our lives when we allow Him to be our friend. He walks beside us every day. We never need to feel loneliness when we are His children.

# February 28

# THE BLESSING OF AFFLICTION

*(Psalms 71:11-12 They say, "God has forsaken him; pursue him and seize him, for no one will rescue him. Be not far from me, O God; come quickly, O my God, to help me.)*

When I read this passage of Scripture this morning, I was reminded of the time when I broke my femur. Bill and I had scheduled a business trip and because of my accident I was unable to go. An atheist acquaintance of ours, who I had been witnessing to, heard about it and inquired about me. Bill related the story to him and his reply was, "Well what does she think about God letting that happen to her?" Bill told him that I felt like God had protected me from it happening while we were traveling.

This man assumed that I was going to doubt my God. But he did not know that sometimes God uses what seem to be bad things, for His glory and for our good. My God came quickly to me during this time and He began showing me His purpose for my life. I wonder if I would ever have come to that point had it had not been for God's grace that used this particular temporary infirmity and time to bring me to the place where He wanted me.

I am eternally grateful to God for getting my attention. I do not see it as a negative accident. I see it as a gift that opened my eyes to the purpose that God had for me all along. Sometimes we can't see things clearly until a storm comes into our life. God never forsakes us. He uses everything that happens in our lives to grow us, teach us, and lead us in the paths of righteousness, so that we will no longer linger in our status-quo, but to step up to the place where He wants us.

The world cannot see God's magnificent grace. His grace goes far beyond any measure that we can imagine. The world questions why God would allow certain things in the lives of Christians. And in all honesty we Christians sometimes question God about such things. But sometimes, God uses those times in our life that others might see as a terrible accident, for a purpose. Sometimes that's what it takes to open our eyes to see His glory in all things.

# March 1

## QUEEN OF QUEENS

*(Esther 2:17 Now the king was attracted to Esther more than to any of the other women and she won his favor and approval more than any of the other virgins. So he set a royal crown on her head and made her queen instead of Vashti.)*

Isn't it absolutely amazing how God will take ugly events and turn them around and use them for His glory? This is what happens in this wonderful book of Esther. Even though God's name is never mentioned in this book, we can see His plan being carried out all the way through.

When I grow up I want to be just like beautiful Esther; not because of her outward beauty but because of her inward beauty. She was a respecter of all persons; she was a devoted daughter; she was an obedient wife; but most of all, she was obedient to God.

When Mordecai asked her to approach the king so that the Jews would not be annihilated he said *("Do not think that because you are in the king's house you alone of all the Jews will escape. For if you remain silent at this time, relief and deliverance for the Jew will arise from another place, And who knows but that you have come to royal position for such a time as this? Verse 14)* Esther's reply was, *("Go, gather together all the Jews who are in Susa, and fast for me. Do not eat or drink for three days, night or day. I and my maids will fast as you do. When this is done, I will go to the king, even though it is against the law. And if I perish, I perish." verses 15-16)*

I want to be so dedicated to my Lord that I would be willing to die to carry out His plan for me. Do you feel like you are in this place at this time for a particular reason? Are you willing to lay your life on the line to carry out the commission God has given you?

# March 2

# ONLY BY GRACE

*(2 Corinthians 4:1, 7 Therefore, since through God's mercy we have this ministry, we do not lose heart. But we have this treasure in jars of clay to show that the all surpassing power is from God and not from us.)*

When God spoke to my heart about writing devotionals, I was astounded and wondered if it was truly from God. I was never a wordy person, at least not on paper; and I certainly wasn"t a bible scholar. But God gave me confirmation that it was truly what He wanted me to do: Since that time I have prayed that He would give me each day what He wanted me to write.. He has never failed me. He is the author, I am just the writer.

We all know that the evil one cannot stand it when we are in a comfortable and secure position in the knowledge that we are where God wants us to be. And so there are days that Satan tries to tell me lies, and undermine my trust and confidence in God's call on my life, by telling me that I am just fooling myself, and that God really did not call me to this particular ministry. But the fact is, I know that I could never write without God's direction. It is only because of God's grace that He has given me this ministry.

Barnes commentary puts it this way: "The purpose of Paul here (verse 7) is, to show that it was by no excellency of his nature that the gospel was originated; it was in virtue of no vigor and strength which he possessed that it was propagated; but that it had been, of design, committed by God to weak, decaying, and crumbling instruments, in order that it might "be seen" that it was by the power of God that such instruments were sustained in the trials to which they were exposed, and in order that it might be manifest to all that it was not originated and diffused by the power of those to whom it was entrusted. The idea is that they were altogether insufficient of their own strength to accomplish what was accomplished by the gospel."

And so I have complete peace once again (and forever, I pray) that I am exactly in the place that God wants me to be, doing exactly what

He wants me to do. And I am here because He put me here for this reason.

Do you doubt God"s call on your life? Call out to Him and ask Him to show you truth and confirmation that you are where He wants you to be. He will answer you in a way that you will know without any doubt.

# March 3

# A LIGHTED PATH

*(Psalms 119:105, 111, 112 Your word is a lamp to my feet and a light for my path. Your statutes are my heritage forever; they are the joy of my heart. My heart is set on keeping your decrees to the very end.)*

I spent the first 42 years of my life running from God. Looking back on those years, I wonder how I ever got along without Him. I believe He sustained me even before I knew Him as my personal Savior. After all he is omnipotent and He knew that I would one day be His. I realize that I had a hunger for Him, a type of hunger that no person or thing could ever satisfy. I am so glad that He continued to pursue me. The peace that I have experienced since giving my heart to Him is a peace that is difficult to explain to those who have never answered His knock on their hearts door. He has led me on a path of peace. Certainly I have things that threaten to take away my peace but He always restores it. His word lights my path that leads me to a peaceful place.

Sometimes our paths are rocky and we trip over obstacles in our way, but God uses His word to protect us from falling. *(Psalms 55:22 Cast your cares on the Lord and he will sustain you, he will never let the righteous fall.)* Sometimes the path is dark and we cannot tell which way to go, but His word lights our path so that we can find the right way. *(John 8:12 When Jesus spoke again to the people, he said, "I am the light of the world. Whoever follows me will never walk in darkness, but will have the light of life.")* Sometimes our path is lonely and it seems there is nobody to help us, but God's Word tells us that He will walk with us all the way. *(Psalms 23:4 Even though I walk through the valley of the shadow of death, I will fear no evil, for you are with me; your rod and your staff, they comfort me.)* Sometimes we are weak and can't seem to walk but God's Word tells us that He lifts us up in His arms and carries us, *(Isaiah 63:9b In his love and mercy he redeemed them; he lifted them up and carried them all the days of old.)* Sometimes our paths are crooked, but God's Word tells us that when we acknowledge Him, he will make our paths straight. *(Proverbs 3:6)*

No matter what your situation is, God's Word will give you the answer that you need. His Word never fails and it never returns to us void. *(Isaiah 55:11 so is my word that goes out from my mouth: it will not return to me empty, but will accomplish what I desire and achieve the purpose for which I sent it.)*

# March 4

# A PORTRAIT OF HEAVEN

*(2Timothy 4:18 The Lord will rescue me from every evil attack and will bring me safely to his heavenly kingdom. To him be glory for ever and ever. Amen.)*

I have always loved paintings with winter scenes, especially those that have a church in them. My husband and I found such a painting many years ago at an antique show. This particular painting is one in which a horse drawn wagon filled with a family is on their way to a church that is in the distance. There is just something about it that gives me a warm, cozy feeling. There is no more beautiful picture to me than seeing an entire family headed to a place of worship.

Every time I look at that painting, I am reminded of how much fun it is to be a Christian; the joy and support of a church family is such a gift from God. To worship together is one of the biggest blessings God gives us. To journey with others who love the Lord is an amazing thing. Sure there will be evil attacks on our life as we go through the days on this earth. And there will be rough roads sometimes: But God will protect us and bring us through each one.

The encouragement we get from our family members is another great blessing. One day I was sharing with one of my sisters that I had been discouraged about a situation, and she reminded me of a Scripture; the perfect Scripture that I needed. God gave me light for my path and peace in His Word through a wonderful Christian sister. What a wonderful support system.

And the map and instructions He gives us in His Word is perfect. He never leads us down the wrong path. We may make a wrong turn, but He will turn us around and direct us to the right way again if we let Him.

Yes, I do get a homesick feeling when I look at that painting because it reminds me of the journey with my Christian family to my eternal home. What a wonderful journey. That painting pales in comparison to what we will see when we get to Heaven. There we will spend eternity with our entire family in the presence of Jesus. What a beautiful world it will be. No more pain or suffering of any kind—and no more tears.

I pray that you have your ticket to Heaven. Jesus paid the price for it. Have you received His gift of Salvation? Will you take that wonderful journey home to the Father who is waiting with open arms?

# March 5

# NEVER TOO OLD

*(Romans 4:19-21 Without weakening in his faith, he faced the fact that his body was as good as dead—since he was about a hundred years old—and that Sarah's womb was also dead. Yet he did not waver through unbelief regarding the promise of God, but was strengthened in his faith and gave glory to God, being fully persuaded that God had power to do what he had promised.)*

I can certainly identify with Abraham. I am now 72 years old, and believe me when I say; I am not who I used to be when I was younger. I can honestly say that my faith is far greater than it has ever been. I, like Abraham, am fully persuaded that God has the power to do everything that He has promised. I don't doubt for one minute that He has his eye and His hand on all things. He knows every circumstance in each and every one of our lives.

It does not matter how old we are, He has a plan for all of us until we depart this earth. If you are beyond the age that you feel like you are no longer a productive citizen—think again and remember Abraham and Sarah. God is never finished with us. He will use us in whatever area He calls us to. Even if you aren't physically able to do many things, you can still use your mind. There is no job more important than that of a prayer warrior, or for that matter, an encourager.

I don't know about you, but it gives me joy to know that God is still using me; more so than ever before. Perhaps it is because I have more faith as I grow older. I know that God is working in and through all things. I believe in His Almighty power and strength because I have witnessed so many insurmountable problems in people's lives that have been met through Christ and His amazing grace. I love the Scripture in *(Hebrews 11:1 Now faith is being sure of what we hope for and certain of what we do not see.)*

Sometimes we cannot see God's power working, but we can be sure that it is. I want to work for the Lord until the day that He calls me home.

## March 6

# ENJOY THE JOY

*(Psalms 28:7 The Lord is my strength and my shield; my heart trusts in him, and I am helped. My heart leaps for joy and I will give thanks to him in song.)*

Before church began one day not long ago, I was discussing with one of my brothers-in-Christ about how much fun it was to serve the Lord. He was telling me that he and his wife had attended a function at a different church than ours, and he said they had talked about the fact they were glad that they attended a church where the people were full of joy. They were comparing the people in our church with the one that they had visited and had noticed that the people were rather sober and did not seem joyful at all.

It just so happened that our pastor was talking about the same thing from the pulpit that same day.

It is fun to be a Christian. I get more joy out of sharing my faith with others, than anything. I do not understand how some Christian people seem to think that you have to be sober in the Lord. No wonder some people are not interested in becoming a Christian. If they don't see the happiness that comes from knowing the Lord Jesus Christ, what would make them want to be like them?

When you think of all of the reasons that we Christians have to be joyful about, it is ridiculous to go about with a sad face. Think about what God has done in our life. He has taken away every sin in our life that has kept us in chains, He has given us strength to do the things that we could never do without Him. He is our shield, our peace, our comfort, our deliverer, our Savior, our friend, and our Redeemer; He is our all in all. He is everything that we need. And yes, He is our joy. As our minister so often says, "That should be shouting ground for us.

I want people to know that my joy comes from the Lord. I want to sing His praises to the entire world. I want my enthusiasm to be inviting to others, don't you?

# MARCH 7

# GOD'S AMAZING PLAN

*(Ephesians 2:9-10 For it is by grace you have been saved, through faith and this not from yourselves, it is the gift of God not by works, so that no one can boast. For we are God's handiwork, created in Christ Jesus to do good works, which God prepared in advance for us to do.)*

Have you ever wondered what God has for you to do? Do you question Him about your purpose in life? For years I wondered what God's purpose was for me. I did not feel like I had any particular gift and I struggled with it. It seemed to me that God used others in certain areas, but I felt like I floundered in the pursuit of seeking the area where God wanted to use me. I took the quiz that is supposed to reveal your talents, but it did not help me. It says to listen to what others say about you, look at the areas that you feel like you excel in. I did all of that and yet I did not discover the place where God wanted to use me. Can you identify?

I was always under the impression that God would use you where you are the most qualified. But I have since learned that it is not necessarily true, although it might be for some people. It was not until I surrendered everything in my life to God that He began to show me what He wanted me to do. And you know, it was in areas that I felt the least qualified for. So I argued with God about those things He asked me to do. But He would always tell me that I can do all things through Him, and that His grace was sufficient. He equipped me with all that I needed to carry out His plan for me. And wonder of wonders, he gave me the love and passion for it. Most especially writing and encouraging others: Things that I could never do on my own. I can never boast in myself because I know and God knows that I could do nothing outside of His grace.

It is amazing that God had this plan for me from the time I was born. And He has a plan for you also. Do not be surprised if it is something outside of your qualifications. God will qualify you for whatever it is that He asks of you.

# March 8

# EVERY DAY ORDAINED

*(Psalms 139:15-16 My frame was not hidden from you, when I was being made in secret, intricately woven in the depths of the earth. Your eyes saw my unformed substance; in your book were written every one of them, the days that were formed for me, when as yet there was none of them.)*

During a time of convalescing from foot surgery, God led me to this Scripture. It touched my heart in such a wonderful, tender way. Just to think that God knew, even before I was born, that I would be going through this period in my life reveals His love for me even more than I had considered. I have felt His love and presence in a powerful way. I could almost feel His loving arms around me. I can honestly tell you that the presence of His Holy Spirit has lifted me higher and higher.

Isn't it amazing that God knows everything that happens to us on a second by second basis? He is there to lead us through every situation. He is there in the good times and the bad times. It is through the times that we are down that He reveals Himself to us in most unusual and wonderful ways. I don't know about you, but is seems as if it is in the times that I feel helpless, that He steps in and takes over. I am reminded that in my weakness, it is He who gives me strength.

It does not matter whether we are weak in body or in spirit—He knows just how to meet our needs: And not just mine, but yours also. He has known every day of our lives long before we live them. What an awesome thought.

We live in a chaotic, unpredictable world, yet we have nothing to fear. Our God will see us through each day and we can have peace knowing that He is in control. No matter what each day brings, nothing can harm those who are covered by His blood.

There are no days in our lives that surprises God—He knew: He knows: And He cares. He will be with us through them all, giving us all that we need to endure.

# March 9

# DO NOT BE VENGEFUL

*(Romans 12:17-19 Do not repay anyone evil for evil. Be careful to do what is right in the eyes of everybody. If it is possible, as far as it depends on you, live at peace with everyone. Do not take revenge my friends, but leave room for God's wrath, for it is written: "It is mine to avenge; I will repay," Says the Lord.)*

I do not believe that there is anybody who has not suffered from the unmerited evil attacks of others. But having that knowledge does not ease the pain for another. It is a fact that there is evil in this world and if Satan can cause dissension in our lives by using others against us, he will surely do it. We do not have any control over those who abuse us by telling lies and attacking our character, but we can have peace and assurance that God knows all about our situations and He will take care of it for us.

I have heard people say that when others attack them they won't get mad, they will get even. But the Scripture above tells us in no uncertain terms that we must not repay evil for evil, but let God handle the situation. We must let go of those things and those people we cannot change: We must wait on the Lord and allow Him to have control of the situation.

It hurts when others attack us, but our Heavenly Father will give us peace as we wait on Him. We don't have to plot evil schemes to get even; that would only lead to useless battles: And we would be no better than our attackers.

Remember the little chant we would use as children when someone would say bad things to us and about us? It went like this-'Sticks and stones may break my bones, but words will never harm me.' When we are children of God, He will fight every battle for us. Satan can only harm us if we allow him to. We must keep our faith and trust in the Lord and not listen to the lies of the evil one; he is out to destroy us but God will save us from his evil schemes.

The best thing we can do is to continue to pray for our enemies. *(Matthew 5:43-44 "You have heard that it was said, 'Love your neighbor and hate your enemy.' But I tell you: Love your enemies and pray for those who persecute you, that you may be sons of your Father in heaven.")*

# March 10

# A CELEBRATION OF LIFE

*(Esther 10:3 Mordecai the Jew was second in rank to King Xerxes, preeminent among the Jew and held in high esteem by his many fellow Jews, because he worked for the good of his people and spoke up for the welfare of all the Jews.)*

I would ask you to go to the book of Esther and read it. You can't find a fictional novel any more exciting than the truthful story in Esther.

What would happen without the Mordecai's of the world? Reading between the lines of this magnificent book of Esther, we can see how God used each person for His will to be done: And none any more than Mordecai. Mordecai was on the job God gave him every day. He was the intercessor used by God to keep the Jews from being annihilated. I can imagine that he spent most of his time in prayer, seeking the Lord's direction.

*(Esther 8:15 Mordecai left the king's presence wearing royal garments of blue and white, a large crown of gold and a purple robe of fine linen. And the city of Susa held a joyous celebration.)* The Jews are celebrating the fact that they were alive. They were very aware of the fact that if it had not been for God and Mordecai, they would not be having this celebration.

I don't know about you, but I am so thankful for all of the fine Christians in this world who are willing to be intercessors. I think about the people in my own life who have interceded on my behalf. God has used them in a powerful way to turn my heart towards Him. There are still many who pray for me on a daily basis that the will of God will prevail in my life. We have much to celebrate when we have those people in our life—those who stand in the gap for us.

# March 11

# EXCESSIVE LIBATION

*(Esther 1:7, 8, 10, 11, 12, 15, 19a Wine was served in goblets of gold, each one different from the other, and the royal wine was abundant, in keeping with the king's liberality. By the kings' command each guest was allowed to drink in his own way, for the king instructed all the wine stewards to serve each man what he wished. "According to law, what must be done to Queen Vashti?" he asked. "She has not obeyed the command of King Xerxes that the eunuchs have taken to her.") "Therefore, if it pleases the king, let him issue a royal decree and let it be written in the laws of Persia and Media, which cannot be repealed, that Vashti is never again to enter the presence of King Xerxes.)*

There is nothing more obnoxious than a drunken person. Excess alcohol can turn a normally nice person into a monster. It has destroyed many homes and families. That is precisely what happened in the case of Xerxes and Vashti. The king had thrown a big bash of a party that lasted seven days, and everyone there, more than likely had drunk their share, which was as much as they wanted. And then Xerxes decided he wanted his wife summoned so that he could show her beauty off. Now how would you ladies feel if your husband sent seven men to summon you at a moment's notice to parade yourself before a drunken crowd? I don't know about you, but I would be highly insulted. So Vashti did what I would have done—she refused. The king was furious and inquired of his wise men (I say cronies) about how he should handle it and they said basically get rid of her and never let her see you again because she has insulted you; and our wives might get the same idea to be like her. Wow! What logic.

It is rather sobering (that's not a pun) when you read this passage. I have given this a lot of thought. How many marriages have broken up because of alcohol abuse, I wonder? Too many I am thinking. When people are under the influence of too much alcohol, they are not them-selves. And they definitely make bad choices. The National Institute of Alcohol Abuse reports that People who have been drinking large amounts of alcohol for long periods of time run the risk of devel-oping serious and persistent changes in the brain. And we know for certain that it leads to changes of personality. Who needs that in a world that is a challenge even in every day sober life? Why do people feel the need to dull their senses? I think it is because they are searching for something that will make them happy and satisfied. We can only find that through Jesus.

# March 12

# COMMIT IT ALL TO GOD

*(Proverbs 16:3 commit to the Lord whatever you do, and your plans will succeed.)*

My niece called me to ask for prayer for her daughter and son-in-law. They have felt a call from the Lord to make a change in their life and their ministry: And they want to know for sure that they will make the right decision. I know exactly what they are feeling because I have been there more than once. It is a scary and serious thing to make huge changes in one's life. We surely all want to know that it is coming from God and not just a flighty idea.

While I was talking to her the Scripture above was brought to my mind. We cannot make a mistake when we commit everything to the Lord. When we seek His will, He will honor our request to hear from Him. It always amazes me when God confirms his call on our life by one means or another. He wants us to succeed in our ministries and without a doubt He will give us success when we commit it all to Him.

I am blessed by being a part of a women's ministry. Each time we are called to a church to encourage other women to a closer walk with the Lord, we first commit everything to Him. We pray for His will in all things: And He has never failed us. We are aware of the fact that we need to always allow God to be in control.

Many times when our church choir gathers together before Sunday services, we are all aghast at how terrible we sound, and we are fearful that we will not do the song justice. But when we pray and commit it to God, he hears our prayers and we realize even as we are singing that He has blessed and honored them. As a matter of fact, it seems as if it is those times that we see are human frailty and put it in God's hands that we receive compliments; and we know that it was because we committed it to the Lord that we were able to carry it off, and not because we just happened to sing the right notes.

I don't know about you, but I certainly do not trust myself. I have to know that I am doing what God wants me to do. It does not matter if we are talking about a ministry or if we are talking about our everyday activities—we should always commit everything to the Lord. Our days belong to Him, and we would not make the foolish mistakes that we often make, if we committed each day and every choice we make to Him. We can trust Him for all things.

# March 13

# OUR ETERNAL HOPE

(Colossians 1:27 Christ in me the hope of glory.)

I have been grieving for the past several days with some relatives who have lost their lovely young daughter, their only child, and with her husband of five years. One never has the proper words to say when the pain is so new and raw. When I spoke with her mother, I just told her how sorry I was and that I was crying with her.

One day soon I will call her to say that because her only child was a Christian she is more alive now than ever before. She had put her hope in Christ. Our hope in Christ is that we will live eternally with him. We, who hope in the Lord, will one day be together with our loved ones who have gone on before us.

I cannot imagine the thought of losing one who had not chosen Christ as their Savior. There would be no hope of ever seeing them again. That would be an unimaginable pain. We, as Christians should always pray for those who do not know Christ—the hope of glory. I am so thankful that my mother prayed for my salvation from the time that I was conceived. I thank God for my Christian heritage.

Oh what peace we have when we have that hope of glory—that promise that we will have eternal life. Death has no sting when we are born again through the blood of Jesus. Those who do not know Christ have no hope of eternal life with Him. But those who did and have departed this world— now know and are experiencing that hope that was promised to them.

Are you a Christian? Do you have that hope that Christ promises us? If the answer is no, I pray that you would surrender your heart to Jesus. He is our hope and our salvation. He is the way the truth and the life, No one comes to the Father except through Him. Ref. John 14:6

## March 14

# THE FAMILY OF GOD

*(Galatians 6:2 Carry each other's burdens, and in this way you will fulfill the law of Christ.)*

I had some foot surgery recently and was told by my Doctor that I could not be on my feet except for bathroom necessities and to set at the table to eat. Now to someone like me, that's a tall order. I am not used to being waited on and it is difficult for me to accept help gracefully. But this was not the first time this has happened to me, so I learned through the first experience that I should accept the help with grace knowing that these precious people truly want to help their sister.

One of the greater benefits of being in the family of God is the love that is shared amongst them. I have seen firsthand how God's people carry one another's burdens. The prayer chain at our church is quite active and is put in effect almost on a daily basis and sometimes more than once a day. God's people care about each other and they show it by putting it into action. Needs are met through that love and concern that we share.

There is no greater love than God's love and He has told us to love one another as He has loved us. Ref. John 15:12 There is a saying "the proof is in the pudding". It is easy to say "I love you," but showing it is a different matter. I am so blessed to be in the family of God. His people love one another and are eager to show it.

# March 15

# ATTACKS FROM THE ENEMY

*(Jeremiah 20:11-12 but the Lord is with me like a mighty warrior; so my persecutors will stumble and not prevail. They will fail and be thoroughly disgraced; their dishonor will never be forgotten.)*

Last night as I was watching the news, I became very disturbed and yes angry as I watched one of the vilest comedians I have ever heard, making terrible remarks about a presidential candidate, simply because he openly proclaims his faith in God. The things he said was unbelievable. Everything that came out of his mouth was vile. He was also making terrible, insulting remarks about women, especially those of faith. It seems like he has an agenda to discredit and insult anyone who proclaims Christianity.

This same evil man has given a million dollars to our current president's campaign. The question was asked if the president should give it back. There is a poll being taken to get the public's opinion. I don't know what you think, but in my opinion anybody with a Godly moral conscience, would not even consider keeping a donation from someone as evil and offensive as this vile man.

As I sat there listening to this man slander these people, I could not help but wonder why God did not strike him down that very minute. But my ways are not God's ways. It could possibly be that God might somehow miraculously reveal himself to the guy and change his heart. I must admit, in my human mind I doubt that his polluted mind would ever be changed. But one thing I do know, if he doesn't repent, he will surely pay the price for insulting and slandering God and His people.

Once again I am reminded that we live in an evil, fallen world. We must keep our armor on and fight against the powers of darkness. We might be persecuted in this world, but God will one day avenge His people.

## March 16

# COMMITMENT AND TRUST

*(Psalms 37:5-6 Commit your way to the Lord; trust in him and he will do this: He will make your righteousness shine like the dawn, the justice of your cause like the noonday sun.)*

As I was preparing for speaking in April, I thought that I had it all figured out. I had prayed about it so I felt fairly confident. But somehow I did not have complete peace, so I continued to pray that God would show me what He wanted me to speak. In the process of writing a devotional, God spoke to my heart and said, "This is what I want you to speak about." All at once, I found the peace and assurance that I was on the right track. Had I not committed it all to God, what I had planned to speak may not have been effective: But because I had committed it to Him, He protected me from doing something other than what He wanted me to. I feel totally confident that God will bless what He has put on my heart.

If we don't commit everything we do to the Lord, it will not only be ineffective, it might just be a disaster. We can do nothing effectively without God, but we can do all things through Him who gives us strength. So that seems to be a no brainer, for me, how about you?

Two things that terrify me are that I would do something without the Lord's blessing, and that I would try to take glory from Him. It is only by His grace that we could do anything. Without Him, we can do nothing. Reference John 15:5

It is only because we have accepted Christ as our personal Savior and only by His grace that we are made righteous. I want my righteousness to shine like the dawn, and the justice of my cause like the noonday sun, don't you.

# March 17

# AN OBEDIENT LIFE

*(Romans 16:19 Everyone has heard about your obedience, so I am full of joy over you; but I want you to be wise about what is good and innocent about what is evil.)*

I have been studying the books of Esther and Ruth simultaneously. Kelly Minter made the following statement in her bible study: 'Faithful obedience and love to God during our earthly years can affect things long after we are gone.' And it has led me on a journey of thought. Ruth and Esther both were women of character who were admired by everyone who knew them. They aren't known for their outward beauty, although I believe they were lovely indeed; they weren't known for their intelligence, although I am sure they were highly intelligent; they weren't known for their education, however we can be certain that they were educated by The Master; and they weren't known for their wealth. What they are known for is their love for God and their obedience to Him.

Now God has gifted people with different things—some with outward beauty—some with great IQ's—others with the opportunity to be educated in the best of schools—and some with great wealth. I think no matter what we have accomplished in our lives, we must realize that it is because of God's grace. And there is no doubt that the world has been affected by some of them. The question is—Are we wise with what God has given us. Are we using it for good or do we use it for evil? Do we use it for our glory or do we give God the glory? When all is said and done; and when our life is over; what do we want people to say about us? How will the life we lived on this earth affect others after we are gone? I don't know about you, but I want them to say about me what Paul said: "Everyone has heard about your obedience, so I am full of joy over you." Ref. Romans 16:19

There is no better legacy to leave behind than the knowledge that one has loved God and was obedient to His call on their lives.

## March 18

# UNLIKELY SERVANTS

*(Matthew 1:5-7 Salmon the father of Boaz, whose mother was Rehab, Boaz the father of Obed, whose mother was Ruth, Obed the father of Jesse the father of King David. David was the father of Solomon, whose mother had been Uriah's wife.)*

If one has never read the bible, they would quickly pass by the above Scriptures. I am quite sure I did that since genealogy has always been a bit confusing to me. But when I seriously started studying God's word; the first time I read this and understood what it was actually saying, it was astounding to me. When I noticed that Rahab was the mother of Boaz, I thought—wait just a minute, I think that Rahab had been a prostitute, sure enough after I checked it out; my memory had served me correctly. And then when I read Solomon's mother had been the wife of Uriah, I did a double take. Isn't she the one who was the reason David committed murder? Indeed she was.

Wow! And you think you have skeletons in your closet. I was reminded of this scripture as I was doing my study in Ruth this morning. Suddenly I thought: How amazing the grace of God is. He can and will use anyone who is obedient to Him. It doesn't matter what their past is, He doesn't look at their past, He looks at the hearts that they have for Him at the time and He plans their future: A future that the average person would never dream possible. I doubt that Rahab or Bathsheba could have ever dreamed that their offspring would be in the lineage of the one who would be the Savior of the world.

If you are a child of God and are feeling unworthy, look in the word of God. Read it and be blessed by those who God used in mighty and powerful ways. He did not always use those who would typically quality. No, he used the most unlikely ones: Those who had a past that most of us would blush at. But not God; He knew the future that He had for them. And He knows the future that He has for you. *(Jeremiah 29:11 "For I know the plans I have for you." declares the Lord, plans to prosper you and not to harm you, plans to give you hope and a future.")*

# March 19

# SHHH! JUST BE QUIET

(Psalms 46:10a Be still and know that I am God.)

Have you ever been so distraught over a hurtful situation in your life that you did not know where to turn? You have prayed and prayed until you didn't know how to pray anymore. I wonder if you have been like me —trying to give God directions on how to handle things. You know, "God if you would do this or if you would do that, then maybe things would get better." Or even worse, try to take things in your own hands and try to fix them. Well duh— how can God help us when we are speaking so loudly we cannot hear His voice?

Why do we seek God's wisdom and at the same time try to control the things that only he can handle? When will we learn to shut up and listen to His voice? When we reach the place where we give up control: and when we finally turn everything over to God, we can be certain that we are in good hands. He hears our hearts and He knows our hurts Even when we cannot seem to be able to pray, He understands even in our groaning's. It is when we step out of His way and allow Him to handle the situation that things will begin to change.

Are there things in your life that you struggle with? Are you fighting the battle by yourself? Maybe you are in God's way. Maybe you need to be still and know that He is God.

# March 20

# PATIENTLY WAIT

*(Psalms 37:7 Be still before the Lord and wait patiently for him; do not fret when men succeed in their ways, when they carry out their wicked schemes.)*

It is so tempting and sometimes very difficult to not jump ahead of God and take control when people are trying to undermine you in any way. After all we are only human and don't we have a right to defend ourselves? The answer to that is yes, God gives us the right to take control of things if that is our desire, but do you really want to do that? Believe me when I say I have been there and done that; and I can assure you that each time I did, I was sorry that I had not waited on the Lord.

When we worry and fret about those people we cannot change, it only destroys our peace. God is the only one who has the power to change people and circumstances. His way, His will, and His timing is perfect. That should be enough for us to put our trust and faith in Him to bring us through our trials with those who are trying to hurt us in any way.

Perhaps you are having a difficult time with someone in your life right now who is trying to hurt you. Don't take things in to your own hands; wait on the Lord to take care of things. Put your faith and trust in Him. Pray, be still, and wait on Him. He will deliver you in His time, in His way, and according to His will. You do not want it any other way.

# March 21

# STANDING FIRM

*(1 Peter 5:8 Be self-controlled and alert. Your enemy the devil prowls around like a roaring lion looking for someone to devour. Resist him, standing firm in the faith, because you know that your brothers throughout the world are undergoing the same kind of sufferings.)*

I love Peter, don't you? He encourages us to always look to God's grace when we are going through trials. It is a fact that we face trials of many kinds; sometimes on a daily basis. Don't find it strange when you are confronted by evil. We will be as long as we live in this life. We can expect it and we must be ready for it.

The evil one looks for ways to try and destroy us. But we must remember that he has no power over us unless we allow him to. We must stand firm in our faith with the armor of the Lord and fight against his attacks. When things are going great in our lives, the evil one cannot stand it: So we must be on guard, because when we least expect it, he raises his ugly head to try and take our eyes off of the hope we have in Christ Jesus.

Satan is no match for Jesus. Through the power of His Name, we can resist everything that Satan throws our way. As long as we remember who we are and whose we are, we can stand firm, knowing that we are protected by God's grace. It is important to know that our brothers and sisters go through trials also. We are not singled out, Satan is not a respecter of people, he is out to try and destroy all of God's children. We need to lift each other up in prayer, knowing that all of us have battles to fight. But praise God, He provides us with the protection that we need.

# March 22

# RESTING IN HIS SALVATION

*(Psalms 37:39-40 The salvation of the righteous comes from the Lord; he is their stronghold in time of trouble. The Lord helps them and delivers them; He delivers them from the wicked and saves them, because they take refuge in him.)*

For the past several days I have been studying psalm 37: And, oh what a wonderful psalm to study. The promises that we find there should still our hearts even in the sinful world that we live in.

Whether we are suffering from the satanic attacks personally or collectively as Christians, it has the same message. His message to us is to trust in the Lord and delight in Him—commit everything to Him— be still and wait on Him—don't be angry— don't fret—turn from evil and do good.

Yes, we live in an evil world. We face challenges and persecution in this world. God has never promised us easy sailing: as a matter of fact He tells us that we will have all kinds of trouble. But He does promise us that He will never leave us, He will never forsake us, He will save us from all of our enemies.

When God sent His Son to die in our stead, we had a choice to accept Jesus as our personal Savior. Those who have made that choice are under the banner of The Lord and His love. We, who are His children, will never have to suffer defeat because The Lord will fight for us, He will protect us, and He will punish those who have hurt us. We will find refuge in Him.

Whose side are you on? If the answer to that question is anything but the side of The Lord, I implore you to turn your life around before it is too late. Even in the middle of this wonderful psalms , Jesus is calling you— in verse 27 *(Turn from evil and do good; then you will dwell in the land forever, for the Lord loves the just and will not forsake His faithful ones.)*

Even churches are buying in to the evil that prevails. They are accepting things that are totally in violation of what the bible says. Many of them are no longer teaching truth.

There are many of God's people throughout the world who are being persecuted and killed because of their stand for Christ. It is disturbing to witness this persecution of the Christians. We feel helpless and perplexed at times, not knowing what to do. But I do not believe that we will suffer this much longer. There will come a time when God will stop all of this. He sees everything that is happening and one day, those who have abused, misused, and persecuted God's people will be revealed and they will be no more.

We are told that God's people will inherit the land and enjoy peace. God's promises are true. We know the end of our story and because of that, we can stand firm in the hope that God has promised us. HALLELUJAH AND AMEN.

# March 23

# WHO DO YOU SERVE?

*(Matthew. 6:24 "No one can serve two masters. Either he will hate the one and love the other; or he will be devoted to the one and despise the other. You cannot serve both God and money.")*

In this world we live in today, people seem to be obsessed with money. They somehow believe that money will insure them of a secure future. But they are so mistaken. We have no control over the economy of this world. We could feel secure one day, and discover that we have lost everything overnight.

It is sad to say that the majority of people do not understand that the only thing that they can be sure of is Christ. They have no clue and seemingly no desire to seek His security. If it doesn't have a dollar sign before it, they just aren't interested.

The happiest people I know are the ones who have a personal relationship with Jesus. They may not have much in material things, but it does not concern them because their hope is in Him. They have found the secret—Christ in them the hope of glory.

*(Matthew 19:23 Then Jesus said to his disciples, "I tell you the truth, it is hard for a rich man to enter the kingdom of heaven.")* Why do you think that is? I believe that it takes their mind off of Godly things. They are so detracted by hanging on to their wealth, and/or making more, that they don't have time for spiritual matters. This Scripture does not say that it is impossible, just hard. There are some wonderful Christian people who are rich, but they don't put their wealth before God. They are not enslaved to it; rather they use it for God's glory and in His service. However, I dare say that they are few and far between.

God said: *(Do not store up for yourselves treasures on earth, where moth and rust destroy, and where thieves break in and steal. but store up for yourselves treasures in heaven, where moth and rust do not destroy, and where thieves do not break in and steal. For where your treasure is, there your heart will be also. Matthew 6:19)*

What is your heart focused on? Who do you serve? Are you storing up earthly possessions or treasures in heaven? We will never take our earthly possessions with us when we leave this world. They will mean nothing at the end of our time on earth. Think about it.

# March 24

# THE TRUE FOUNDATION

*(Ezra 3:1, 3, When the seventh month came and the Israelites had settled in their towns, the people assembled as one man in Jerusalem. Despite their fear of the peoples around them, they built the alter on its foundation and sacrificed burnt offerings on it to the Lord, both the morning and evening sacrifices.)*

When the Israelites came together to rebuild the temple; they came together as one. The above Scripture says that they built an altar on its foundation and made sacrificial offerings to the Lord on it

There are so many beautiful churches in the world today: Beautiful to look at but I wonder how many were built on the foundation of Jesus. I wonder how many of the builders came together as one and prayed that the church be built on the rock of salvation—Jesus. I fear that far too many are just beautiful buildings, full of beautiful things, but lacking in all the things that God's church should be built on—Christ Himself. If the buildings we worship in are empty of The Holy Spirit, we have wasted a lot of time, energy and money. Some people have been blinded by the builders of those kinds of churches and have given sacrificially to a lost cause. *(Psalms 127:1 Unless the Lord builds the house, its builders labor in vain.)*

What kind of church do you worship in? Is it just a beautiful building void of The Holy Spirit? It is not the building that we should worship; it is the Foundation of that building. If it is built on anything less than the foundation of Jesus Christ, you are in the wrong church.

# March 25

# A SPIRIT OF DIVISION

*(Ezra 3:11-13 With praise and thanksgiving they sang to the Lord; "He is good; his love to Israel endures forever." And all the people gave a great shout of praise to the Lord, because the foundation of the house of the Lord was laid. But many of the older priests and Levites and family heads, who had seen the former temple, wept aloud when they saw the foundation of this temple being laid, while many other shouted for joy)*

When the builders laid the foundation of the temple of the Lord, the Levites gave praise to God. Scripture tells us that the shouting was so loud that it was heard from far away. Can you just imagine what it must have sounded like? The young ones were shouting with joy but many of the older ones were weeping because they remembered days of old. Isn't that just the way it is today?

Some people do not like change. Especially we older people: We want things to stay just like they have always been; while the young people want change. They don't want things to stay the same forever. Music is a major reason trouble starts in a church. The young want more modern music, and the old want the old standard hymns. Shouldn't we, as a church reach out to them all? I think God would want us to feed every age. As long as the music honors and glorifies God, I see no reason why we should boycott any of it. I for one love the old hymns and they will always be my favorite. At the same time there are many of the praise songs I absolutely love. The words honor God and invite His Holy Spirit. The young should learn to like the old hymns and the old should learn to like the new music. After all we are all in the same family and we should love and respect each other. We certainly don't honor God when we squabble about such a small thing. We come to worship and to praise and honor God with our hearts, not to grieve Him with an ugly spirit of conflict about what kind of music we have. We should unite, not divide.

This devotional may not please everyone. There will be those young and old alike, who will take offense at what I am writing, but I must write what God puts on my heart and today it is this. I don't mean to offend anyone; I just want us to glorify God in ALL things.

# March 26

# BEARING FRUIT

*(John 15:5 I am the vine; you are the branches. If a man remains in me and I in him, he will bear much fruit; apart from me you can do nothing.)*

This is an amazing Scripture. It tells me that God is my source for all things. He gives me the nourishment that I need to be able to bear fruit, and not only for that reason; but I need Him to survive spiritually. I would be dead in my sin if not for His grace that grafted me in as His child.

I am very aware of the truth that I could never do anything without Him. He is the source of my very life. I am so in awe that God loved me so much that He gave His life for me, and made me in to a new person. A person that recognizes that it is only by His grace that I am who He says I am. I no longer have to feel like a failure. It is through His blood that I have been saved; and only by His grace alone, and not by anything that I have done to merit it. And because of His grace, I can do all things through Him, who nourishes me and gives me the strength.

I don't know about you, but I am so thankful that God is the one who nourishes me spiritually. There are a lot of good preachers and teachers, but Jesus is our life blood. He is the only one who can provide the nourishment we need to survive. It is only because He nourishes us that we can bear fruit. I love the picture of me being a branch on the tree that gave me eternal life, don't you?

# March 27

# INCOMPARABLE DELIGHT

*(Psalms 37:4 Delight yourself in the Lord and He will give you the desires of your heart.)*

The desires of my heart today are definitely not the same as the ones I had before I accepted Christ as my Savior. The desires then were all of the flesh. You know what I'm talking about— those things of the world that we think will make us happy. A nice home with beautiful furnishings, a nice car, pretty clothes, money to travel, etc. I would venture to guess that if you weren't/aren't a Christian you can identify with what I am talking about.

I have to confess that I had most everything I desired; but you know what? They did not make me happy. The reason they didn't was because my delight was not in the Lord. My desires totally changed when I gave my life to Christ. My delight was in Him and my desires became those things that were spiritual. I desired to learn more about Him and His will for my life. I discovered that my happiness and contentment was in Him. He began giving me those desires. He began to show me things that I could never see before. My life and desires were revolutionized. Today He leads me in the paths of righteousness for His name's sake. My delight is in Him day and night.

What are the desires of your heart? Do you delight in the things of the world? Or do you delight in the Lord? Perhaps you have everything that you could possibly want, but you are still not happy. I dare to say that you never will be unless your delight is in the Lord. The only way you can obtain that is through knowing Jesus as your personal Savior. It is only then that you will find true and lasting happiness. The delight you will find in Him is incomparable.

# March 28

# COMFORT IN PRAYER

*(Psalms 77: 1, 11, 12 I cried out to God for help; I cried out for God to hear me. When I was in distress I sought the Lord; at night I stretched out untiring hands and my soul refused to be comforted. I will remember the deeds of the Lord; yes, I will remember your miracles of long ago. I will meditate on all your works and consider all your mighty deeds.)*

I wonder how many of you have struggled with the fact that you have been praying for a long time for a certain person or circumstance to be changed; and yet they still remain the same. I would imagine that most of you will be able to identify with me. And if you can, I would guess that you, like me, have suffered from the same discouragement that I have. Is that not true? Do you ever wonder if God has heard your prayer and if so, is He ever going to answer it? I don't understand why God doesn't immediately answer our prayers, but I do know that He hears them and in His time and in His way He will answer them.

When we read God's word, and when we remember all of the deeds He has done; and all of the miracles He has performed in the past, how can we consider the thought that He will not answer our prayers? He is not an uncaring God. He is our God who loved us so much that He gave His only Son to die on the cross for our sins. With that kind of love, why would we think that He does not care enough to hear and answer our prayers?

When I consider all of God's marvelous ways, I am encouraged. When I consider God's promises to me, I am comforted. I will not be discouraged because God has not yet answered my prayers, because I am assured that In His time, He most assuredly will.

*(Philippians 4:6 Do not be anxious about anything, but in everything, by prayer and petition, with thanksgiving, present your requests to God. and the peace of God, which transcends all understanding, will guard your hearts and your minds in Christ Jesus.)*

Let's pray, believe, and wait with thanksgiving that God will answer our prayers.

## March 29

# LET YOUR PERSONALITY GLORIFY GOD

*(Psalm 139:14 I will praise you, for I am fearfully and wonderfully made; marvelous are your works and that my soul knows very well.)*

I have a six year old granddaughter that has probably the most loving personality that I have ever encountered. And she shares that love generously and profusely. Everybody that knows her sees her wonderful qualities and marvels at her loving and magnanimous way.

I recognize the importance of her always channeling that kind of love in the right direction. There are many people with her type of personality that can easily be taken advantage of as they get older. And I pray each day that she would always recognize where and to whom she would direct her love.

Thinking about it, I began to be aware of the fact that we are to use our lives to glorify God in all things. He has given us each a different personality. We have a great responsibility to channel them in the right direction. One can use their personality to their advantage, or they can use them to glorify God.

There are some people who are born leaders. They, above all, have the responsibility to lead in the ways of God. Yet how many leaders in this world use their charismatic personality to lead people down the wrong path.

Considering the fact that God has uniquely made us and has called us to do His work, I think we should certainly be doing the work that would glorify His name. It would be a terrible thing to misuse our personalities to mar the person that God designed us to be, don't you? *(1 Peter 4:11If anyone speaks, he should do it as one speaking the very words of God. If anyone serves, he should do it with the strength God provides so that in all things God may be praised through Jesus Christ. To him be the glory and the power for ever and ever. Amen)*

# March 30

# NURTURED BY GOD

*(1 Samuel 1:27-28 I prayed for this child and the Lord has granted me what I asked of him. so now I give him to the Lord. and he worshipped the Lord there.)*

I think we are all familiar with Hannah's story. She had been barren for many years, but she did not give up hope. She continued to pray that God would open her womb and give her a child. She promised God that if He would give her a child, she would give him back to the Lord for His service. God heard and answered her prayer, and Hannah stood true and firm on her promise to the Lord. As soon as Samuel was weaned, she took him to Eli to be nurtured in the ways of the Lord.

Now you mothers and grandmothers are probably like me—wondering how you could put your baby in the care of another. It would be an extremely difficult thing to do. But Hannah knew God and she trusted in Him. We know the rest of the story of what a Godly man Samuel became.

I think every Christian mother prays for her children. But at the same time we are reluctant to turn them completely over to the Lord. It is hard not to try to control the lives of our children. After all, we gave them birth— surely we have the right to be in control— right? No, that is not right. Our children have minds of their own and we have no control over them once they are grown. They make their own decisions. Only God can help them make the right ones. We have to let go and let God take control.

We must learn that God is the only one who can show them the way. We can pray and we can encourage them to seek His way and His will, but we must surrender them to God. We must let them go. We can trust God. Hannah gave her son to God to nurture him, and we must do the same. Who knows what Godly men or women will come forth through the nourishment of the Lord?

# March 31

# A RESURRECTION VISION

*(Acts 4:1-2 The priests and the captain of the temple guard and the Sadducees came up to Peter and John while they were speaking to the people. They were greatly disturbed because the apostles were teaching the people and proclaiming in Jesus the resurrection of the dead.)*

The Sadducees rejected the belief in resurrection; so of course they were greatly disturbed. The world today is full of Sadducees, although that isn't their title. I can remember when I was a young girl learning the meaning of Sadducees: This is how I remembered 'Sadducees did not believe in the here-after so that was why they were 'sad-you-see'. Those who do not believe in the resurrection and Heaven are for certain the saddest people in the world. There is no hope for their future.

There are many people who do not believe that Jesus even existed. Some believe but have never accepted Him as their personal Savior. And some just simply don't care to hear about Him. Their minds are set on the things of this life with never a thought or concern about eternity.

I had the pleasure of attending a Women's Conference this past weekend. While there, a woman collapsed and was taken away from the building in an ambulance. I never found out whether it was a life or death matter. But I said to my friend who was with me. "If she died, what a way to go." How marvelous it would be to leave this world while singing praises to God—and be ushered into Heaven

The older I get the more anxious I become to be resurrected into the presence of Jesus. There is nothing to fear about death when we are people of God. As a matter of fact it will be a victorious time for the Christians. The struggles of this life will be over on our resurrection day.

Do you celebrate Easter with joy because of what it means to you personally? Are you ready for your resurrection? Do you know where you will spend eternity? Jesus paid the price for our sins when He was crucified—but death did not keep Him in the grave—He rose again and is in Heaven with the Father—and His people will also. What a wonderful future.

# April 1

# PRAY CONTINUALLY

*(1 Thessalonians 5:16-18 Be joyful always; pray continually; give thanks in all circumstances for this is God's will for you in Christ Jesus.)*

Do you ever wonder how in the world you can cover every prayer request that is given you? Or for that matter, do you ever wonder how you will ever make it through your own prayer requests? I must confess that I have been overwhelmed at times with everything that I need to pray for. There just does not seem to be an end to the things that we ought to pray about.

As I was pondering on this very thing this morning, God brought the above Scripture to my mind. God says to pray continually. How is that possible? If we took every thought that comes to our mind throughout the day and turned it into a prayer, wouldn't that be praying continually? What about that sandpaper person in our life that just seems to continually rub us the wrong way? Instead of getting angry, we could pray right on the spot that God would give us the grace to ignore the barb and ask Him to convict them of their abrasive way. And what about the things we say to others that might be hurtful. Do we quickly ask God to give us a sweet spirit before we open our mouths to speak? Do we spend our time worrying about the circumstances around us that we have no control over? Do we agonize over a financial issue, a marital problem, our job, our children, our world situation, or anything else? We could take that opportunity to give them to God the very moment that they enter our mind instead of carrying them around with us allowing them to rob us of our joy.

God says to give thanks in all circumstances for that is His will for those who are in Christ Jesus. God allows things to come in to our lives for a reason. So instead of asking "Why me God", perhaps we should give Him thanks for using all things to grow us in to who and what He wants us to be. We can trust Him in every circumstance and in all things. Satan wants to destroy our joy so he brings things to our mind through out the day to try and discourage us. When that happens let's pray that God will remind us that all things work together for our good because we are His people and give Him thanks.

There of course are those times that we need to go into our prayer closets and cry out to God. But I know I forget that I need to pray without ceasing. How about you?

Instead of trying to bring all of our prayers of thanksgiving and our prayers of petition to God in an hour of prayer, maybe we could remember to pray about everything that enters our mind at that particular minute. I like that idea, how about you? That way we would stay in a continual prayerful mode.

## April 2

# GUARD YOUR HEART

*(Proverbs 4:23 Above all else, guard your heart, for it is the wellspring of life.)*

Proverbs is full of wise sayings: And the above verse is probably one of the wisest. Whatever we harbor in our hearts will surely affect our everyday life. If we harbor any kind of evil, the evidence of that will show. Anger, perverse speech, un-forgiveness, slander, and any other kind of evil will be transparent. We will not be able to hide it. And the worse part of it all is, we will never have peace as long as we allow those things to take control of our heart.

There are many people who carry bitterness in their hearts, because they are unable to allow Christ to change their heart. They would rather wallow in their evil thoughts and self-pity, than to seek wisdom from God. Satan has a field day, when we allow our hearts to entertain this kind of evil. And unless we allow God to teach us His ways, unless we seek His wisdom and His peace, our hearts will never change.

On the other hand when we seek wisdom from God and keep our hearts pure of evil thoughts, surely the evidence will show. *(Philippians 4:8 Finally, brothers and sisters, whatever is true, whatever is noble, whatever is right, whatever is pure, whatever is lovely, whatever is admirable—if anything is excellent or praiseworthy—think about such things.)* If we continually think on good things, we will not have room for evil to take hold of our hearts.

# April 3

# TRUTH OR CONSEQUENCES

*(Proverbs 9:8 Do not rebuke a mocker or he will hate you; rebuke a wise man and he will love you.)*

There are many in this world today who are determined to go their own way—even when they know that they are making the wrong choices. They have loved ones who have tried to counsel them and counselors who have tried to talk with them about their destructive choices. All of this is to no avail to those who will not listen. Many times they mock the ones who are trying to instruct them in the right way. They hate the wise advice that is given to them. They would rather listen to lies than the truth.

People can choose to do their own thing, ignoring the word of God with contempt. The world speaks louder to them because that is what they want to hear. They might get by with their mocking for a while: But their foolishness will eventually lead to destruction.

On the other hand, wise men and women embrace truth and wisdom. They seek the ways of the righteous. They love those who instruct them wisely. They seek wisdom because they know that it is through truth that they will find the right way to live.

It is frustrating to try and help those who will not listen to wisdom. The verse above says not to rebuke the mocker or he will hate you. That is a sad thing to ponder. But it is a fact that we cannot ignore. We have no influence over those who will not take wise advice. Verse 12 in this same chapter tells us that those who are wise will be rewarded, but the mocker will suffer alone.

It boils down to this: will we choose to embrace wisdom or does our desire to go our own way keep us ignorant of the ways of God. It is a choice we ourselves make. One leads to life and the other to destruction.

# April 4

# COMPLETE FAITH AND TRUST

*(Proverbs 3:5-6 Trust in the LORD with all your heart and lean not on your own understanding; in all your ways acknowledge him, and he will make your paths straight.)*

Most days I totally put my faith and trust in God. But I have a confession to make, there are times when in my human weakness, I do not understand why God allows things to happen. It is during those times when I take my eyes off of the Lord that all I can see is the negative aspect of a situation. That is when I start considering ways that I could change them. That is totally in opposition of what the above Scripture tells me. Can you identify?

If I were to write all of the Scriptures in God's word that tells us to trust in the Lord for all things, I would not have enough paper to claim them all. Our entire peace and happiness depends on how much faith we put in the Lord. We will never understand all things, but when we put our faith in God and acknowledge Him in all things, He will make our paths straight. We do not have to know the reason for everything, or how God will make our paths straight. All we have to do is to trust Him.

Are you like me? Are there days when you simply cannot see God working out the circumstances in your life? Well, let me tell you, He knows everything that is going on in your life and in my life. He knows all about our troubles, and He has the answer for all things. But if we do not acknowledge Him and put our faith and trust in Him, we will not find the help that He wants to give us. Our will gets in His way.

I am aware of the fact that Satan tries to destroy my peace and I become angry with myself for ever allowing him to tell me lies. It is very important that we see the truth; and the truth is found in the Word of God and His promises to us. We can trust in Him for all things. Let's claim that promise everyday so that the evil one will not take control for even one minute.

# April 5

# OPEN YOUR EYES

*(2 Kings 6:15-17 When the servant of the man of God got up and went out early the next morning, an army with horses and chariots had surrounded the city. "Oh no, my lord! What shall we do?" the servant asked. "Don't be afraid," the prophet answered. "Those who are with us are more than those who are with them." And Elisha prayed, "Open his eyes, LORD, so that he may see." Then the LORD opened the servant's eyes, and he looked and saw the hills full of horses and chariots of fire all around Elisha.)*

I love this passage of Scripture. When the servant to the man of God (Elisha) went out and discovered that they were surrounded by an army prepared to fight, he was terrified. He was greatly intimidated by what he saw. But Elisha assured him that there was more with them than the ones that were surrounding them. When God opened his eyes he saw what Elisha had already seen, help surrounding them.

Does this story sound familiar to you? Oh not the same circumstances, but the fear that threatens to overcome us because we cannot see the truth. When we pray that God will open our eyes, He will illuminate the truth through the Holy Spirit. I wonder how many of you have been in this kind of situation. I can tell you I have been there many times. In fact just recently I was concerned about a situation in my life, and fearful of the outcome. I prayed about it, and I was overwhelmed when God led me to the very Scripture that He knew I needed to read. He shed His light on it and I was overwhelmed with the peace and knowledge that He gave me.

We would walk in darkness always if it were not for the Spirit shedding His light on us. I believe that's why this world is in such fear of the unknown today. To contemplate the evil things that threaten to annihilate us is more than our finite minds can comprehend. But God enlightens the people that seek Him through His word; and they find peace. The truth is an illumination to the fact that we have nothing to fear. We are surrounded by the protection that He gives us. Nothing can harm us. No matter what happens in this life, we are assured of eternal life with Him.

## April 6

# OUR ETERNAL HOPE

*(Colossians 1:27 To them God has chosen to make known among the Gentiles the glorious riches of this mystery, which, is Christ in you, the hope of glory.)*

I was forty-two years old when I experienced the mystery that is mentioned in the above scripture—that being Christ in me—my hope of glory. What a difference that made in my life. Had it not been for God's grace and Jesus sacrifice, I would never be here writing about this today.

You can imagine my happiness the day my little seven year old granddaughter, Tahlia made the choice to give her heart to Jesus. I must admit that I prayed that she was old enough to realize what she was doing. She is ten now and I have watched her faith and love for the Lord increase daily. This ten year old prays for the salvation of others. I no longer wonder whether or not she was old enough to make the decision to follow Christ, because it is apparent.

It is by God's grace and Jesus sacred blood that we can have the hope of glory. The Holy Spirit seeks us out, but it is up to us to make the choice to follow Him. It does not matter how old we are, if we are sincerely seeking His love and grace, He will pardon our sins.

I pray that if you have never experienced salvation, that you will make that choice today. Without Jesus, there is no hope for your future.

# April 7

# PRIDE BEFORE THE FALL

*(2 Chronicles 26:16 But after Uzziah became powerful, his pride led to his downfall. He was unfaithful to the Lord his God, and entered the temple of the Lord to burn incense on the altar of incense.)*

The life of Uzziah is very disturbing. He was only sixteen years old when he became king and he reigned in Jerusalem for fifty two years. It is recorded that he was instructed by Zechariah in the fear of the Lord. As long as he sought the Lord, God gave him success in all that he did. One would think that he would never turn his back on God with a record like that. Unfortunately that is not the case. He became a very powerful king and as a result his pride took control and he became unfaithful to the Lord. That's why I say his life is very disturbing. Because of Uzziah's sin the Lord afflicted him with leprosy until the day he died.

We ask ourselves how someone like Uzziah can become so prideful that they start taking credit for themselves rather than giving all of the glory to the Father. I think there is a very loud warning to the people of God. We must realize that it is only through God's strength and power that we have success in all that we do. We have no right to take glory for that which God has done through us. It is by His grace and by His power that we can boast of anything that we have done. Will we leave this world praising God for the work that he has done? Or will we go out of this world with the sinful scars of taking glory for ourselves?

## April 8

# PROCEED WITH CAUTION

*(1 Corinthians 10:11-13 These things happened to them as examples and were written down as warnings for us, on whom the fulfillment of the ages has come. So, if you think you are standing firm, be careful that you don't fall! No temptation has seized you except what is common to man. And God is faithful; he will not let you be tempted beyond what you can bear. But when you are tempted, he will also provide a way out so that you can stand up under it.)*

Have you ever seen someone come up to a stoplight that has already turned to yellow but they speed right on through the light? I just witnessed that yesterday; and it happened to be a semi that did it, and the light turned red before he made it through. He could have killed himself or someone else because he did not heed the warning light. I would be less than honest if I said I have never done that. I wonder how many accidents have occurred because of this very thing. I would imagine that there have been lives lost as a result of this particular careless choice. Stop lights are there for a reason—Red means stop—Green means go—Yellow means to proceed with caution: It does not mean hurry up and beat the red light. We all have intelligence enough to know when we see a yellow light to be very careful. It is for our own protection.

I wonder how many of us have been warned to proceed with caution as we have journeyed through this life. I don't know about you, but there have been many times that in my heart I heard a warning to stop what I was thinking—what I was about to do—or what I was about to say. There are times when I have proceeded with caution and other times I have given way to my own will and sped right on through to a disastrous end. Why are we so foolish that we would not heed a warning to proceed with caution? We are all tempted at times, but God gives us warnings in our spirits. We have a choice to make at that point: We can race right on through the warning, or we can recognize that danger might be just ahead.

# April 9

# DON'T ACT LIKE SUPERMAN

*(1 Corinthians 2:1-5 And so it was with me, brothers and sisters. When I came to you, I did not come with eloquence or human wisdom as I proclaimed to you the testimony about God. For I resolved to know nothing while I was with you except Jesus Christ and him crucified. I came to you in weakness with great fear and trembling. My message and my preaching were not with wise and persuasive words, but with a demonstration of the Spirit's power, so that your faith might not rest on human wisdom, but on God's power.)*

I was listening to a woman who is a mentor and encourager to other women. She relayed a story about a woman (I will call her Sue) that she had mentored for a couple of years. She said the first year Sue did not have much to say. But the second year she began to open up. It was very revealing to the one who had been her mentor. Sue told her that the first year her mentor seemed like Superman, and she was just not able to identify with her. But the second year she became like Clark Kent, and she began to see the work that God had done in her life. And she was able to connect and understand what she was saying.

The above Scripture addresses this very issue. If Christians, who are trying to mentor and encourage others, don't reveal the fact that we are who we are because of Jesus, people will not be able to identify with us. We must let those who we are trying to encourage know that we are only vessels used by God. It is only because of what He has done in our life that gives us the authority to encourage others. We are nothing without God and His grace. And we are not qualified to do anything outside of His grace. He is the one who calls us and He is the one who qualifies us. It is only by the Spirit's power that we are made strong enough to encourage others.

None of us are Superman or Superwoman; just like Paul, we should resolve to know nothing except Jesus Christ and Him crucified. It is through are weakness that He makes us strong. If we are acting like we have all of the answers, others will not be able to identify with us. If they see that we are just humans working through God's grace, that saved us and made us into the person that He wants us to be, they will be able to see that it is only because of Christ that we can encourage them. We should let them know that we do not have the answers to life's problems, but we know the One who does.

Are we Supermen or Superwomen? Absolutely not: We are weak in our human flesh. The Holy Spirit is the power in whom we get our strength.

## April 10

# ATTAINING YOUR GOAL

*(2 Corinthians 5:9-10 So we make it our goal to please him, whether we are at home in the body or away from it. For we must all appear before the judgment seat of Christ, so that each of us may receive what is due us for the things done while in the body, whether good or bad.)*

There was a book written entitled '100 Things To Do Before You Die.' The author talked about all of the things on this earth that were goals for him: Included among them were things like going to the Academy Awards, and experiencing the Running of the Bulls along with 98 other worldly things. The author of this book died at the age of 47 by hitting his head in a fall. It is told that he only accomplished half of his goals.

I find the story of this man so sad. I don't think that any of the things that he accomplished meant a thing. Nothing is said about accomplishing anything for the Lord, which leads me to think that he was not a Christian. We all have things that we would like to do and places that we would like to go in this life. There is nothing the matter with that unless it takes precedence over what we want to accomplish for God.

Our goals as Christians should be what God has called us to do. Any other goal will not count when our life is over. Only what is done for Christ will matter. We will stand before the judgment seat to receive what is due us, whether good or bad. I don't want to face the embarrassment when I stand before the judgment seat having to explain why I pursued only the things I desired on earth do you?

I love the Lord and my desire to hear from Him when I see Him face to face is, "Welcome home my good and faithful servant." *(1 Peter 1:8-9 Though you have not seen him, you love him; and even though you do not see him now, you believe in him and are filled with an inexpressible and glorious joy, for you are receiving the goal of your faith, the salvation of your souls.)*

My questions to you are these—what is your goal; what are your priorities; have you put your faith in Christ; do; you love Him; or are you interested only in pursuing your earthly desires? What will be important when your life is over? Will it matter if you have accomplished all of your earthly goals?

# April 11

# A DISCIPLE OF CHRIST

*(Matthew 4:18-20 As Jesus was walking beside the Sea of Galilee, he saw two brothers, Simon called Peter and his brother Andrew. They were casting a net into the lake, for they were fishermen, "Come, follow me," Jesus said, "and I will make you fishers of men." At once they left their nets and followed him.)*

When one considers those that Jesus chose to come along with Him as His disciples, you have to wonder why He chose such ordinary men. There were surely people more educated, and more capable of being His disciples. And the fact that they immediately left their nets to follow Him is amazing as well.

God knows exactly who to call to follow Him. And He knows who will be obedient to His call. It does not matter to Him whether or not you have a formal education; He wants people who love Him and those who are dedicated to follow Him, no matter where it might take them. Jesus taught them all that they needed to know to accomplish the things that He was calling them to do. They even performed miracles in His name. What an absolutely amazing thing.

I have often wondered why God has chosen me to write devotionals when I have had no formal education in writing, nor am I a bible scholar. But He teaches me daily as I read His word. He is the one who gives me the Scriptures, stories, and inspiration as to what to write and how to write it. I could certainly not do anything without Him. He is my teacher, and it is because of His call on my life, and His guidance and direction, that I am sitting here this morning writing this devotional.

I would guess that there are people who think I am audacious because I write without a formal education in that field. And they probably ask themselves why I feel qualified to write devotionals, when I have never been to seminary. I want to assure them that I could never write these on my own imagination. It is Christ who empowers me to do the things that He has called me to do. Just like His disciples, I am a plain uneducated ordinary woman who wants to follow where Jesus leads me simply because I love Him.

Do you feel like God is calling you out for a purpose? Are you hesitant because you do not feel qualified? Don't be; God will qualify you, He will educate you, He will teach you and He will empower you to complete the work that He has called you to do. He just wants you to be obedient to His call to be one of His disciples.

# April 12

# RESTORED YEARS

*(Joel 2:25-26 "I will repay you for the years the locusts have eaten—the great locust and the young locusts and the locust swarm—my great army that I sent among you. You will have plenty to eat, until you are full, and you will praise the name of the Lord your God, who has worked wonders for you; never again will my people be shamed.)*

The book of Joel describes the invasion of Judah by a plague of locusts that destroyed everything in its path and impoverished the people. Joel urged the people to turn to the Lord.

As I was preparing to give my testimony at a conference that's coming up, God reminded me of the Scripture above. I went to the book to refresh my memory; I was overwhelmed by how great our God is. His mercy never fails and His forgiveness never ends. This devotional is not about the situation that they were in at that time, or for that matter for the situation that our country is in today: It is about what God has done in my life.

The greatest regret in my life is the fact that I did not walk with the Lord for the first 42 years of my life. Satan is always there to remind me of my past failures. That is what was happening as I was working on my testimony. I began to once again anguish over the 42 years that I had not served God. But my God is far greater than the evil one. And it was His Spirit that gave me the comfort of the Scripture above. I recognize those former days as that of the locusts. They threatened to devour everything around me. But God pursued me and I repented of my sins.

He has given back to me those years that the locusts had eaten. He has given me food that has filled me up to overflowing. I am praising God for His love and forgiveness; and for His willingness to restore those wasted years to me. I cannot take back those years, but God has given me these last years of my life to praise His Holy Name. I have never in my life felt such aliveness and exuberance.

The evil thoughts that Satan brings to my mind in trying to discourage me will never be able to put me to shame, because God has promised me that He will not let that happen because of the wonders He has worked in my life.

# April 13

# THE FALACY OF FOOLS

*(Proverbs 17:12 Better to meet a bear robbed of her cubs than a fool in his folly.)*

I think everyone knows how vicious a bear can be when they feel threatened. . And none more so than a mother bear protecting her cubs. It would be absolutely foolish to go in pursuit of one. They would turn on you with a viciousness that one could never overcome. If they got a hold of you, they would tear you to pieces. Very few people have survived a vicious attack from a bear that is out to defend her cubs.

The Scripture above says that we would be better off facing such danger as being in the presence of a fool in his folly. There are so many people who become involved with those who do evil things. They do not see the danger of the relationship that they are entering, and most of the time they are caught up and trapped in the lifestyle of the fool.

One of the definitions of a fool is: someone who does not behave in an intelligent or sensible way. And folly is described in this way: a way of thinking or behaving that is stupid and careless, and likely to have bad results.

Have you ever done a study of a fool in the bible? If you haven't, you should. It is very enlightening: And definitely not at all flattering. In Proverbs 1:7 it says that fools despise wisdom; 12:23 the heart of fools blurts out folly; 13:19 fools detest turning from evil; 13:20 a companion of fools suffers harm; 14:9 fools mock making amends for sin. 14:24 the folly of fools yields folly.

I can remember that my mother would always chastise us if we referred to anyone who was a fool. At the time I could not understand why it disturbed her so much; now I totally understand why. When you consider the fact that fools mock making amends for sin: it is the ultimate insult to be called a fool, if you are a Christian. I sure don't want to be called a fool, do you?

## April 14

# PROTECT THE INNOCENT

*(Exodus 23:6 "Do not deny justice to your poor people in their lawsuits. Have nothing to do with a false charge and do not put an innocent or honest person to death, for I will not acquit the guilty.)*

There are so many different opinions about whether Christians should bring lawsuits against another. But in this passage of Scripture, it seems pretty clear that an innocent man has the right to defend himself. It also appears that we should have nothing to do with those who bring false charges against another.

If one is guilty of a charge, God says He will not acquit them. But the ones who are innocent of false charges should not be ridiculed and trampled under the feet of others. Some people stand in judgment and persecute the innocent just because they have been accused. Before we accept false charges as truth, we need to understand that God's word says that it is wrong. He even says that we should not deny them the right to defend themselves.

If we see one of God's people being falsely accused, let's stand up for them. Let's pray that they would be exonerated and that they would be reinstated to their rightful place. Praise God that He is our defender. Let's stand with Him to protect the innocent.

## April 15

# RESISTING TEMPTATION

*(Hebrews 4:14-16 Therefore, since we have a great high priest who has gone through the heavens, Jesus the Son of God, let us hold firmly to the faith we profess. For we do not have a high priest who is unable to sympathize with our weaknesses, but we have one who has been tempted in every way, just as we are—yet was without sin. Let us then approach the throne of grace with confidence so that we may receive mercy and find grace to help us in our time of need.)*

In Matthew 4 we read that Jesus was led into the desert by the Holy Spirit to be tempted by the devil. Isn't that an astounding thing to think about? Why in the world would The Holy Spirit lead Jesus into such a situation? The answer is—He did it for us. Jesus came to earth in the flesh so that He could experience the same earthly things that we do. He was tempted just like we are, yet he did not sin. As a result, He can identify with the temptations that we are faced with.

Every one of us has faced temptations in one way or another, sometimes on a daily basis. We do not have to give in to the temptation. Every time Satan tempted Jesus, He would respond with quoting Scripture. We can do the same thing. When we are tempted in any situation, we can look to the Scriptures. What does it say about the situation? There is an answer for all things in God's Word. Check it out before you make any decision that may lead you in to sin. The Holy Spirit will empower us to resist temptation.*(No temptation has seized you except what is common to man. And God is faithful; he will not let you be tempted beyond what you can bear. But when you are tempted, he will also provide a way out so that you can stand up under it. 1 Corinthians 10:13)*

Don't give in to temptation. It is not the temptation to sin that matters; it is the choice you make. We have the power in the name of Jesus to resist any temptation that we may confront.

## April 16

# QUALIFYING THE UNQUALIFIED

*(Jeremiah 1:6-7 "Ah, Sovereign Lord, "I said, "I do not know how to speak; I am only a child." But the Lord said to me, "Do not say, 'I am only a child.' You must go to everyone I send you to and say whatever I command you. ")*

Wow! I can certainly identify with Jeremiah in this verse. For some reason God has called me to speak. Of all the people in the entire world, I feel the less qualified for this commission. You are hearing from a woman who is fearful of being up in front of people to do anything—let alone speak to an audience. Yet this is what God is calling me to do. Once again, God has asked me to do something that I could never do on my own. But I have learned that God's grace will see me through. *(And God is able to make all grace abound to you, so that in all things at all times having all that you need; you will abound in every good work. 2 Corinthians 9:8)*

Have you ever been in that position before? Not speaking necessarily, but going out to accomplish what God has called you to do when you feel that you are incapable of doing what He has asked? Do you ever wonder why He chose you instead of someone who is much more qualified? I sure have. Do you think it just might be that He wants the ones who are not qualified, to show His grace and greatness? I don't know about you, but I can do absolutely nothing without Him. But He assures me that I can do all things through Him, because His grace is sufficient.

I am always fearful of what I am going to say. I have no words of my own to speak but here again in this marvelous book of Jeremiah, He stills my uneasiness; *(Then the Lord reached out his hand and touched my mouth and said to me, "Now, I have put my words in your mouth. Jeremiah 1:9).*

## April 17

# THE CONSEQUENCE OF REJECTION

*(Jeremiah 2:27 They say to wood, 'You are my father,' and to stone, 'You gave me birth.' They have turned their backs to me and not their faces; yet when they are in trouble, they say 'Come and save us!')*

Don't you think that the Israelites should have learned something by now? How many times had God rescued them from their troubles? They would honor and worship God for a while and then they would turn and follow worthless idols. The Lord speaks through Jeremiah reminding the people of how He had always rescued them and yet they would turn their backs on Him.

Does this sound familiar to you? There are those today that seek God only when they are in deep trouble and need His help. They don't consider Him any other time. When things are going well, they pursue their own 'gods', not giving God a thought. And the minute they find themselves in a position beyond their control, they immediately turn to God and ask Him to come and save them. Jeremiah reminds them that it was because of their apostasy that their troubles have assailed them. The same message applies today. If we reject God, we are bound to have troubles.

When you see the things that are going on today in our world, and pointedly in our own country, don't you wonder how long it will be before God says, "Enough is enough". I sure do, it is a puzzle to me how God can be so patient. God's grace goes far and beyond any human mind can comprehend.

# April 18

# REPENT AGAIN

*(Jeremiah 3:12 Go, proclaim this message toward the north: "Return, faithless Israel," declared the Lord, 'I will not be angry forever. Only acknowledge your guilt—you have rebelled against the Lord your God, you have scattered your favors to foreign gods under every spreading tree, and have not obeyed me,'" declares the Lord.)*

The love and grace of God is amazing. Even after the Israelites had once again rebelled against God and gone after other gods, He was willing to forgive them if they would repent of their sins.

Does that not speak volumes to you? It sure does to me. Instead of God telling us that we have stumbled once again, so He is through with us; he tells us that if we repent of our sins, He will forgive us and bring us back into fellowship with Him. Take notice that He tells us to acknowledge our guilt. How can we establish fellowship with God if we have sinned and we are not willing to admit it and ask Him for forgiveness? All He asks of us is to come to Him and acknowledge our guilt.

We cannot hide our sins from God. He knows everything we think, say and do. I think He grieves when we turn our backs on him to follow in the paths of the unrighteous. We are held captive when we are trapped in our sins. But we do not have to stay in that place. He wants to bring us back to the place where He wants us.

Nothing can take the place of sweet fellowship with our Lord. We all stumble at times, but God is willing and able to restore us back to the relationship that we once had with Him. What an amazing God we serve. No other love can compare to His love for us.

# April 19

# GOOGLELING WISDOM

*(Jeremiah 9:23-24 This is what the Lord says: "Let not the wise man boast of his wisdom or the strong man boast of his strength or the rich man boast of his riches, but let him who boasts boast about this: that he understands and knows me, that I am the Lord, who exercises kindness, justice and righteousness on earth, for in these I delight," declares the Lord.)*

There is a lot of information to be had from the Google bar on one's computer. Just about anything you want to know about a subject or a person can be found there. There is much wisdom to be gained through some of the things that we read from Google. But one must be very careful about taking what we read as the gospel truth.

Sometimes we can be impressed by those who are wise, strong, or rich. But will what they have to offer help us to secure our future; No, of course not. They may boast about what they have accomplished in this life, but at the end of their time on this earth, it will make no difference at all. If they have put their trust in their own accomplishments instead of seeking God and His wisdom, they will be lost.

If we do not acknowledge the fact that God is Lord of all, who we are and what we have done in this life will be for naught. What kinds of things do you Google? Are you looking to find the things that you think will help you in this life? Or are you looking for things that will count when you leave this world. You may be wise, you may be strong, and you may be rich, but God does not delight in those things. He delights in the one who understands who He is and what He is all about.

When we know Christ, we can boast in Him and all that He has done for us. But we can never boast about whom we are and what we have accomplished in this life on our own—for it will mean nothing when we leave this world.

If you want to find wisdom, Google 'the bible', or better yet pick it up and read it. It is the only resource that will point us to the cross. And Christ is the only way to eternal life. When we know Him as our personal Savior, we have found the wisdom that pleases Him.

# April 20

# BEWARE OF FALSE WITNESS

*(Proverbs 19:5 A false witness will not go unpunished, and he who pours out lies will not go free.)*

I just finished reading the story of a man that had served 25 years in prison for the murder of his wife. As it turned out, through DNA evidence that was found on a bandana last year, it was revealed that it had blood and hair from his wife but none of his. DNA evidence was not used at the time. Since then DNA from that same bandana was matched to a man who is now serving time in prison for another crime.

When they interviewed this innocent man and his family, they all said that they had prayed for the past 25 years that he would be exonerated. He had proclaimed his innocence all along. The only witness to the murder was their then, 3 year old son. The little boy had described the murder but because of his age, they did not consider his credibility. He had said that his father was not there.

I cannot imagine the anguish that this man has gone through for these wasted years. He has missed precious time with his son: And the hurt that he must have felt knowing that others believed the lie that he had murdered his wife, who he had loved with a passion, must have been unthinkable.

The man who is guilty of the murder has robbed 25 years of the life of this innocent man. By not coming forward and admitting his guilt he has, in a sense lied. He will suffer the consequences of his lies. Unfortunately it will not restore the lost years of the innocent man. But I believe that because of the innocent man's faith in God, those years somehow will be restored to him through the happiness of the years that are ahead. *(Joel 2:25 "I will repay you for the years the locusts have eaten—the great locust and the young locust, the other locusts and the locust swarm—my great army that I sent among you.)*

# April 21

# SAFE IN THE ARMS OF LOVE

*(Psalm 4:8 I will lie down and sleep in peace, for you alone, O Lord, make me dwell in safety.)*

As I was sitting in a restaurant the other day waiting for a friend, I happened to see a mother sitting holding a sleeping baby in her arms. I was mesmerized by the beautiful scene as I watched his mother bestowing kisses on his little head. He was so content in her arms that he wasn't even aware of the noise and chaos around him. Her love for him was visually evident; as was his trust in her. It absolutely blessed my heart as I thought to myself that is a picture of true love. That little child was allowing his mother to comfort him even in sleep. He felt completely safe in her arms.

I have been thinking about that tender scene ever since. I relate that to how God loves on us at all times: Even when we are unaware of it. There are times that we suffer anxiety and worry and can't seem to find rest, but God is there to comfort us through it all, just as a mother comforts her child. God even compares His comfort to that of a mother's. *(For this is what the Lord says: "I will extend peace to her like a river, and the wealth of nations like a flooding stream; you will nurse and be carried on her arm and dandled on her knees. As a mother comforts her child, so will I comfort you; and you will be comforted over Jerusalem. "Isaiah 66:12-13)*

Isn't it comforting to know that we can dwell in peace and safety in the arms of Jesus? Even in all of the chaotic times surrounding us. *(You will keep in perfect peace him whose mind is steadfast because he trusts in you. Isaiah 26:3)*

# April 22

# SEEKING GODLY COUNCIL

*(1 Kings 22:8 The king of Israel answered Jeshoshaphat, "There is still one man through whom we can inquire of the Lord, but I hate him because he never prophesies anything good about me, but always bad. He is Micaiah son of Imlah." The king should not say that Jehoshaphat replied.)*

When Ahab, the king of Israel was seeking advice from the prophets as to whether he should go to war against Ramoth Gilead or not, he was told by the false prophets to go ahead. But Jehoshaphat, king of Judah asked if there was not a prophet of the Lord that they could inquire of. The above Scripture was the response Ahab gave to Jehoshaphat.

Isn't that the way it is in so many cases today. When we are at war in our spirits about which way to turn in our life, we have a tendency to want to hear from the people who say what we want them to say. They aren't really looking for the truth because then they might have to do the thing that they don't want to do. They would rather take the advice from a false prophet as they would from those who walk with God and seek His wisdom. In fact most times they won't even talk to those who might reveal truth to them. Ahab said he hated Micaiah because he never said anything good about him. The translation there is that he never said anything that Ahab wanted to hear.

It is so frustrating when we see those around us choosing to go their own way, sometimes through the advice of others simply because they don't want to hear the truth. Wrong decisions can cost us everything: It ended up costing Ahab his life even though he had been warned about what would happen to him. It is a very dangerous thing to consult the wrong people about our future. Why don't people want to hear the truth? Because it might interfere with what they really want to do. Are you facing a crisis in your life today? Are you seeking Godly council, or are you listening to those who support your desire. Search for the truth because it is the only way that you will find God's will for your life.

# April 23

# A TRULY REPENTANT HEART

*(Romans 6:1-4 What shall we say, then? Shall we go on sinning so that grace may increase? By no means! We died to sin; how can we live in it any longer? Or don't you know that all of us who were baptized into Christ Jesus were baptized into his death? We were therefore buried with him through baptism into death in order that, just as Christ was raised from the dead through the glory of the Father, we too may live a new life.)*

Make no mistake about it, when we accept Christ as our Savior we are a new creation. Why then do we see those who claim to have received Christ and even gone through the ceremony of baptism; yet their way of life has not changed at all? They still live the same old way that they did before their so-called conversion.

*(For we know that our old self was crucified with him so that the body of sin might be done away with, that we should no longer be slaves to sin—because anyone who has died has been freed from sin. Romans 6:6-7)* As Christians, we should want to obey the word of God, we should want others to see the change that has occurred in our lives. The desire to sin should not linger in our hearts to the point of fruition. The evil one will continue to tempt us to sin, but God is much greater than him. He will give us the strength to turn away from the sin that prevailed in our lives before Christ. *(Romans 8:12-14 Therefore, brothers, we have an obligation—but it is not to sinful nature, to live according to it. For if you live according to the sinful nature you will die, but if by the Spirit you put to death the misdeeds of the body, you will live, because those who are led by the Spirit of God are sons of God.)*

If you have gone through the motions of salvation, but have not changed your old sinful ways that have you in bondage, may I suggest that perhaps you really did not accept the forgiveness that Jesus has offered you: If you do not have the desire to turn away from your sin, something is wrong. It is a serious question to ask yourself. God saves a repentant heart always, and along with His forgiveness, He gives us the desire to change our sinful ways. Do you really want to change? Have you honestly opened your heart to salvation? Pretending to be a

Christian will not be good enough, you must honestly and truly repent and accept what Jesus offers you—forgiveness and eternal life.

# April 24

# ENVY=JEALOUSY=DESTRUCTION

*(Galatians 5:19-21 The acts of the sinful nature are obvious: sexual immorality, impurity and debauchery; idolatry and witchcraft; hatred, discord, jealousy, fits of rage, selfish ambition, dissensions, factions and envy, drunkenness, orgies, and the like. I warn you, as I did before, that those who live like this will not inherit the kingdom of God.)*

Wow! The sins listed above are wrapped up in one package. Few of us have been involved in most of them, but what about envy and jealousy? This is truly something to think about.

I have seen so many friendships end as a result of envy and jealousy. Some people become so jealous of others that they resort to lies that lead to the destruction of another's reputation. Or they are so eaten up with envy and jealousy that they cannot enjoy the friendship that is offered to them. Why do we allow envy and jealousy to invade our spirits? Could it be that we are insecure in our own skin? Or is it because we have not found our identity in Christ? If we are secure in Him, we will let go of the envy and jealousy that we harbor in our hearts.

Many marriages are destroyed by unmerited jealousy. We cannot let jealousy take hold in our hearts. It will eat away at us until it destroys the peace that God has for us. Make no mistake about it, if we are so insecure that we must tear others down, and ruin marriages and relationships, it is because we have a spiritual problem.

I believe we have all been envious at some time in our life, but as children of God we must overcome that destructive sin.

*(Galatians 5:22-23 But the fruit of the Spirit is love, joy, peace, patience kindness, goodness, faithfulness, gentleness and self-control. Against such things there is no law.)* Let's ask ourselves if we exhibit any of these fruits when we suffer from envy and jealousy. I personally don't think we can, do you?

## April 25

# WE ARE CALLED EVANGELISTS

*(Mark 16:15 He said to them, "Go into all the world and preach the good news to all creation.")*

Wow! I have just realized that I am an evangelist. I have always thought that an evangelist was one who has been formally educated in theology and had a degree. But suddenly I have seen the truth of who an evangelist is. The dictionary describes it this way—(a) someone who travels around trying to persuade people to become Christians. (b) Someone who is very enthusiastic about something and likes to tell other people how good it is.

The most exciting thing that has occurred to me is the fact that even though I am a simple, ordinary woman; and even though I don't have a degree, it does not keep me from evangelizing. When Jesus spoke the words above, He was speaking to His disciples, the men who chose to follow Him, ordinary men. Jesus taught them all they needed to know to evangelize. God has called each of us to go out into the world and evangelize. He equips us with all that we need. We must proclaim His love and mercy to the world so that they might obtain the hope of glory. We cannot save them, only Jesus Christ can do that; but God wants to use us as vessels to spread His word, and point others to His saving grace..

That is quite staggering, isn't it? It is a command and one that should be taken seriously. When something good happens to us concerning our life, we are always anxious to tell others. And what better thing than the treasure we have in knowing Christ as our personal Savior. We should be shouting that good news from the rooftops.

Let's remember that we are evangelists. And let's not miss the opportunity as we go out in the world, to proclaim Christ: For we are certainly those who are enthusiastic about Jesus; and if we are not, we certainly should be.

## April 26

# ARE YOU PLEASED WITH YOUR NAME?

*(Luke 1:3-4 Therefore, since I myself have carefully investigated everything from the beginning, it seemed good also to me to write an orderly account for you, most excellent Theophilus, so that you may know the certainty of the things you have been taught.)*

What is in a name? Names are something that our parents give to us when we are born. Sometimes we are not happy about the one that they have chosen. I wonder if Theophilus was pleased with his name. I probably would not have been. But when one considers what that name means, it changes the entire picture Theophilus is of Greek origin, and it means 'loved by God'. What a more wonderful name than that.

Little is known about Theophilus, but when Luke addresses him it is with great respect—most excellent Theophilus, which indicates to me that he was a great and powerful man. The Scripture leads me to think that Theophilus was questioning Luke about his opinion of Christ and His life. There had been several different accounts of Christ's life, but none any more clearly than Luke's. He goes into great detail about Christ and who He was, why He came, and what He accomplished through His life, death and resurrection.

Certainly it was the Holy Spirit that led Luke to write this wonderful gospel. But could it be that He used Theophilus to inspire Luke to write it? It could be, don't you think? I believe Theophilus had questions and Luke went to great lengths to find the truth and to write it down. It, of course has been passed down from that generation to this one and it will go on and on until the end of time.

The meaning of the name that was given Theophilus is proven I think. He was so loved by God that He wanted him to know the gospel truth about Him. Would Luke had written it otherwise? Maybe and maybe not—God has a purpose for everyone and this was one of His purposes for Luke. We never know who God might use to inspire us through the Holy Spirit. Luke said that he was writing it for his friend, but look how it has been used for all of us today. God certainly did love Theophilus and He loves us also. We have benefitted from the call on Luke to write this book.

No matter what our name is or what it means, if we call ourselves Christians, we must live up to that name if we want to honor God. We become new creations when we are born again. Christian is the most wonderful name of all because we are named after our Savior. And like Theophilus, we are loved by God.

# April 27

# A TRUE FRIEND

*(Proverbs 27:6 "Faithful are wounds of a friend.")*

How would you describe a friend? I think a friend is one who is loyal through good times and bad times; one who loves you unconditionally, one who will uphold you to those who wrongfully use you; one who is willing to tell you when you do or say something that is wrong. In other words; *(a friend who loves at all times.) Ref. Proverbs 17:17*

If you saw a friend start to cross the street in front of an oncoming vehicle, wouldn't you yell out a warning to them? Of course you would. It is the same when we see one of our friends doing something that will eventually harm them or someone else. And likewise, we should not be offended by a friend who would point out to us those things that would harm us or someone else. True friends are willing to take the risk of anger to save another from calamity.

I am not saying that we pick on everything that we think is a character flaw in a person. I don't think that's what this Scripture is saying. I believe it is speaking of spiritual matters. To help a friend out, we must be honest about sinful actions in the lives of our friends. We should lovingly speak to them about such things. Yes, we might take the risk of their anger, but if it will save them from disaster, it is worth the risk.

I truly believe that we have very few friends of this kind in our life. And if we have only one, we should treasure them above all others. If I have a friend who is willing to speak truth to me that will save me from making a huge mistake, I thank God for that person. If they are a true friend, their words may wound us, but their intention is to save us from harm. Friends help each other out. *(Proverbs 27:17 As iron sharpens iron so one person sharpens another.)*

# April 28

# SERVING IN LOVE

*(Romans 12:9-13 Love must be sincere. Hate what is evil; cling to what is good. Be devoted to one another in brotherly love. Honor one another above yourselves. Never be lacking in zeal, but keep your spiritual fervor, serving the Lord. Be joyful in hope, patient in affliction, faithful in prayer. Share with God's people who are in need. Practice hospitality.)*

There is a wonderful woman in our church named Martha. She serves the church well in the position that she has, but there is another part that she plays that people probably don't see. She loves and serves those around her who are in need. I rarely see her when she does not have an elderly person with her. I was in Wal-Mart yesterday, and there she was again: She had brought a woman who does not have a car to shop for her needs. The woman with her proudly told me that she was going home to prepare something to take to a meeting and that Martha was going to pick her up and take her. Martha fits the above Scripture perfectly. She is retired from her regular job, but believe me she is not retired from serving the Lord. I am blessed every time I run into Martha because I see her heart for the ministry she has in helping others. She is never too busy, too proud, or too tired to practice hospitality to those around her.

We could all take a lesson from Martha. God has instructed us to love and serve others. If we were as enthusiastic and dedicated as she is, it would be a much better world. Martha has found her purpose and she pursues it with a dedication that some never find. We are never too old, and we should never be too busy, too proud or too self-centered to ignore the needs around us. Let's be eager to serve others wherever and whenever needed.

# April 29

# THANKS TO GOD ALWAYS

*(1 Thessalonians 5:18 Be joyful always; pray continually' give thanks in all circumstances, for this is God's will for you in Christ Jesus.)*

Sometimes when I read this Scripture I say, 'Come on God, are you serious? How can I give thanks when there are so many things going on that are so worrisome; things that I have no control over; those things that are tearing my world apart?" Can you identify? Not only does the Scripture say to give thanks, but it also says to be joyful, and to pray continually.

How is all of this possible? It is possible only when we put our faith and trust in the Lord for all things. We can be joyful when we realize that God is on our side and that all things work together for our good when we are His people. We can give thanks because we know that no matter what the circumstances, God has allowed it in our lives for a reason. We don't have to know the reason; we just have to have faith in Him. *(Now faith is being sure of what we hope for, and certain of what we do not see. Hebrews 11:1)* We can pray continually knowing that God hears every word and that He will answer in His time and in His way.

So let's do as the Scripture says. We can do it because God is on our side. Let's praise the Lord and give Him thanks for the things we cannot see.

## April 30

# IT'S ALL ABOUT JESUS

*(John 14:6 Jesus answered, "I am the way and the truth and the life. No one comes to the Father except through me.)*

It makes me cringe when others say that every religion is ok because they are all trying to do the right thing. I am here to tell you that the only way to Heaven is through Jesus Christ. Religion has nothing to do with it. We might consider ourselves religious people, we might go to church every Sunday, we might pursue good things, and we might do good works. But the fact of the matter is, if we are not Christians (believers and followers of Christ) we will never spend eternity in the presence of God.

You may think this is rather harsh. But I am only quoting exactly what Jesus said. Sometimes it takes harsh words to penetrate the hearts of others. Jesus assured Philip that whoever has seen Jesus has seen the Father. We are never going to see Jesus through the lies and deception that so many religions teach. It is only through the Holy Spirit and His conviction in our hearts that we will find Jesus. And it is through our acceptance of Jesus that we see God.

I feel like Paul when he said, *(For I resolved to know nothing while I was with you except Jesus Christ and him crucified. 1 Corinthians 2:2)* Like Paul, I do not come with eloquence or superior wisdom. I come to you with the truth of who Jesus is and why He came to this earth. Christianity is the only religion that is based on a perfect man, that being Jesus, who gave His life for our iniquities; the only religion that will count at the end of our life on this earth. And don't let anyone convince you otherwise.

In what and in whom do you believe? If the answer is not Jesus, you are lost.

# May 1

## A COMPASSIONATE FATHER

*(Jeremiah 31:20 Is not Ephraim my dear son, the child in whom I delight? Though I often speak against him, I still remember him. Therefore my heart yearns for him; I have great compassion for him," declares the LORD.)*

We parents know the depth of the love that we have for our children. It breaks our heart when they turn against us. But all they have to do is to say they are sorry for the things they have done, and we are willing to accept their apologies and forgive them. There are times that their actions will temporarily ruin the relationship. But there is always hope that it will be restored.

God's love for us is never ending. Sometimes we hurt God with our rebellious ways, and sometimes He shows his anger and disappointment to us by putting us in exile, just as He did to Ephraim. Have there been times that you have displeased God? Have you felt the exile that your disobedience and rebellion has brought in to your life?

Matthew Henry's commentary says it this way: 'Ephraim (the ten tribes) is weeping for sin. He is angry at himself for his sin, and folly, and forwardness. He finds he cannot, by his own power, keep himself close with God, much less bring himself back when he is revolted. Therefore he prays, Turn thou me, and I shall be turned. His will was bowed to the will of God. When the teaching of God's Spirit went with the corrections of his providence, then the work was done. This is our comfort in affliction that the Lord thinks upon us. God has mercy in store, rich mercy, sure mercy, suitable mercy, for all who seek him in sincerity.'

As I read this Scripture this morning it really touched my heart. The knowledge that God is willing to accept our repentance, even after we have sinned against Him shows how much He loves us. There was a time, even after I became a Christian, when I was in exile just because of my rebellious ways, but God forgave me and brought me back into a closer relationship with Him that I had never had before: A relationship that I could never have imagined.

## May 2

# SHAPING OUR COUNTRY

*(Jeremiah 18:5-10 Then the word of the LORD came to me. He said, "Can I not do with you, Israel, as this potter does?" declares the LORD. "Like clay in the hand of the potter, so are you in my hand, Israel. If at any time I announce that a nation or kingdom is to be uprooted, torn down and destroyed, and if that nation I warned repents of its evil, then I will relent and not inflict on it the disaster I had planned. And if at another time I announce that a nation or kingdom is to be built up and planted, and if it does evil in my sight and does not obey me, then I will reconsider the good I had intended to do for it.)*

I have written devotionals on the potter and the clay before. In those particular ones I was referring to individuals who had gone astray but God had reshaped them into the people that He wanted them to be. This devotional however is entirely a different slant of what God's word has to say about the potter.

In the Scripture above He, through Jeremiah, is addressing the nation of Israel. The message is very clear—the way he shapes countries is dependent on their obedience to Him. His word is the same today for us.

For many years America was known as a Godly nation. But I wonder today if the world sees us in that light. The values in our country have changed drastically. We have allowed evil to slip into our midst until it threatens our reputation as a Godly nation. It makes one wonder if it is too late to do anything about it.

I do not believe it is too late. But just as it was true for Israel back when Jeremiah was warning them, it is also true for us. We can, through prayer and obedience to God, turn this thing around, to the point that God would remold us once again into a Christian nation. *(2 Chronicles 7:14 If my people, who are called by my name, will humble themselves and pray and seek my face and turn from their wicked ways, then I will hear from heaven, and I will forgive their sin and will heal their land.)*

America has been the recipient of the blessings God bestowed on us from the time it was founded, simply because He was in the center. But because of our disobedience and because we have turned our back on Him, I believe He is going to remove that blessing if indeed He hasn't already. God wants to bless this country once again, but He will not if we do not obey Him. We will eventually be destroyed if we pursue our rebellious ways.

## May 3

# DANGER IN THE PULPIT

*(Jeremiah 26:7-8 The priests, the prophets and all the people heard Jeremiah speak these words in the house of the LORD. But as soon as Jeremiah finished telling all the people everything the LORD had commanded him to say, the priests, the prophets and all the people seized him and said, "You must die!)*

Can you even imagine the anguish that Jeremiah must have felt when he was told that he must die for the things that he had been prophesying? Jeremiah spoke only those things that God told him to speak. Don't you think he had his times of questioning God about the fact that nobody seemed to listen?

Jeremiah was a prophet used by God to warn the people of the plight they would be facing because of their disobedience. As I read this book I cannot help but identify it with what is going on in our country today. One can see that what Jeremiah spoke in his day, is appropriate for us today.

There are some preachers who are brave enough to stand in the pulpit and preach the message that God gives them to preach. Yet, how many people really listen? I feel certain that those brave ministers think sometimes that they are preaching to the choir. Jeremiah is called the 'weeping prophet' because he wept over the fact that the people he preached to would not listen to the word of God. I wonder how many of God's preachers today also weep over those who will not listen to the truth. I would venture to say that most of them do.

There are those today in other countries who lose their lives because they preach the truth. We still live in a country where there is freedom to speak the word of God. But I wonder how long it will be until we will lose that freedom. Will there come a time when the lives of the ministers who preach the truth of God's word will be in jeopardy? There are many false priests and prophets out there today who are preaching lies to the people. Will they be the first ones to cry out against those men who are called by God?

The Scripture above leads me to believe that they were the ones who incited the people against Jeremiah.

Let's pray for the Jeremiahs of this world, those who speak God's word through the power of the Holy Spirit. The pulpit is a dangerous place for some of those who speak the truth, simply because it is not politically correct.

And the pulpit is a dangerous place for those who stand in it telling lies to the people. For one day God's wrath will consume those who misuse His word.

# May 4

# PENALTY OF LIES

*(Jeremiah 29:30-32 Then the word of the LORD came to Jeremiah: "Send this message to all the exiles: 'This is what the LORD says about Shemaiah the Nehelamite: Because Shemaiah has prophesied to you, even though I did not send him, and has persuaded you to trust in lies, this is what the LORD says: I will surely punish Shemaiah the Nehelamite and his descendants. He will have no one left among this people, nor will he see the good things I will do for my people, declares the LORD, because he has preached rebellion against me.'")*

Knowing that God and His word are as alive and active today as when Jeremiah was alive, this is quite a warning to those false prophets of today: And we certainly do have them. They are standing in the pulpits of many churches, spewing their lies; lies about God and His word. There are many that are privy to be on television where they have a large audience.

Shemaiah had disguised himself as a messenger of God and was giving the people false hope by the lies that he was telling them. And many people loved the lies that he told. It is the same today with some men and women who say they speak the word of God. No they don't, they speak what the people want to hear.

Jeremiah on the other hand was not popular with the people because He spoke the words that God wanted him to speak. He spoke the truth. We must be aware of the people we listen to. We must check them out in God's Word to see whether or not what they say is true. If it isn't, you had better run away from their false teaching as quickly as you can: For if you believe their lies, and not the truth, you will perish along with them.

I know it is not a popular thing to speak the truth of God's Word in this world today, and I thank God for those people who are willing to preach the truth. It is not a popular thing to proclaim that we are Christians in this world either, but we must stand up and tell others about God's saving grace, even though we may be hated for our stand.

## May 5

# NOTHING IS IMPOSSIBLE

*(Genesis 18:13-14 Then the Lord said to Abraham, 'Why did Sarah laugh and say, "Will I really have a child, now that I am old?" Is anything too hard for the Lord? I will return to you at the appointed time next year, and Sarah will have a son.")*

Sarah laughed at the thought of having a baby at her age. It was impossible—or so she thought. But as we know she did have the child that God promised Abraham. In all honesty, don't you imagine that if we were told that we would have a baby at Sarah's age, we too would laugh? It would seem to us that it would be impossible.

The fact of the matter is, there is nothing impossible with God. He performed miracles many times that we read about in the bible. He still performs miracles, some we don't even recognize or acknowledge. He makes people walk again who have been told that they would never be able to. He raises people up who have been told they have only a few weeks, months or years to live. And they live long lives. I could go on and on about miracles I have seen and read about; and I will guess that you could too. Yet we still doubt.

So many times we pray for something or someone thinking that what we are asking will never happen; that it is impossible. Just like Sarah we doubt that God will be able to do something that we deem impossible. We put God in a box when we doubt His Holy power. God is able to do all things, no matter how impossible we in our finite minds believe. We pray and then think that our prayers far exceed the power of God.

I will ask you the same *question* that God asked Abraham *"Is anything too hard for the Lord."* The answer is no—there is nothing to difficult for Him. If you doubt that God is unable to answer your prayer, think again and remember Sarah.

## May 6

# LED BY THE GOOD SHEPHERD

*(Psalm 23 The LORD is my shepherd; I shall not want.)* Everyone knows that a good shepherd leads his sheep to safe places; he sees that they are fed—not too much, and not too little. He sees that they have water to drink. He sees that they have everything they need.

*(He maketh me to lie down in green pastures: he leadeth me beside the still waters.)* The good shepherd sees that his sheep rest in the safest and best of places, and he leads them to calm waters, not raging ones.

*(He restoreth my soul: he leadeth me in the paths of righteousness for his name's sake.)* Our Shepherd restores our wounded hearts, and leads us back on the paths of righteousness for Jesus sake.

*(Yea, though I walk through the valley of the shadow of death, I will fear no evil: for thou art with me; thy rod and thy staff they comfort me.)* There may be times that we will walk in dangerous places, and there will come a time when our bodies will face death, but we have nothing to fear for the Holy Spirit is with us at all times to comfort us.

*(Thou preparest a table before me in the presence of mine enemies: thou anointest my head with oil; my cup runneth over.)* Even when evil people are around us, Our Shepherd feeds us in the midst of our enemies. He anoints us with His Spirit until our hearts are overflowing with joy that nothing can suppress.

*(Surely goodness and mercy shall follow me all the days of my life: and I will dwell in the house of the LORD for ever.)* God's mercy is great and His mercy will follow us until the end of time.

It appears that David wrote this psalm during his later years. He had been a shepherd in his younger years; and he knew the attributes and what it took to be a good shepherd. He recognized his Good Shepherd and how He had led him through every path into the righteousness of God. He was praising God through this psalm for leading him through every thing that he had experienced in his life.

This psalm is used probably more than any other passage of Scripture at funerals; and it gives us hope for eternity. But it is just as much for the living. What joy we have in the knowledge of being led daily in the paths of righteousness. If we allow Jesus to be our Shepherd, we will find rest and peace even on the rough paths.

## May 7

# PURITY BY CHOICE

*(Psalms 119:9-10 How can a young man keep his way pure? By living according to your word. I seek you with all my heart; do not let me stray from your commands.)*

We rarely hear about those young people who choose to walk with the Lord: Those who seek His word and ask for God's guidance, protection, and direction to keep His commands. Once in a while we will hear about one who has done something that has brought them worldly fame.

I have been blessed this week as I have observed young people in our church, from the age of 4 on up, show the knowledge that they have learned about God and His word. Two of them are my grand-daughters, and of course I am blessed to think that they are learning and hiding God's word in their heart. As I reflect on what God is doing in all of their young hearts, I consider the fact that God is preparing them to be who He wants them to be.

One young college student that I have been so impressed and blessed by; has set a goal to be a ball player aside to serve God where He has called him to serve. He ministers to other young people and encourages them to turn from their worldly ways to find the truth of God and His purpose for their life. This young man takes one day a month to pray for others. He will always email me to ask if there is anything that I would especially like him to pray for. It takes courage in this world today for young people to make the decision to follow Christ. But the benefits far outweigh the applause of the world.

Psalms 119:9-10 gives the formula of how a young man or woman can be pure in a world where the word purity is rarely used. If we see young people who are choosing to walk with the Lord, we should encourage them every time we get a chance. They will be a light to the world around them if they continue in their pursuit of God's will for their life. And that my friend is a true rarity and blessing.

# May 8

# IT'S UNBELIEVABLE

*(Jeremiah 33:3 Call to me and I will answer you and tell you great and unsearchable things you do not know.)*

This is one of my favorite verses: One of the first ones that really spoke to my heart as a new Christian. But it was years before I really experienced the fullness of the message: Mostly because, I had not totally surrendered everything to God. Like many others, I sometimes feel that this verse was written just for me. And of course it was, as well as all Christians.

In my wildest dreams I would never have imagined the things that God has shown me. I was so intimidated and felt so unqualified in most everything. And quite frankly, it was true. I was unqualified. I could never be doing the things that God has called me to do if it were not for God's grace.

I know that many of you can identify with me. It is only when we get serious about our purpose in life—it is only when we call out to God to reveal that purpose, and it is only when we surrender everything to Him, that He will show us these things. He does not force us to do anything. But He graciously guides us to the unsearchable things we do not know when we ask Him to.

I can tell you for a fact, that when God calls you and you respond to His call, you will find peace and happiness beyond anything you have ever known. I am not saying that you will not have any more struggles and problems in this world: As a matter of fact, you might just have more. But God provides us with the protection that we need, He will fight for us when we are totally dependent on Him. He has promised that He will never leave us unprotected.

Have you called out to God to show you those unsearchable things that you do not know? Don't be afraid, surrender all to God and go for it. God will not disappoint you. He will hear your call and He will answer it in ways that will be unbelievable to you.

# May 9

# PATIENTLY WAITING

*(Psalm 27:13-14 I am still confident of this: I will see the goodness of the Lord in the land of the living. Wait for the Lord; be strong and take heart and wait for the Lord.)*

I am not a patient person by nature. I am one of those people who want things done now. And as we all know that rarely happens; especially if they are things that are totally out of our control. Although I have many faults, this is probably one of the biggest. So this verse is a real challenge for me. Can you identify?

It is not easy to wait for our prayers to be answered. But I know that God's timing is perfect and I also know that He hears and answers our prayers, unless of course my will or others get in the way. So I can rest assured, even in my anxious heart that my wait will not go on forever. This Scripture tells us that we can be confident that we will see the goodness of the Lord in the land of the living.

One commentary says that: 'The waiting place is where our faith is built up.' God will not keep us waiting forever. He knows our frustrations, and He will give us the patience to wait on Him when we put our faith and trust in Him. The knowledge of the fact that we will eventually see His goodness should be a comfort to us all.

We do not serve a God that turns His back on those who seek His face. We serve a God that hears our prayers and knows our anxious heart, and He assures us that we will see His goodness. What a wonderful thing to ponder. We should not be discouraged because we don't see things happening on our time frame. We just need to be patient and wait on the Lord. His way and His timing are perfect.

Are you anxious about something in your life? Have you sought the Lord? Then just wait patiently, with full confidence that you will see His goodness.

# May 10

# ASKING WITH BELIEF

*(Mark 9:23 "If you can" said Jesus. "Everything is possible for him who believes.")*

Sometimes there are trials and tribulations in our life that seem to be insurmountable: Things that are completely out of our control. Have you ever faced that kind of situation? If you haven't, you must be one of the very few. Most of us at some time or another have faced those kinds of trials. And most of us have tried to fix things that have gone wrong, but to no avail. There are some things that only by God's intervention can change.

In the above Scripture Jesus was speaking to a father whose son was possessed by an evil spirit. He brought him to Jesus and said, "If you can do anything, take pity on us and help us." And Jesus replied, "If I can? Everything is possible for him who believes."

Now we all know that this situation was definitely one that only Jesus could do anything about. It was truly an impossible situation for the boy's father to handle. When we deal with people, we absolutely have no control, especially if there is an evil spirit within them.

Many times parents are in anguish over their children who seem to be obsessed by sin in their life. They try their best to try to change them, but they are bound and determined to go their own way. There comes a time when they give up trying, and finally give their children to God.

That's what this father did. He sought Jesus out; he brought his son to Him; and when he finally told Jesus that he believed and to help him overcome his unbelief, Jesus healed his son. That 'if' became "I believe".

My mother prayed for me for years before I became a Christian. I know that she believed that one day I would accept Jesus as my Savior. We must pray for our children with assurance and belief that the Holy Spirit will penetrate their hearts and send the evil spirit that is in them fleeing. We need to get rid of that 'if' in our heart and have faith in the power of Jesus Name.

## May 11

# WALK BY FAITH

*(2 Corinthians 5:5 -7 Now it is God who has made us for this very purpose and has given us the Spirit as a deposit, guaranteeing what is to come. Therefore we are always confident and know that as long as we are at home in the body we are away from the Lord. We live by faith, not by sight.)*

I don't know if you remember the old song 'This World Is Not My Home' or not: But I sure do. And the words in it are so true if we are Christians; we are only passing through this time on earth. The home we live in now is temporary, but we can look forward to our eternal home. Our eternal home was purchased for us through the blood of Jesus. Just think of it, we have a home provided freely to us: A beautiful home that will make this one on earth pale in comparison.

We are not able to see our future eternal home, but we know it is there awaiting our arrival because God has promised it to us, and His promises are true. We live by faith in Christ that we are guaranteed that permanent home with Him. Wow! I don't know about you, but it certainly makes me anxious to think that I will one day be living in a home where I will live with my Heavenly Father.

What about you? Do you have the assurance that your home is ready for you in Heaven? What an exciting thought. Don't miss out on such a glorious hope. *(Colossians 1:27 To them God has chosen to make known among the Gentiles the glorious riches of the mystery, which is Christ in you, the hope of glory.)* Have you found the answer to that mystery? If you haven't, I would like to introduce you to Jesus—He is our hope of glory. He is the only way to our eternal home. He wants to prepare a home for you.

# May 12

# THE TEACHING MOTHER

*(Proverbs 31:1 The sayings of King Lemuel—an oracle his mother taught him.)*

I cannot tell you how many times I have read Proverbs 31. I am amazed that until yesterday, this 1st verse in chapter 31, had not registered with me. I was astounded by it. King Lemuel was writing about the things his mother had taught him. He obviously learned from the example that she set being this Godly woman. He knew, therefore, of what he was writing about. And God's grace inspired him to share it with the world.

Proverbs 31 is a wonderful pattern of what a Godly woman should be. I cannot read it without thinking about my wonderful Christian mother. From the time I could understand words, I was taught about Jesus. She not only taught me through words, but she taught me through being an example. It is very possible that I might not even be a Christian today if it were not for my Godly mother pointing the way to Jesus.

What a responsibility we have as mothers. When our children are youngsters, they spend more time with their mother than anyone else. It is then that we should teach them about Jesus. It is the opportunity that we should not miss. Their little minds absorb things like a sponge. As they grow older it is more difficult to teach them the things of God.

Those of you, who know me well, know that I was not serving the Lord at this crucial time in my children's lives, and it is my biggest regret. I cannot go back and change the mistakes I have made. I have to be satisfied with teaching them as much as I can now. The problem is, I lost the opportunity to do so when they were youngsters.

I don't know about you, but the most wonderful thing that could ever happen to me is if my children and my husband would rise up and call me blessed. Not because of anything I have done, but because they recognize that Jesus is my guiding force and guiding light. I am thankful that God has forgiven me of my sin. And I pray that I will not miss the opportunity to set a Godly example to my children and my grandchildren from this day until the day I die.

I encourage all of you mothers, no matter how old your children are, teach them what you have learned about Jesus and His amazing grace.

# May 13

# WOEFUL SIN

*(Isaiah 5:20 Woe to those who call evil good and good evil, who put darkness for light and light for darkness, who put bitter for sweet and sweet for bitter! ESV)*

As I read this passage of Scripture this morning, I could not help but identify it with what is going on in our country today. The things that we have been taught from God's word since the beginning of time, is now being trampled on. Evil has taken hold of many people's minds. Truth has been set aside in favor of lies.

Even many of those who have walked with the Lord for many years, have now decided that His word is not prevalent for today. So they are buying into Satan's lies. Those things that are abominations to the Lord are now being sanctioned by those who have been blinded by the evil one.

Some have lived in darkness their entire lives, and others have traded God's light for the darkness of evil. But there will be a day of reckoning for all. Those who think that they have seen a new modern light; a light that says everything is ok; will one day discover that their eyes have been blinded by the evil one of this world. Scripture says: "Woe to them".

# May 14

# THE LIVING WORD

*(1 Peter 1:23-25 For you have been born again, not of perishable seed, but of imperishable, through the living and enduring word of God. For "All men are like grass, and all their glory is like the flowers of the field; the grass withers and the flowers fall, but the word of the Lord stands forever.")*

We read in Jeremiah: 36; that God had told Jeremiah to write everything that He had told him concerning Israel, Judah, and all the other nations, from the time that God had been speaking to him. So he had Baruch write it in a scroll as he dictated all that God had told him. Since Jeremiah was restricted and could not go to the Lord's temple, he told Baruch to go and read it to all the people.

When King Jehoiakim was told about it, he demanded to see the scroll. As his secretary read three or four columns, the king would take them and throw them in the fire; that continued until the scroll was burned. The entire thing had been destroyed, or so the king thought.

But God told Jeremiah to take another scroll and write it again. Can you imagine having to reconstruct that much material? It would have been impossible to remember everything that he had written in that scroll if it were not for the power of the Holy Spirit.

People have tried over and over, in one way or another to try and destroy the word of God: But God's Word will never be destroyed. Not then and not now. His word is imperishable. *(John 1:1 In the beginning was the Word, and the Word was with God, and the Word was God.)* How then can anyone think that it could be destroyed?

His Word enlightens us and it teaches us. It is through His Word and by His grace that we are saved. Of course the evil one does not want God's word to be heard, so he tries to destroy it, but to no avail. *(Hebrews 4:12 For the word of God is living and active. Sharper than any double-edged sword, it penetrates even to dividing soul and spirit, joints and marrow; it judges the thoughts and attitudes of the heart.)* GOD'S WORD IS ALIVE.

## May 15

# UNANSWERED PRAYER

*(Jeremiah 7:16 "So do not pray for this people nor offer any plea or petition for them; do not plead with me for I will not listen to you.)*

I have been studying the book of Jeremiah for a while now. It can be a very confusing book; and I confess that there is much in it that I do not understand. But God's Word jumps out to me in certain areas and this certainly is one of them. In the time that I have spent in this story of the 'weeping prophet', I learned that God told Jeremiah three times (Jeremiah 7:16; 11:14; and 14:11 to cease praying for the people of Judah because he would not answer his prayer.

I think many of us believe that if we pray long enough and hard enough God will answer our prayers. Jeremiah loved the people of Judah and grieved about what was going to happen to them, and he tried to warn them. He constantly prayed that they would listen to him. God spoke to and through Jeremiah, and Jeremiah was obedient in every way to God. But no matter how close we are to the Lord and no matter how much we pray, there are times that our prayers are not answered. Not because of what we have or haven't done, but because of the wills of the people that we pray for.

There was a time that I fasted and prayed for someone's marriage to be saved. I was certain that God would answer my prayer, but I had not considered that each one of us has our own choices to make. That marriage broke up in spite of all of my prayers and fasting. God wanted that marriage to be spared even more than I did, but the couple did not listen to God or to my warnings to them. They went against the Word of God and disobeyed.

God does not make us robots, He allows us to choose our own way, even though His word warns us against making the wrong choice. That is why God told Jeremiah that He would not answer his prayer. The reason why is found in verses 12-15 (read it). The bottom line is this—God spoke to them but they did not listen.

Don't be discouraged because God does not always answer your prayer. It is not your fault. It is because of the disobedience of those who you are praying for.

# May 16

# EVIL STALKS

*(Proverbs 17:4 A wicked man listens to evil lips; a liar pays attention to a malicious tongue.)*

It was quite an exciting time last week as the world received the news that the man who was responsible for mass murder was killed. This man was full of hatred for innocent people. Not only was he full of hatred but he instilled that same hatred in thousands of people. These people who followed him are controlled by the same evil in their hearts, because they have bought into the lies of this evil man. He spent his lifetime teaching others to hate and to kill the innocent.

I believe that we are all aware and alert to the fact that just because one evil man was killed, it doesn't mean that evil attacks are going to end. We are not safe from the desires of the evil intent of these kinds of people. We must be on our guard as a nation, realizing that another attack on our country could come at any time. We need to be prepared to fight and defend our country.

We must be aware of the fact that all evil comes from Satan. He tries to destroy us with his evil attacks on our own personal lives. He is always roaming around trying to find the people he can attack; with the intent of destruction. *(1 Peter 5:8-9 Be self-controlled and alert, your enemy the devil prowls around like a roaring lion looking for someone to devour. Resist him, standing firm in the faith because you know that your brothers throughout the world are undergoing the same kind of sufferings.)*

We don't have any control of the evil in the world, but we do have control over the evil that attacks us personally. We don't have to listen to his lies; we don't have to fall in to his trap; we have the power to resist him through Christ. *(James 4:7 Submit yourselves, then to God. Resist the devil, and he will flee from you.)* Do you know the quickest way to cause Satan to flee, is to call the name of Jesus out loud? There is power in the name of Jesus and the evil one cannot stand against Him. God is far greater than the one trying to destroy. You will withstand every attack if you allow Jesus to fight your battles.

I urge you to stay alert and be ready because you can be assured that evil will knock at your door. Don't open it—call out to Jesus to fight for you.

## May 17

# CROUCHING SIN

*(Genesis 4:6-7 Then the Lord said to Cain, "Why are you angry? Why is your face downcast? If you do what is right, will you not be accepted? But if you do not do what is right, sin is crouching at your door; it desires to have you, but you must master it.")*

Wow! This is a Scripture that we all especially need to heed. When we are born again, we become new creations: The old has gone and the new has come. But that does not mean that Satan doesn't try to bring us back to the place and the person we used to be. He will work overtime to try and win us back—to try to enslave us again. We must continually keep our guard up so that we will not be enticed to sin once more. When we are tempted, we know it. We need to run as fast and as far away as we possibly can.

We know right from wrong; why then do we put ourselves in a position to be tempted to fall? If we have a weakness, we know what that weakness is. We must never allow ourselves to go near that temptation; we should immediately turn away and not allow the evil one to lead us back to a life of sin. That is what his mission is—to take back control of our lives and enslave us once again. He will try and tell us that we can handle the temptation—I have news for you, the only way that one can handle temptation, is to let God have control of our life. We will never be able to conquer it on our own. And when we intentionally allow ourselves to go where we know we will be tempted, we are giving Satan an open door to enter once again.

If you are struggling with a desire to go back to your old habits, your old ways, your old sins. Run to Jesus and ask Him to restore you to the place where He brought you to. Don't allow Satan to enslave you again.

# May 18

# FRUITS OF LABOR

*(Psalms 128:1-2 Blessed are all who fear the Lord, who walk in his ways. You will eat the fruit of your labor; blessings and prosperity will be yours.)*

Gone are the days when a man was the bread winner and the wife was the bread baker. Gone are the days when Christian parents (for the most part) took time for God: They made time to gather their family around and read God's Word and pray with one another. Gone are the days when they missed church only if weather or sickness was an excuse. Gone are the days when they put God as top priority in the family unit.

We live in a fast paced world today where other things have usurped God's position in the family. We are so caught up in outside activities that we don't have time left to worship. There are plays, games, trips, television, work, etc. that tire us and leave no energy left for the only thing that can give us peace and contentment. Many mothers are too busy to take the time to teach their children the ways of God. Many fathers are so busy working that they don't have time for their family: Busy, busy people laboring in one way or another to fill the time that should be given to the Lord.

We should not labor only for earthy food, but for spiritual food that will return the fruit of righteousness. What kind of fruit will your labor return? Will you gain money, power, and position to show off the fruits of your labor? Or will you walk in God's ways spending time in His presence that will lead to blessing and prosperity. Not monetary prosperity necessarily but prospering in the truth and knowledge of our Lord that leads to a fulfilling and successful life.

The things of this earth are temporary but the things of God are eternal. Which blessings to you want, those for today—or those that will last forever?

## May 19

# A ROYAL FAMILY

*(1 Peter 2:9 But you are a chosen people, a royal priesthood, a holy nation, a people belonging to God, that you may declare the praises of him who called you out of darkness into his wonderful light.)*

The world was astir as the Royal couple walked down the aisle to exchange their wedding vows a short time ago. I have no idea how many people were riveted to the occasion, including me. But I know it must have been millions. There is always such a fascination surrounding royalty. The lavishness of this particular wedding was extreme. Nothing was spared in the pursuit of having the best of everything. There were many crowding the streets just to get a glimpse of the royal couple.

Do you realize that we Christians are in The Royal family? We are sons and daughters of The King of Kings and the Lord of Lords. The world does not become excited about our royal position. They are not at all impressed, for they do not see material lavishness in the lives of most of God's children. What they do not know and see is the lavishness of His love for us: The enjoyment and honor of setting at His banquet table; the abundance of the royal food that we are privy to in His Word; the joy of seeing a commoner become a member of His Royal family: The wonderful fellowship of those that belong to Him. They do not know the joy of being a part of God's Kingdom. Absolutely nothing can compare to The Royal family of God.

I would not trade my position with that of any earthly royal family, would you? I am so looking forward to meeting my bridegroom face to face one day. Have you prepared yourself for that occasion? *(Matthew 25:30. "But while they were on their way to buy the oil, the bridegroom arrived. The virgins who were ready went in with him to the wedding banquet. And the door was shut.")* Don't miss the wedding banquet because you are unprepared.

# May 20

# THE OVERCOMERS

*(Philippians 4:13 I can do everything through him who gives me strength.)*

Before I knew Christ as my personal Savior, I had one of the most inferiority complexes in the world. It was even difficult for me to meet new people because I just knew that they would not like me and that they would find out how stupid I was. Satan held me in chains for years with that inferior feeling. If you have ever suffered from this terrible affliction, you will be able to identify with me. The moment I invited Christ in to my life I was a totally different person. He gave me confidence and a feeling of worth.

Satan cannot stand it when God takes control of our life. He tries his best to take back that control by bringing back our past inadequacies. And so there are times when he tries to attack and destroy my confidence once more. The other day was one of those days. I was to sing a solo at church, and before I sing, God usually puts something on my heart to say in preparation to the message in the song. The Scripture He gave me was one that I was very familiar with, but when I opened my mouth to quote it—half way through it my mind went blank. I could not think of one of the words. Now at one time I would have been destroyed to the point that I could not even have finished what I had set out to do; but I immediately felt God's hand of protection over me and my spirit was calmed. I was able to get through the song.

This story might not sound so amazing to you, but believe me, with my former insecurities, it was a miracle in my life. As I was thinking about it later, I thought about how Satan had tried to undermine me by saying, "See, I told you that you are not who you think you are. You are so inferior and people are going to see that." But guess what—because of Christ, I am an overcomer. I can withstand anything that the evil one brings in my path, because God fights my battles and He wins every time.

Are there things in your past that Satan tries to defeat you with? Well, take heart, knowing that through Christ you have won the battle. He will fight for you. He will not let you be defeated.

## May 21

# THE BEST LAID PLANS

*(Proverbs 16:3 Commit to the Lord whatever you do, and your plans will succeed.)*

From the time we are little we begin to have aspirations about our future. As children we have dreams about being like those who make an impression on our young minds. By the time we are in high school, we begin to start seriously thinking about our future education. Then in college there is usually a choice about what direction we will take; and we pursue that final plan for our future.

Once we get settled in our occupation, then we start making plans for the things that we want in life. The pursuit of material things so many times consumes our thoughts. Sometimes our aspirations become loftier than what the possibility of reality offers: And then what? Do we alter our plan, do we chuck the whole thing, or do we react the way God wants us to—by committing it to Him.

Many times our plans don't pan out the way that we would like them to. But God has a perfect plan for us. If only we would allow Him to carry out that plan. Sometimes the plans we make work out and other times they don't—but God's plan will always succeed.

We can get so caught up in our own plans that we crowd God out of the equation. We need to seek God first. *(Luke 12:31 But seek his kingdom and these things will be given to you as well.)* The problem with a lot of people is the fact that they don't put God first in their lives. Those plans that they have been making has taken first place rather than God.

What about you? Do you seek God's will for your life first? Or do you pursue your plan without consulting Him? You can be sure of one thing: If it is God's will your plan will succeed and if it isn't His will, believe me, you don't want it.

## May 22

# LISTENING TO GODLY WISDOM

(Jeremiah 42:1-2a Then all the army officers, including Johanan son of Kareah and Jezaniah son of Hoshaiah, and all the people from the least to the greatest approached Jeremiah the prophet and said to him, "Please hear our petition and pray to the Lord your God for this entire remnant.)

Jeremiah was a prophet and this remnant that was asking him to intercede on their behalf to God, told him that they would obey whatever God told them to do. And Jeremiah, as always, went to the Lord with their petition. But when he brought back to them the answer that God gave them, he was called a liar, (Ref. Jeremiah 43:2) and they disobeyed God and went to Egypt anyway; even after the warning that God had given them through Jeremiah that they would die by the sword, famine and plague if they disobeyed Him and went where they wanted to go: And the rest is history.

There are so many people who have gone their own way seeking things that they want: But when they get into trouble they go to Godly people assuring them that they have had enough, and that they want to change their disobedient ways. But when they hear from them what God's word says; they retreat back into their own way of life.

We are not any different than those men in Jeremiah's time. They constantly disobeyed what God's word had told them to do. But this time, they said that they would listen. And of course they didn't. If we reject the word of God, just as they were warned, we will perish.

It is in the word of God that we find truth and wisdom to live a life pleasing to God. It supplies everything we need to know how to live an abundant life. It is a dangerous thing to reject His word.

Maybe you have been living your life your way but feel like you want to change. You might want to consult a wise Godly person to pray for you and to give you good council. By all means go to them, but when they tell you what God's word says; don't reject it and turn back to where you were before. God listens to those intercessors who pray for you, but if you don't listen to their wise words, you will fall right back in to your disobedient ways, that will eventually destroy you.

# May 23

# WORK WITHOUT GROANING

*(Jeremiah 45:When Baruch son of Neriah wrote on a scroll the words Jeremiah the prophet dictated in the fourth year of Jehoiakim son of Josiah king of Judah, Jeremiah said this to Baruch: "This is what the Lord, the God of Israel, says to you, Baruch: You said, 'Woe to me! The Lord has added sorrow to my pain; I am worn out with groaning and find no rest.' The Lord said, 'Say this to him: "This is what the Lord says: "I will overthrow what I have built and uproot what I have planted, throughout the land. Should you then seek great things for yourself? Do not seek them. For I will bring disaster on all people, declares the Lord, but wherever you go I will let you escape with your life.")*

Baruch was a faithful servant and what we would call a secretary to Jeremiah. He wrote everything down that God spoke through Jeremiah. Suddenly instead of a message to the people; in this shortest chapter of this book, what God spoke through Jeremiah was directed solely to Baruch. Up until this point Baruch quietly and faithfully did his job. But now it seems he is doing a bit of complaining. Baruch *said "Woe to me! The Lord has added sorrow to my pain; I am worn out with groaning and find no rest."* Is that an 'ouch, that hurt' moment for you? It is for me.

I don't know about you, but there are times when I feel like the things I do are not making any difference at all. We should not dwell on how God will handle any situation. He will do what He will do, regardless of what we think He should or should not do. Our job is to continue the work that He has called us to do without doubt or complaint. We may have the idea that what we do is little and will make no difference at all. But I don't believe God sees anything as little. We must not seek great things for ourselves, but rather be content in the job that God has given us to do. Whatever He calls us to do, if we do it with faith and trust in Him, He will be pleased. We should not become weary and start complaining.

One commentary says "'Do not let us sit down supinely... and wait for God to do what He will never do. He brings things to a certain point and leaves men to do the rest. God works in His own way, and it is for us to find it out. Get into the groove of this, and God will work with us and prosper our endeavors, if it seems good to Him so to do. And an enlightened man will not wait till he can do a great thing. If a man waits till he can do a great thing, he will never do anything. Do the little things faithfully and these may grow to great. Things that are considered great are made up of many little's, and the man who scorns the little will never reach the great."

# May 24

# A DOWNCAST HEART

*(Psalm 42:11 Why are you downcast, O my soul? Why so disturbed within me? Put your hope in God, for I will yet praise him, my Savior and my God.)*

I love music and I love to sing. For years I would not sing solos because I was so afraid. But one day, I felt like the Holy Spirit was telling me to start singing solos and I finally worked up the courage to do just that. Now you must understand that I do not have the best voice in the world, but God gives me certain songs to sing because of the message that they bring.

On Mother's Day, I thought I was all geared up to sing a wonderful song. I felt confident that I could get through it without falling apart. Well guess what, I couldn't and when I finished, I was embarrassed and deflated. By the end of the day, I told myself that I would never sing another solo again.

Like David, my soul was downcast. But thank God, He is in the restoration business. I am so grateful that I have a Christian family that encourages me. It was because of their words of encouragement that I changed my mind. God does not give us a spirit of fear. That comes from the evil one. He will do anything and everything that he can to try to trip us up and destroy our confidence in whatever we are doing.

We must not allow Satan to cast a shadow on our Spirits. We are not perfect, nor will we ever be. God does not expect perfection from us: But He does expect us to be diligent and obedient in whatever He has called us to do. I will continue to sing as long as He wants me to, and as long as He gives me the songs to sing. I cannot be concerned about what others think about my imperfect voice or how I am performing. I do not want to be a performer—I want to spread the word of God through the message of the song.

## May 25

# PLANTED IN THE RIGHT PLACE

*(Psalm 1:2-3 But his delight is in the law of the Lord, and on his law he meditates day and night. He is like a tree planted by streams of water, which yields its fruit in season and whose leaf does not wither. Whatever he does prospers.)*

The reason I was inspired to write this devotional is because I have been amazed that I have been successful in growing a beautiful fern for the past 2 years. As I was wondering why, for the first time in my life, I have been successful with those ferns—God reminded me that it is because I had found the right spot for it to flourish.

I am not and never have been a gardener. My parents were and I have friends that are. They study about when, where and how to plant each particular item. And unless unforeseen circumstances happen beyond their control, their gardens will show the measure of their knowledge. Their gardens will be beautiful.

Our spiritual lives are the same. If we study the book that will tell us how and where God wants to plant us, we will flourish. But if we go out on our own, and try to plant ourselves in the wrong places, our efforts will die: we might survive but the beauty of the Lord will not show.

When we meditate on God's word, Scripture tells us that we are like a tree planted by streams of water. We are nourished and we will be fruitful in the proper season; whatever we do will prosper. What a picture, don't you think? It should encourage us to look into God's word and find the place where God wants to plant us.

# May 26

# ACKNOWLEDGING GREATNESS

*(Psalms 47:7 For God is the King of all the earth; sing to him a psalm of praise.)*

During Music Award ceremonies the other night, Carrie Underwood sang 'How Great Thou Art' to an audience that does not normally worship in music to the Lord. It was a full house of those who entertain the world with secular music. I did not personally see the show, but since then I have had emails with the song she sang on youtube.com.

It was totally amazing as I watched the audience and their reaction to that wonderful song. There is no doubt their hearts were moved. I sat there thinking how God's Holy Spirit can move even in those places that you would least expect. And when they gave a standing ovation, I felt like they were not applauding the singer as much as they were applauding the greatness of God. I saw many tears flowing down the cheeks of some that the cameras were on.

I thought about God's word that tells us one day every knee will bow and every tongue confess that Jesus Christ is Lord. I was encouraged to think that there must have been some in that enormous audience that had a life changing experience just because they understood How Great God is. I pray that as a result of that song being sung that people will allow the words to ring in their hearts and minds forever.

I believe that Carrie Underwood surely must be a Christian—She prefaced the song by saying, "I hope the floodgates are open, I don't know if I can get through this song." That intimates to me that she knows first hand how great God is. I thank God that He will send His Holy Spirit wherever and whenever He pleases. I believe with my heart that He used that particular singer in that particular moment to open the hearts of all to the reality of His greatness. Praise His Name.

# May 27

# GIFTED TEACHERS

*(1 Timothy 4:13-14a Until I come, devote yourself to the public reading of Scripture, to preaching and to teaching. Do not neglect your gift.)*

One day just before Easter, I happened to see my 9 year old granddaughter's spelling test lying on the dining table in their home. I picked it up to look at it and I was amazed. These were a few of the words the teacher had given them to learn: Resurrection, Betrayal, Calvary, Forgiveness, and Salvation. I was so blessed by them. I stood there in awe of the lesson that those children learned through that test. They not only learned to spell the words, they were taught the meaning; and I realized that she must have used them to focus on the entire Easter story.

My youngest granddaughter was in the Easter play performed on Chapel day. I was blown away—not just because of her performance—which of course her grandma was proud of—but because of the message of the story. I am quite emotional about the things of God—so when the play was over, Ellison, being the observant little girl that she is—walked over to me and said. "Grandma was you almost ready to cry." And I told her yes I was, because the play touched my heart.

How blessed I am to think that my grandchildren are being taught by Christian teachers who are free to sing the praises of God and to teach the children about Him. I wish that every child could have the advantage of being educated in the same way. I have seen first hand how my granddaughters have been taught not only the academic necessities, but also the Word of God. I have observed and heard of their love and respect for the teachers who have taught them thus far.

I am so thankful and blessed by the fact that we have a Christian school in our town. I am glad that we are still free to make the choice to send our children there. And I wonder how much longer we will have a choice. It is deplorable that we live in a world where there seemingly is no room for God. He is being kicked out of the public domain because some are offended by His Name. How sad that Our Lord and Our Savior is no longer wanted in the very world that He Created.

# May 28

# QUESTIONING IN TRUST

*(Psalm 13 How long, O Lord? Will you forget me forever? How long will you hide your face from me? How long must I wrestle with my thoughts and every day have sorrow in my heart? How long will my enemy triumph over me? Look on me and answer, O Lord my God. Give light to my eyes, or I will sleep in death; my enemy will say, "I have overcome him"; and my foes will rejoice when I fall. But I trusted in your unfailing love; my heart rejoices in your salvation. I will sing to the Lord, for he has been good to me.)*

When our children are little, it seems as if they are full of the why, when, where, how, and how long questions. God's children are the same way. We ask Him the same questions over and over again. Do you wonder if He gets weary of hearing them? I believe God has far more patience with us than we do our children.

I think this is a psalm that all of us can identify with; at least I certainly can: therefore it comforts my heart to know that David also suffered from pain that came as a result of someone else's actions against him. It is always an encouragement to know that others have come through pain victoriously as a result of God's loving care on their life.

Sometimes we ask God how long He will allow us to linger in our hurtful circumstances. Yet we know God and His attributes, so we can rest assured that He knows all about our situation and He will deliver us in due time.

After all, hasn't He always shown us His amazing grace? Yes, He has and He always will. Even in those times that we may feel temporarily defeated, we can be sure that He is walking right beside us, giving us the ability to persevere. We know and have the assurance that we can put our faith and confidence in His grace.

# May 29

# ETERNAL LIFE

*(Romans 6: 17-23 But thanks be to God that, though you used to be slaves to sin, you wholeheartedly obeyed the form of teaching to which you were entrusted. You have been set free from sin and have become slaves to righteousness. I put this in human terms because you are weak in your natural selves. Just as you used to offer the parts of your body in slavery to impurity and to ever-increasing wickedness, so now offer them in slavery to righteousness leading to holiness. When you were slaves to sin, you were free from the control of righteousness. What benefit did you reap at that time from the things you are now ashamed of? Those things result in death! But now that you have been set free from sin and have become slaves to God, the benefit you reap leads to holiness, and the result is eternal life. For the wages of sin is death, but the gift of God is eternal life in Christ Jesus our Lord.)*

Wow! In light of what we just read, why would we want to ignore the gift that Christ offered us when He gave His life blood that we might have eternal life explained in this passage of Scripture. It certainly seems like a no brainer to me. However, I must admit to you that I lived the first forty-two years of my life ignoring this marvelous gift. I was blinded to the truth of who God is; my picture of Him was certainly skewed.

I thought God was a stern God who would punish me if I did one wrong thing. I was so confused about Christianity in general that I decided that I wanted no part of it. I knew that I could never be perfect, so I was not going to even try. What a shame that I waited 42 years to realize that God is not what others say He is. He is who He says He is. God does not expect perfection from us. There is only one person who has ever been perfect or will ever be: His name is Jesus and He paid the price for our sins.

Don't listen to the lies of Satan that keep you from surrendering your heart to Jesus. Don't linger in the sins that will keep you from spending eternity in Heaven. When we give our hearts to Jesus, we become righteous; not because of anything we have done but because of His grace.

You will never know complete peace and happiness until you receive the gift of salvation. Nothing in this world can fill that desire. Take my word for it friend. I sought happiness in all of the wrong places, but none of it satisfied my soul. Oh I was not what you might call a hard core sinner, but God does not rate sin. What He wants from us is to recognize who Jesus is and why He came and to accept Him as our personal Savior. He forgets our past sins.

## May 30

# ONLY BY HIS GRACE

*(Romans 7:24-25 What a wretched man I am! Who will rescue me from this body that is subject to death? Thanks be to God, who delivers me through Jesus Christ our Lord!)*

Can you identify with what Paul is speaking about here? There are some people who think that if you sin at all you are not a Christian. I would certainly disagree with them. For if we depend on ourselves, we cannot live a life free from sin. Now just wait a minute if you take offense of what I say. Hang in there with me.

Do you ever lose your cool and say things that you should not say? Do you ever have a thought that does not honor God? Have you ever committed a sin of omission? Those of you who have not committed any of these sins; please reveal yourself because you must be the only person in the world who can say that.

None of us are perfect. The only perfect one that ever lived died on the cross for our sins and rose again so that we might have eternal life. We have a sinful nature and it raises its ugly head often. But God's grace will remind us of whom we are in him. If you are like me, you're attitude stinks sometimes, but God does not renounce us as His children. There are times when He must chastise us but He will not forsake us for our human frailties.

I do not believe Paul is talking about those sins that are blatantly contrary to what God says a Christian should be. If we are going our own way in everything we do, we must ask ourselves whether or not we are really a Christian, or did we just go through the motions.

Just like Paul, sometimes I do what I do not want to do. But the Spirit reminds me and sets my heart and my mind straight. We are not perfect because we are of the flesh but, God knows what is intentional and what comes from our human nature, and He forgives us our short comings. Only by His grace, He delivers us through Jesus Christ our Lord.

# May 31

# TAKE REFUGE AND BE BLESSED

*(Psalm 2:10-12 Therefore, you kings, be wise; be warned, you rulers of the earth. Serve the Lord with fear and rejoice with trembling. Kiss the Son, lest he be angry and you be destroyed in your way, for his wrath can flare up in a moment. Blessed are all who take refuge in him.)*

In light of what is happening in the world today, one can surely see that most of the kings and rulers of this world have either not read God's word, or they have and just don't care what it says. It seems to me that most of them make their own rules and do not consult the word of God whatsoever. But it is plain in this chapter what will happen to those who do not take His word to heart.

It is truly a sad thing to watch as our own country slides down the slippery slope of sin. What in the world can we do to stop the madness that is overtaking our county and our world? As Christians we are told to pray with a pure heart. And we must continue to do so. However, we certainly do not have control of others.

It seems as though things look rather bleak. But praise God, no matter what happens the scripture tells us that those who take refuge in God will be blessed. I don't know about you, but it takes the worry out of the equation for me. Of course I continue to pray that our country will turn back to the Christian values that our United States was founded on, but it gives me great comfort to know that no matter what happens I will be ok. I am hidden in the shelter of His arms.

Are you frightened of the future? You need not be, if you know who and where you are in Christ. If you belong to the family of God, if you have been washed in the blood of Jesus; you are one of the blessed. Hallelujah and Amen.

# June 1

# THE BEAUTY OF CREATION

*(Psalm 8:9 O LORD, our Lord, how majestic is your name in all the earth!) ESV*

My husband and I are both sky watchers. It is like looking at a new painting every minute. As one watches the clouds roll by, or just gazing into the beautiful cloudless blue sky, I realize that God has ordained the magnificence I see. I can remember as a child laying on my back looking up to see the clouds and imagining what I saw. It was one of my favorite pass times.

My husband and I were returning from a trip just the other evening, and we were marveling at the beauty of the sunset. And when I got home I had an email that was one of the most gorgeous pieces of time lapse photography that I had ever seen. It was showing God's creation in its pure unadulterated beauty of flowers, hummingbirds, bees and bats.

I have pondered much on these wonderful things that God created simply for our enjoyment. And I think of the Scripture *(When I look at your heavens, the work of your fingers, the moon and the stars, which you have set in place, what is man that you are mindful of him, and the son of man that you care for him? Psalm 8:3-4 ESV)*

How on earth can anyone deny that our beautiful world was created by God? There is nothing or no human who could conjure up such beauty. It is ludicrous to think that this all came in to being through happenstance. But the most dreadful thing is the fact that those who deny God and His wonderful ways will never enter heaven's door. As beautiful as God created this world, I cannot even imagine the beauty that we will see in heaven, can you? What a wonderful thing to look forward to.

# June 2

# MAGNIFICENT MIDWIVES

*(Exodus 1:15, 16, 17, 21 The king of Egypt said to the Hebrew midwives, whose names were Shiphrah and Puah, "When you help observe them on the delivery stool, if it is a boy, kill him; but if it is a girl, let her live." The midwives, however, feared God and did not do what the king of Egypt had told them to do; they let the boys live. And because the midwives feared God, he gave them families of their own.)*

Webster's dictionary describes a midwife as:
1: a person who assists women in childbirth
2: one that helps to produce or bring forth something

Can you imagine a king who would order the annihilation of all baby boys? It is appalling to think that someone would want to kill an innocent child—yet it happens every day all over the world. The only salvation for many of those babies who would otherwise be killed, are those who stand in the gap and fight for their lives. I am going to call them midwives. It might not be the midwife that the above Scripture talks about—but they are just like Shiphrah and Puah; they are standing in the gap for those babies whose lives are threatened.

I recently had the pleasure of walking in a fund raiser for Door of Hope: An organization that is dedicated to saving the lives of those unborn children. I thought about those people who have dedicated their time and energy to save those precious ones that others seek to kill. What a wonderful ministry! I truly believe that because of their efforts—many babies are going to be born, who would otherwise be killed. Who knows but what those children will be like Moses—leaders in the kingdom of God. Even if they won't be a Moses—God has a plan for each one of them. The audacity of those people who seek to murder the ones that God has created in the womb is deplorable.

God bless those who are standing in the gap for these threatened babies. They are truly magnificent midwives.

# June 3

# A TRUE FRIEND

*(1 John 1:6 If we claim to have fellowship with him yet walk in darkness, we lie and do not live by the truth.)*

While I was having breakfast in a hotel one morning, I overheard a conversation between two men. They were discussing the talents of an engraver and one of the men said, "He is the best in his field, I am not just saying that because he's my friend--in fact I don't even like him." Now wouldn't you say that is an oxymoron? How can you say someone is your friend but you don't like them? I immediately thought how terrible it was that someone would make a statement like that about a friend. Then I realized that the engraver might have been a friend of the man speaking, but the man speaking certainly was not a friend of the engraver, he just pretended he was.

How many times I wonder, have people called Jesus their friend but they really do not like him. They may even admit that He is Holy but they don't treat Him as their true friend because they don't really know Him as their Lord and Savior. If we will admit it, we were all guilty of that before we allowed Jesus to come in to our hearts. I think we can honestly say that we did not love Him because the conviction that He put in our hearts was something that we did not like and did not want to address.

*(John 15:14 You are my friends if you do what I command.)* Are you truly a friend of God--or do you just say that you are? Words are cheap if they aren't from the heart. Our declaration of being a friend is worth nothing if we don't like them.

# June 4

# PRAYING FOR PROTECTION

*(John 17:15 My prayer is not that you take them out of the world but that you protect them from the evil one.)*

The only way that one could live a life without trials and troubles would be to die. Jesus knew that and did not ask that we be taken out of this world, but that God would protect us from evil. He did not ask that we would not have trials, He knew that we would. It is through trials and tribulations that we grow in faith and trust. It is when we grow that we are able to carry out His plan for us—that is to tell the good news of Jesus. He knew that He would be going to HIs Father soon and was praying that we would be prepared for all things.

When we pray for our friends and loved ones, do we always pray for God's will? It is definitely a mistake not to do that. God knows the future for each one of us—and He is the only one who can protect us from having our own way. Sometimes we think because we don't see an answer to our prayer, God is saying no, or that He just isn't listening. But that is not the case. He hears everyone of our prayers, and He will answer in His time and in His way. Who knows what we could be protected from by not having our prayers answered right away? Can we be sure that we are not praying for something that God knows is not what would benefit us? Sometimes what seems like the perfect thing to pray for is the very thing that could harm us in some way.

When we pray let's pray as Jesus did—that we and those for whom we are praying will be protected from the evil one. Sometimes evil disguises itself as good—Only God knows. So let's put our faith and trust in Him when we pray. We can trust Him with the knowledge that He knows what's best.

# June 5

# AWESOME REST

*(Proverbs 19:23 The fear of the Lord leads to life. Then one rests content, untouched by trouble.)*

There are many versus in the bible that speaks of the fear of the Lord. This fear that is spoken of does not mean to be afraid of God: To the contrary, it means to be in awe of Him and His holiness: To reverence Him above all things. I believe that only those who have that personal relationship with Him can understand this fear. Every one of God's attributes is awesome. When we think about His omnipotence, His omniscience, and His omnipresence and His absolute Holiness, we cannot help but fear Him. It is that fear that leads us to eternal life.

We can rest contentedly in Him. It does not matter how many storms rage around us. It does not matter how many trials and troubles we have in this life—they cannot touch us. Our minister has said so many times that even if someone threatens to kill us, we have nothing to fear—in his words, "What can they do except to hurry our time to be with Christ, and what better place is there?"

What a wonderful realization. We can face anything that comes our way knowing that we will never be overcome. God is with us in and through every situation in our life. He is an awesome God. Even when we face fatal diseases, we do not have to fear: Because death was conquered through Christ's resurrection.

# June 6

# PERSEVERING THROUGH TRIALS

*(Genesis 41:51-52 Joseph named his firstborn Manasseh and said, "It is because God has made me forget all my trouble and all my father's household." The second son he named Ephraim and said, "It is because God has made me fruitful In the land of my suffering.")*

I just love the story of Joseph. The courage and determination that was Joseph's is such an encouragement for us today: An encouragement to keep on keeping on even through the severest trials.

Joseph was sold into slavery by his own brothers. He was purchased by Potipher, one of Pharaoh's officials and taken to Egypt. Potipher took him into his household, and was so impressed with him, that he promoted him to his attendant and was put in charge of his entire household. Potipher was more than jubilant as he saw how his household was being blessed under the management of Joseph— until the day that his wife made a false accusation about Joseph. Then Potipher burned with anger, and Joseph was thrown into prison.

Through all of the terrible things that happened to him, Joseph persevered in his faith. He did not even consider giving up when his own family betrayed him. In fact the Scripture said God caused him to forget them. He did not waver in his faith when he was thrown in prison for something that he was not guilty of. He persevered and was released from prison and Pharaoh put him in charge of the entire land of Egypt. God made him fruitful in the land of his suffering.

Do you get discouraged when others betray you? Do you want to give up when others falsely accuse you? So many Christians have the idea that they should never have to face adversity. Most people at some time in their life will suffer at the hands of others cruelty. But we can see from the life of Joseph that God used all of these things that happened to him and turned them around for good.

We are no different than Joseph, No matter what we go through, God is right beside us to deliver us to ultimate victory. Don't be discouraged, just keep on keeping on. God will deliver you.

# June 7

# THE GREEN EYED MONSTER

*(Genesis 37:17a-18 So Joseph went after his brothers and found them near Dothan. But they saw him in the distance, and before he reached them, they plotted to kill him.)*

If you are familiar with the story of Joseph, you know that his brothers were terribly jealous of him. So jealous in fact, if it had not been for one of them stepping in to save him, they would have killed him. That is a pretty extreme action as a result of a jealous nature.

Not many people would resort to murder because of their jealousy toward another. However, there is no pretty picture to paint when it comes to jealousy. It is one of those sins that can be covered up outwardly, but nurtured in one's spirit. It is like a disease that becomes so aggressive it can destroy the mind.

What makes a person jealous of another? In Joseph's case it was because his father was partial to him above the other siblings. Many family relationships have been destroyed because of that. Some people are jealous of others looks, possessions, talents, personalities, etc. But let's think about it—nobody should be jealous of another. God has made us each differently. So if we carry jealousy, it is an offense to God. Jealousy can be destructive to another if that jealousy is unchecked. But most of all it is destructive to the person who carries it in their heart. It wastes a lot of time and energy, and it certainly isn't something that God is pleased with. If we are Christians we should not be acting like worldly people who can be consumed with jealousy. *(1 Corinthians 3:3 You are still worldly. For since there is jealousy and quarreling among you, are you not worldly? Are you not acting like mere men?)*

Do you have a problem with jealousy? Let it go. Being jealous of another does not help you in any way. Be content with who you are—the person that God made you to be. So what if someone has something you don't have—you probably have something they don't have. Jealousy is a chain that Satan puts on people to cause all kinds of problems. Ask God to take away every jealous bone in your body.

# June 8

# SAY WHAT?

*(Deuteronomy 11:26-28a See, I am setting before you today a blessing and a curse--the blessing if you obey the commands of the Lord your God that I am giving you today; the curse if you disobey the commands of the Lord your God and turn from the way that I command you.)*

I wonder how many mothers could count the times that they have said to their children, "Because I said so". It was a phrase that dominated my speech when my children were growing up. It seemed as if they had to have an explanation of why they couldn't do this or that. Or they questioned one of my commands. I would try to explain to them that whatever command I gave them was for their own good. And by not obeying they could get in all kinds of trouble. When I finally realized that none of my explanations were satisfactory to them, I responded to their questions of why with, "Because I said so." Why can't children just obey their parents without question?

Why can't we as Christians obey The Lord without question? Because we are just like our children—we want an explanation as to why God is asking us to do something—and sometimes we ignore the warning not to take a wrong path. We should have learned from trying to teach our own children obedience; that everything God asks of us is for our own good. But unfortunately we don't view that as being the same with our Father. We sometimes demand answers instead of being obedient to God without question. And sometimes when we just ignore His command and rebel against Him—we get in to severe trouble.

God has our best interest at heart and He would never command us to do anything that would harm us. Just like we expect our children to be obedient to our commands without question, we should be obedient to Him just because He says so.

# June 9

# LISTENING AND UNDERSTANDING

*(Matthew 13:14-15 In them is fulfilled the prophecy of Isaiah:"You will be ever hearing but never understanding; you will be ever seeing but never perceiving. For this people's heart has become calloused; they hardly hear with their ears, and they have closed their eyes. Otherwise they might see with their eyes, hear with their ears, understand with their hearts and turn, and I would heal them.")*

Do you ever become frustrated when you try to explain God's Word to some people and they just don't seem to understand, or they simply don't want to hear what you have to say? I sure do, because I have been there and done that. There was a time when I was hearing but not understanding, because I didn't want to. I'm sure that those who were trying to make me understand would walk away with a sigh and a prayer in their heart that The Holy Spirit would lead me to the truth. God answered those prayers and I finally received Him and His Word in all of its fullness. When we see that those we talk to about spiritual things do not perceive what we are saying, we should pray that The Holy Spirit will enlighten them.

What is even more frustrating is hearing others who claim to know and understand the Scriptures so blatantly misquote it. How many times have you heard even ministers misconstrue God's word? I have often wondered how and where they get the messages that they come up with. Their understanding seems to be so different from my own. Oh there are times when we may have a different view of a certain passage; however I am talking about those who are mis-construing His word for their own purpose to either prove a point or to substantiate sin. It is good to be able to quote Scripture, but when we take it out of context it changes the entire meaning of the Scripture. We must see the whole picture to be able to discern what God is saying to us.

The above Scripture sheds light on why some discern what they are reading and others don't. Their heart's become calloused and they have closed their ears and eyes to the truth. Are we using God's Word to glorify Him? Do we listen to those who are misconstruing His Word;

we had better check it out ourselves and see if it is counterfeit. It is a bad thing to intentionally misuse God's Word.

# June 10

# LOOKING TO THE FUTURE

*(Isaiah 43:18-19 "Forget the former things; do not dwell on the past. See, I am doing a new thing: Now it springs up; do you not perceive it?)*

I have a dear friend who absolutely will not forget about her past sins. She thinks she has conquered it only to get caught in the trap again—that trap that Satan sets for those who will not or cannot believe that God has not only forgiven their sin, but does not even remember it anymore.

It is frustrating for those who know her and love her, to see her suffer in these chains that bind her. She doesn't seem to realize that the moment she received Jesus, she was freed from her chains. She will never be at peace if she doesn't once and for all tell Satan to leave and not return in the name of Jesus. I was listening to Dr. David Jeremiah this morning and he made a statement that was so inspiring. He said, "When the devil wants to tell you about your past, you tell him about his future."

If you are continually being reminded of your past sins, just remember that God doesn't remember your sin—and that those thoughts come from Satan. Tell him that he is not going to control your thoughts any more. Let him know that you have been washed clean by the blood of Jesus and that you are moving on to a future of hope and contentment.

# June 11

# SAVED FROM THE ENEMY

*(Psalm 18:16-19 He sent from on high, he took me; he drew me out of many waters. He rescued me from my strong enemy and from those who hated me, for they were too mighty for me. They confronted me in the day of my calamity, but the Lord was my support. He brought me out into a broad place; he rescued me, because he delighted in me.)*

There are so many people who are confronted by those who are led by an evil spirit, and some almost on a daily basis. David was one of them. This entire chapter in Psalm addresses his situation. David was hunted down like an animal by Saul. But David sought the Lord's help and He rescued him and He delivered him from his enemy: And all because God delighted in him.

I know many people today who suffer from those who want to hurt them in one way or another. But God will not let His people suffer forever. When we walk in the fullness of God, He will rescue us from all of our enemies. The first sentence of this wonderful chapter says—*I love you, O Lord, my strength.* Our love for God and His love for us is what set us apart from those who are controlled by the evil one, God is our strength, He is our rock, and he is our deliverer.

We can be assured that God will deliver us from our days of trouble. He loves us more than we can ever comprehend. He desires our devotion to Him, along with our faith and trust. Even on those days that our enemies try to destroy us in one way or another, He is there. He is aware of everything that is going on. Look up to Him; cry out to Him in your distress. He will rescue you.

# June 12

# A HUMBLE HEART

*(Psalm 25:8-10 Good and upright is the Lord; therefore he instructs sinners in the way. He leads the humble in what is right, and teaches the humble his way. All the paths of the Lord are steadfast love and faithfulness, for those who keep his covenant and his testimonies.)*

God is such a gracious God. It does not matter what sins we have committed in the past; when we humble ourselves before the Lord He will direct our path. Our lives are totally changed when we walk in the paths of righteousness. God covenants with us, when we confess our sins and determine to walk in His ways.

God's love is steadfast and sure for those who keep his covenant. God's word instructs us in how we should live our life. It is through our humbled hearts that we can be taught the ways of the Lord. Without that humbleness we cannot and will not be able to walk in the paths of righteousness. Our spirits must align with His, or we will be an obstinate people, not conforming to His way.

When we humble our hearts and confess our sins we are made new. God teaches us a new way to live our life. We should no longer live by worldly standards, but by God's. *(Do not be conformed to this world, but be transformed by the renewal of your mind, that by testing you may discern what is the will of God, what is good and acceptable and perfect. Romans 12:2)*

# June 13

# STRENGTH IN WEAKNESS

*(Exodus 4:10-12 Moses said to the Lord, "O Lord, I have never been eloquent, neither in the past nor since you have spoken to your servant. I am slow of speech and tongue." The Lord said to him, "Who gave man his mouth? Who makes him deaf or mute? Who gives him sight or makes him blind? Is it not I, the LORD". Now go; I will help you speak and will teach you what to say.")*

When the Lord told Moses that he wanted him to lead the Israelites out of Egypt, he argued with the Lord because he felt that he was lacking in areas that would not allow him to be successful in the challenge that God had presented him. He had a lot of 'what ifs'. Even after God showed him that he would give him the ability to do miraculous things, he was still doubtful that he could do it.

Have you ever been faced with a challenge from God? Has he ever asked you to do something that you feel you are unqualified to do? I have—several times. And if we tried to do it on our power we would surely fail. But God qualifies us himself. We can do all things through Christ. That is a promise from the Lord. *(2 Corinthians 12:9-10 But he said to me, "My grace is sufficient for you, for my power is made perfect in weakness." Therefore I will boast all the more gladly about my weaknesses, so that Christ's power may rest on me. That is why, for Christ's sake, I delight in weaknesses, in insults, in hardships, in persecutions, in difficulties. For when I am weak, then I am strong.)*

# June 14

# WORN OUT AND WEARY

*(Matthew 11:28-29 Come to me, all who labor and are heavy laden, and I will give you rest. Take my yoke upon you, and learn from me, for I am gentle and lowly in heart, and you will find rest for your souls.)*

I spend the majority of my time reading and writing. My days start very early and for some reason or another, I feel like I should be spending all of my time doing what God has called me to do; and if I don't, I feel guilty. Lately I have taken time to relax and do some of the things that do not require a lot of study—and yes, you guessed it—I feel guilty.

This morning as I began to pray that God would show me what to write in the way of a devotional, this is what He brought to my mind. God is not a task master; He is a loving shepherd who leads His flock in the paths of righteousness. He tells every one of us who labor and are heavy laden to take His yoke upon us and learn from Him. He is gentle and lowly in heart and we will find rest for our souls.

Sometimes we suffer burn out because we put such a heavy burden on ourselves. That is not God's way—He does not put on us so much that we become weary. Yoke, used as a verb means to join, couple, link, or unite. What a beautiful picture when we relate it to the verse above. When we unite with God, He will give us strength for each day. But when we push ourselves beyond what He desires of us, we are bound to wear ourselves out.

*(Mark 6:30-32"The apostles gathered around Jesus and reported to Him all they had done and taught. Then, because so many people were coming and going that they did not even have a chance to eat, He said to them, 'Come with Me by yourselves to a quiet place and get some rest.' So they went away by themselves in a boat to a solitary place".)* Jesus saw that they needed rest and He told them to go with Him to a quiet place for some rest.

Notice He says to go with Him to that quiet place. We won't find rest unless we rest in Jesus. It is in those quiet times when our spirits are refreshed that we can once again find the strength to carry on the job that God has called us to do.

# June 15

# BE PATIENT

*(Psalm 27:14 Wait for the Lord; be strong and take heart and wait for the Lord.)*

Do you ever get discouraged when things you have been praying for just never seem to change? I believe all of us could answer yes to that question. I read the following statement the other day that was written by some unknown person, and it made a tremendous amount of sense; 'When you are going through difficulty, and wonder where God is—Remember the teacher is always quiet during the test.'

There are times in our life that we wonder where God is and why He doesn't step in to stop the madness that is going on in our life and/ or in our world. If God answered our prayers as soon as we call on Him, would we learn to put our faith and trust in Him? James 1:2-3 says—(*Count it all joy, my brothers, when you meet trials of various kinds, for you know that the testing of your faith produces steadfastness.*)

We learn to live by faith and trust in God when we face trails that we know are out of our control. God may be quiet at times, but we can be sure that He has not forsaken us. We need to be still and know that He is God, as He tells us in Psalm 46:10. (*Isaiah 40:31 But they who wait for the Lord shall renew their strength; they shall mount up with wings like eagles; they shall run and not be weary; they shall walk and not faint.*) Our hope is in the Lord, He is not slow in answering our prayers—His timing is just different than what we think it should be.

# June 16

# DEFILING THE TEMPLE

*(Ezekiel 44:6, 7, 9 Say to the rebellious house of Israel, "This is what the Sovereign Lord says: Enough of your detestable practices, O house of Israel! In addition to all your other detestable practices, you brought foreigners uncircumcised in heart and flesh into my sanctuary, desecrating my temple while you offered me food, fat and blood, and you broke my covenant. This is what the Sovereign Lord says: No foreigner uncircumcised in heart and flesh is to enter my sanctuary, not even the foreigners who live among the Israelites.)*

One morning, I was watching a news station and there was a debate between two ministers. I was appalled by what I heard. One of the ministers was telling about how his church had invited the Muslims to utilize their church to worship in while their mosque was being built across the street. He used the Scripture that you should 'love your neighbor' as the reasoning behind it. What an absolute dangerous and destructive thing to take one Scripture and use it to sin. The other minister was saying that he thought it was wrong in a more diplomatic way than I would have. I wonder if this so called minister has ever read the above Scripture—or perhaps he is one of those who believe that the Old Testament does not apply to us today. God's Word is the instruction book for all Christians to live by—His entire word. I can't imagine a minister who is washed in the blood of Jesus to allow such a thing. I am absolutely enraged by this. What kind of an example does this set? It certainly does not honor our Lord and Savior.

Yes we are to love others and point them to the way of Christ but certainly not at the expense of desecrating our Sanctuaries. We must be sure that we are listening to the right people—those who preach the word in spirit and in truth.

# June 17

# A FORGIVING SPIRIT

*(Matthew 6:14-15 For if you forgive men when they sin against you, your heavenly Father will also forgive you. But if you do not forgive men their sins, your Father will not forgive your sins.)*

The Scripture above is a warning that comes directly from Jesus, and it is very explicit. There are no if, ands, or buts about it. Have you ever said or done anything in your life to someone that you wanted forgiveness for? I would venture to say that there is nobody who could say no to that question. We have all been there at one time or another. I wonder how many times people have asked someone for forgiveness while all the time they are harboring un-forgiveness toward another. Does that seem like the right thing to do? Jesus says if we don't forgive others, He won't forgive us. Does that work the same in our life? Should we refuse to forgive someone while they have an un-forgiving attitude toward another? And how can we truly forgive someone if they don't ask for it?

This is all something to think about and ponder over. According to God's Word, He will not forgive me if I don't forgive others. In that respect I believe my obligation is to forgive the person who has hurt me and it is up to them to make the choice as to whether or not to forgive others. I will forgive them for what they have done to me, but God will not forgive them if they don't do the same to others. We cannot harbor un-forgiveness in our heart toward anyone and expect God to forgive us—that is the bottom line.

Is there someone you are harboring un-forgiveness in your heart toward? Do you want God to forgive you? Then you must forgive others, you have no other choice if you want forgiveness from Jesus— these are not my words, but His. Many marriages and family relationships have been destroyed because of those involved holding grudges, hatred, and un-forgiveness in their heart. And I believe that those relationships will never be healed if everyone concerned is not willing to forgive.

# June 18

# THE DEFENDER

*(Zechariah 3:1-2 Then he showed me Joshua, the high priest standing before the angel of the LORD, and Satan standing at his right side to accuse him. The LORD said to Satan, "The LORD rebuke you, Satan! The LORD, who has chosen Jerusalem, rebuke you! Is not this man a burning stick snatched from the fire?")*

Have you ever noticed that as soon as you commit yourself to something the Lord has asked you to do, suddenly Satan is right there beside you trying to tear you down with his lies and discouragement? I think all of us can identify with the picture God gave to Zechariah. I know every time I surrender to obedience to God, the evil one shows up. But look at what the Scripture says—The Lord is right there rebuking him. He has rescued us from the burning fire into His safety and security. We are over comers when we have Christ as our Redeemer.

Isn't it wonderful to have the knowledge that we need not fear the one who tries to destroy us? As I read the Scripture this morning, I praised the Lord for the reminder that He gave me—the reminder that God will protect me from what Satan tries to rob from me. If he had his way, I would be reduced to helplessness. But God is greater than the one who is in the world trying to destroy me and you. What a wonderful picture this is. Just imagine!!! God is right beside us to rebuke Satan at all times. Let's remember when the evil one tries to tear down our defenses; he cannot win because God is there to protect us.

# June 19

# A GARMENT OF WHITE

*(Zechariah 3:3-4 Now Joshua was dressed in filthy clothes as he stood before the angel. The angel said to those who were standing before him, "Take off his filthy clothes." Then he said to Joshua, "See, I have taken away your sin, and I will put rich garments on you.")*

Don't ever fly on an airplane dressed in white. I did that once and unknowingly I sat in a seat where apparently the person who had sat before me had been eating chocolate. Not only was it on the seat, but it was also on the seat belt. When I went to the bathroom and looked in the mirror, I was horrified at what I saw; The entire front of my slacks was stained with chocolate. I quickly wet some towels and tried my best to wash the chocolate off; the more I tried the worse it got. I walked back to my seat with my arms held in front of me in hopes that nobody would notice, not realizing that it was on my back side also.

The scripture above tells us when we come to Jesus dressed in our filthy rags. He takes away our sin and clothes us with the rich garments of righteousness. When Jesus clothes us in His righteousness, those around us see it. We should wear those clothes proudly in the name of Jesus, and keep those garments clean.

Are we keeping our garments clean? Or are we letting the sins of the world soil our garment of righteousness? Others are watching how we live our lives. Can they see that our garments are white as snow? If we allow are garments to become soiled, we cannot scrub them enough to make them clean, we will only make a bigger mess. Only God can make them clean again. If you have allowed your garment of righteousness to become soiled, allow Jesus to clean you up and put you back in right relationship with Him.

# June 20

# A REASON TO LIVE

*(Isaiah 1:18-20 "Come now, let us reason together, says the Lord: though your sins are like scarlet, they shall be as white as snow; though they are red like crimson, they shall become like wool. If you are willing and obedient, you shall eat the good of the land; but if you refuse and rebel, you shall be eaten by the sword; for the mouth of the Lord has spoken.")*

This Scripture is as real today as it was in Isaiah's time. God says the same thing to us—"come let us reason together". How can anybody refuse to reason this out? Why would anybody refuse the offer of having their sins washed away by the blood of Jesus? I ponder that question on a regular basis as I watch so many people ignore God and His word.

This world we live in today is only a temporary home. And we are the ones who will make the decision as to what will happen to us when our time has come to leave this sinful world.

It does not take a scholar to figure this whole thing out. It is simple and direct and to the point. We can accept the offer of salvation, or we can reject it. The choice is ours.

I have a friend who is a very intelligent man and he is a very nice, generous person. He has all of the qualities that the world would consider good. But he lacks one thing—the willingness and obedience to read and believe in Jesus and His word. Although I have taken every opportunity to try and reason with him about the most important thing in life, he refuses to listen. I have used every example that God has put on my heart to try and convince him, yet he is still obstinate. It breaks my heart to see friends and family refuse to reason out the choice that they have for their future. Have you reasoned these things out? Have you chosen to receive what Jesus has offered you—eternal life in Heaven?

# June 21

# DISAPPEARING IDOLS

*(Isaiah 2:17-19 The arrogance of man will be brought low and the pride of men humbled; the LORD alone will be exalted in that day, and the idols will totally disappear. Men will flee to caves in the rocks and to holes in the ground from dread of the LORD and the splendor of his majesty when he rises to shake the earth.)*

I am always amazed at the way people idolize others: And it begins at a very young age. Movies, television, magazines and many other venues are used to infiltrate the lives of the ordinary public. Movie stars, TV stars, sports figures, models, wealthy people, corporate figures, political figures—you name it; there will be those who are in awe of their 'idol'.

And there are those who idolize themselves: Those proud people who have gained wealth, power and/or fame from their accomplishments or perhaps their beauty. They bask in the glory of themselves and the lives they lead. They never give a thought to the one who has given it all to them.

This is what the Lord says about them in Isaiah 2:*12 (The LORD Almighty has a day in store for all the proud and lofty, for all that is exalted and they will be humbled)*. One day, there will not be one person alive who will not recognize the splendor of God's majesty. They will understand that those they have idolized, whether it be themselves or someone else was all foolishness. They will be humbled before the Lord and they will flee trying to hide from Him.

The first commandment in the bible is this—*(And God spake all these words, saying, I am the Lord thy God, which have brought thee out of the land of Egypt, out of the house of bondage. Thou shalt have no other gods before me.Exodus 20:1-3)*. What is there in this commandment that we do not understand? It seems pretty plain to me, how about?

# June 22

# FAITH IS THE VICTORY

*(Matthew 14:28-30 "Lord, if it's you," Peter replied, tell me to come to you on the water." "Come, he said. Then Peter got down out of the boat, walked on the water and came toward Jesus. But when he saw the wind, he was afraid and, beginning to sink, cried out, "Lord, save me.")*

Isn't this just like us. We ask God to do something for us and He does. Then the storms of life come along and we become fearful and our faith starts to sink. I have been there, have you? I ask myself why I would allow myself to doubt what God has done for me. I believe the reason is the evil one tells us lies. He cannot stand for us to be victorious in the things that God has done in us and through us. So we take our eyes off of Jesus and momentarily allow the lies of Satan to take over.

*(Without faith it is impossible to please God, because anyone who comes to him must believe that he exists and that he rewards those who earnestly seek him. Hebrews 11:6).* I want to share with you that I have been fighting the same battle for the past several months. Satan has been trying to accuse me with the intention of trying to destroy my faith and confidence in what God has done in my life. There have been many mornings that I lay face down, crying out to God. It seems to be a never ending battle, but God is there to lift me up the minute I say "save me Lord". I tell you this so that you will know that you are not the only one who is attacked by Satan. As Zechariah 3 tells us—God is on one side and Satan on the other trying to accuse us-The Lord is rebuking him every time he tries to destroy our confidence. We do not have to fight these battles—God fights for us. He is always there to save us from drowning.

Are you letting God fight your battles, or you allowing Satan to drown you in the sea of defeat? I tell you the truth, I know that you don't have to be defeated—God is there with you every minute of every day. He wants to fight your battles and win the victory for you. Let Him.

# June 23

# EVERLASTING LIFE

(John 3:16 "For God so loved the world that he gave his one and only Son, that whoever believes in him shall not perish but have eternal life.)

The other night I had a terrible dream about the death of one of my loved ones. When I awoke and realized it was a dream, I was so relieved. Immediately God spoke to my spirit and said, "Laura, many people are suffering from the loss of loved ones, pray for them." God reminded me of the family last week that had lost 6 of their 7 children in a fire, and the earthquake victims, and all others who are suffering

In 1982, my husband was facing by-pass surgery. I was so scared that I was going to lose him. I started to pray for his healing when God spoke to my heart and said, "You need to be healed first." Now I was raised in church and I knew immediately that He was speaking of the healing of my spirit. God used those circumstances to bring me to a personal relationship with Him. Without the healing of our spirits, there is no hope for eternal life. Oh, our bodies may be healed for a time on this earth, but it is eternity that really matters.

I have seen the importance of being ready to meet our Lord and Savior. Without Jesus, we have no hope of spending eternity in Heaven. But when we know Him as our personal Savior, we have the assurance that we will spend eternity with Him and also with our loved ones who have gone on before us. Death loses its sting when we are Christians. When God calls His own home, we will be more alive than we ever were in this world. And so I pray for all of the survivors of the earthquake and every other person in this world who are suffering—that if they have not prepared their hearts—if they have not met Jesus as their personal Savior—they would do that before it's too late.

As a Christian I can't think of anything worse than losing a loved one that has not given their hearts to the Lord. I know it hurts to lose anyone, but having the knowledge that we will spend eternity with them in Heaven in the presence of Jesus takes away the despair of losing them forever.

Jesus gave His life in order that we will gain eternal life. He rose again to live for eternity with His own. (1 Corinthians 15:54-55 When the perishable has been clothed with the imperishable and the mortal with immortality, then the saying that is written will come true. Death has been swallowed up in victory." "Where, O death is your sting?") If you have not prepared your heart, please do it now before it is too late. Life is just a breath away. Life on this earth is short—life after death is for eternity. Where will you spend eternity?

# June 24

# WHEN THE TIME IS RIGHT

*(2 Peter 3:8-9 But do not forget this one thing, dear friends: With the Lord a day is like a thousand years and a thousand years are like a day. The Lord is not slow in keeping his promise, as some understand slowness. He is patient with you, not wanting anyone to perish, but everyone to come to repentance.)*

There are so many people who are concerned about the coming of the Lord. There have been those who have predicted that time and have ended up with red faces. Then in these last days there are those who scoff at the entire matter saying (*"Where is this coming he promised? Ever since our fathers died, everything goes on as it has since the beginning of creation." 2 Peter 3:4).*

I know when He is coming again. He is coming when He says the time is right. I honestly and truly believe in my heart, that His return will be the day when His omniscience knows that everyone that He has waited on to come to Him, has come. God does not want anyone to perish, so He will wait patiently until all of His children have come to Him. I believe that is the day when He will say "It is time". What about you?

Surely if we knew the exact day, we would prepare for it; and none of us know when that day will be—so shouldn't we be ready to go? There will not be time to make that decision once He decides to come for His bride. His word says in a twinkling of an eye he will come. *(1 Corinthians 15:51-52 Listen, I tell you a mystery: We will not all sleep, but we will all be changed—in a flash, in the twinkling of an eye, at the last trumpet.)*

Are you ready for that day? Don't be one of those scoffers who think you have plenty of time because the Lord surely isn't coming soon. He could come today. I pray that you will be ready.

# June 25

# THE GIFT

*(1 Corinthians 12:4-11 There are different kinds of gifts, but the same Spirit. There are different kinds of service, but the same Lord. There are different kinds of working but the same God works all of them in all men. Now to each one the manifestation of the Spirit is given for the common good. To one there is given through the Spirit the message of wisdom, to another the message of knowledge by means of the same Spirit, to another faith by the same Spirit, to another gifts of healing by that one Spirit, to another miraculous powers to another prophecy, to another distinguishing between spirits, to another speaking in different kinds of tongues, and to still another the interpretation of tongues All these are the work of one and the same Spirit, and he gives them to each one, just as he determines.)*

There are so many that want to argue about the gifts of the Spirit, especially about the gift of speaking in different languages. There are even those that say if one doesn't have the gift of tongues they aren't filled with the Holy Spirit. Now I am not here to discuss the meaning of these 'tongues', I am hear to say that it is untrue that if one does not have that particular gift they aren't filled with the Holy Spirit. I don't see how anyone can say such things if they read the above scripture. If they have read it, and they still say it, they sure do put a different spin on it than I do. I believe that this Scripture is very clear about all of the gifts and from whom they come from.

First of all I believe when we come to know Christ as our personal Savior we receive the Holy Spirit at that precise time. The trinity is God the Father, God the Son, and God the Holy Spirit. How can we separate them? Our individual spiritual gift may not be shown to us immediately, but in due time God will reveal those to each of us according to His liking. He does not see one gift any greater that another.

Further on in this chapter it tells us that the body is a unit, made up of many parts and those parts form one body. We were all baptized by one Spirit into one body. There should be no quarrels about such matters. If you think your gift is better than someone else's—you are very, very wrong. Let's respect each other for who we are in Christ. And for Heaven's sake let's not look down on another.

God gave us the gift of eternal life through Jesus Christ. That is the only gift that we should be concerned about. If we have accepted that gift, God will show each of us our Spiritual gifts.

# June 26

# SACRIFICIAL OFFERING

*(Hebrews 10:5-7 Therefore, when Christ came into the world, he said: "Sacrifice and offering you did not desire, but a body you prepared for me; with burnt offerings and sin offerings you were not pleased. Then I said, 'Here I am—it is written about me in the scroll—I have come to do your will, O God.")*

There are many churches who observe the season of Lent. The 40 days leading up to Easter, known as Lent, are set aside as a time for reflection and self-denial in preparation for the celebration of Easter.

Now I want to say right up front that I am not condemning those churches or those people who choose to do that: I think it is a very good thing to do if one really understands what it is all about. If their great desire is to use those 40 days to pursue a closer relationship to Jesus the Savior of the world; and to give sacrificial offerings in love and with surrendered spirits; then it is a beautiful thing.

I believe there are many who have the idea that if they give up something for Lent, it will help to make them more holy in God's eyes. But God's Word says in *(Psalms 51:16-17 You do not delight in sacrifice, or I would bring it; you do not take pleasure in burnt offerings. The sacrifices of God are a broken spirit; a broken and contrite heart, O God, you will not despise.)*

Do you honestly think that if you give up a certain food, or a certain drink, or even a certain habit for a period of 40 days that it will please the Lord? I believe the only way that it will please God is if it is in pursuit of worshipping Him and searching out His will for your life. In fact I have to wonder if it isn't an insult to Him, if you're doing it for any other reason. I have actually heard people laugh and make light about the things they give up for Lent. With that attitude, they certainly aren't pursuing God's will for their life, nor are they honoring the Lord.

Jesus gave the supreme sacrifice: He gave His life that we might live. There is no other sacrifice that can do that. We could give up everything in our life but it will not make us Holy. The only way we are Holy is by accepting Jesus. And then serve Him, honor Him, and make our sacrifices of praise to Him with a broken and contrite heart. That is what He will be pleased with.

I have to ask this question: Shouldn't we be making sacrifices with a broken and contrite heart to Him on a daily basis; 365 days out of the year and not just for 40 days?

# June 27

# SELF DECEPTION

*(1 Timothy 4:1-2 The Spirit clearly says that in later times some will abandon the faith and follow deceiving spirits and things taught by demons. Such teachings come through hypocritical liars, whose consciences have been seared as with a hot iron.)*

I was listening to a wise minister the other night; and he was talking about self-deception. He made the statement that a person who willfully deceives himself will eventually develop a hardened heart; and when that happens, the Holy Spirit will convict them less and less. What a dangerous place to be in. These types of people fall prey to the lies of Satan. They become so caught up in his lies that they start believing them. One has to question whether or not they were ever really a child of God or an imposter.

When we accept Christ as our personal Savior, it seems to me that there should be a change in the heart that inspires us to learn more and more about the attributes of God; and we should have the desire to follow His plan for our life and allow it to develop to fruition. To say you are a Christian does not make you one. If you don't have the desire to seek His wisdom and His ways then you should ask yourself—"Am I really a Christian. Was my heart in it when I asked for forgiveness, or did I just simply go through the motions? Am I truly a Christian or am I an imposter?"

These are serious questions in serious times. We must not let Satan deceive us. Our future is at stake—it is a question of where we will spend eternity. This wise man said, "A good way to measure our position in Christ is this—1. Has God called us to serve Him? 2. Has He empowered us to do it? 3. Do we give all of the glory to Him? This is a very good measuring stick. If we can answer yes to all of these questions, I believe that we are truly walking in the spirit and truth of who we are in Christ Jesus.

Satan is a liar. *(John 8:44 You belong to your father, the devil, and you want to carry out your father's desire. He was a murderer from the beginning, not holding to the truth for there is no truth in him. When he lies, he speaks his native language, for he is a liar and the father of lies)*

God is truth. (John 3:21 But whoever lives by the truth comes into the light, so that it may be seen plainly that what he has done has been done through God.)

Who do you believe? And whom will you serve?

# June 28

# DO YOU QUALIFY?

*(Ephesians 3:20 Now to him who is able to do immeasurably more than all we ask or imagine, according to his power that is at work within us, to him be glory in the church and in Christ Jesus throughout all generations for ever and ever. Amen)*

I would guess that there are many Christians that are facing fear right now because of something God has put on their heart to do. And I would guess that they are arguing with God because they don't feel qualified to do it. Are you one of these people? Are you letting the evil one lie to you? God does not give us a spirit of fear—His perfect love casts out fear. God will supply all of your needs to do the things that He has asked you to do. Of course there are many things that we could never do on or own—but through Christ we can do all things.

I understand the fear and the arguments that you are having with the Lord—I have been there and done that. Most of us are not qualified for what the Lord asks of us. But He is the one who teaches us and qualifies us. He would never ask us to do something and then turn away to let us figure it out on our own. It would never work if the Lord isn't the one showing us the way. If we were setting our sights to do something on our own it would be a disaster. We can do nothing without the power of the Holy Spirit. He is the one who empowers us to do things that we could never even imagine.

What a wonderful God we serve: The one who loves us and calls us for His purpose in our lives and then walks us through every step of the way. I don't know about you, but I am so humbled by the fact that He loves me so much that He would call me to serve Him in any particular way and then take the time to teach me all I need to know to carry out His purpose.

# June 29

# BLESSED IMPERFECTIONS

*(Jeremiah 18:5 Then the word of the Lord came to me: O house of Israel, can I not do with you as this potter does? So are you in my hand O house of Israel.)*

I have a friend who is close to being a perfectionist. She expects far too much of herself. She is multi-talented and can do many things. She is not afraid to step out and reach for the stars. But when she thinks she is not doing a perfect job, she gets very upset with herself and will not rest until she reaches the perfection that she thinks is necessary. She will not be convinced that everything does not have to be perfect. She recently was working on a video for a special retiree's celebration. Everything was going perfectly well until the program on her computer decided that it was not going to cooperate. She spent several days and nights agonizing as she tried to diagnose the problem. We committed it to prayer and God heard and answered. The job was done and those that saw the finished product raved about it. ("But we have this treasure in jars of clay to show that this all-surpassing power is from God and not from us." 2 Corinthians 4:7)

As I was thinking about her situation I thought about how God molds us in to the person that He wants us to be. When we consider that we are only clay in the hands of God, we can be assured that the way He molds us is the way He wants. He does not expect perfection, but He does expect us to step out and do what He has given us the talent for.

There is never a piece of pottery that is perfect and the potter is aware of that. But the pottery is still beautiful in the eyes of others. God does not look at our flaws; He looks at the imperfect vessel and loves it,

Do you hesitate on stepping out of your circle of comfort because you are afraid that you might do something that is less than perfect? Go for it and trust God even if what you do is not exactly the way you want it. The important thing is that you do the best you can. He will bless you through your imperfect ways because of your obedience to step out and use the talent that He gave you.

# June 30

# SHATTERED DREAMS

*(Romans 12:2 Do not conform any longer to the pattern of this world, but be transformed by the renewing of your mind, Then you will be able to test and approve what God's will is—his good, pleasing and perfect will.)*

I believe that every one of us have had dreams of one kind or another—dreams of the perfect job—dreams of the perfect mate—dreams of traveling throughout the world—dreams of the perfect house—dreams of a perfect life—dreams of this and dreams of that. And some have even taken their dreams to God in prayer; asking Him to bless them with that dream. But how many have actually asked that it be according to His will? How many of us have been content to wait on His answer?

The following is a wonderful poem that is so enlightening.

As children bring their broken toys
With tears for us to mend,
I brought my broken dreams to God
Because He was my friend.

But then instead of leaving Him
In peace to work alone,
I hung around and tried to help
With ways that were my own.

At last I snatched them back and cried,
"How could you be so slow?"
"My child," He said, "What could I do?
You never did let go."
- Author Unknown

Does this sound familiar to you? It sure does to me. We search for the will of God and then let our will get in the way. Why can't we realize that God's will is perfect and if the dreams that we have are not according to His will—we surely don't want them. The world wants its own way but we Christians should want God's way and no other. Our minds should be transformed so that we will accept the will of God. Don't you think?

# July 1

# SPEAKING IN SPIRIT AND TRUTH

*(Psalms 119:129-130 Your statutes are wonderful; therefore I obey them. The unfolding of your word gives light; it gives understanding to the simple.)*

A woman I know recently gave her testimony to some Christian women to critique, in preparation of speaking to a group. When she completed her testimony, they said that it was good, but that she needed to change some of the 'churchy words'. She was confused about what they meant and when she asked if they could clarify the words that they were referring to, they said. "Well like Satan, sin, and vision." They expounded on how some people would not understand such words and that she should change them in such a way that they could. She did not respond at that time except in her thoughts, "Well there goes my testimony." By the next morning she realized that the Lord had answered her prayer as to whether or not He wanted her to speak for them. And the answer was an absolute no.

She was shocked when they suggested that she change important and profound words in the bible. She had great respect for these women, but she was not willing to compromise the Word of God for anyone. She does not want to speak in an arena where she would have to water down the Word of God. How do you change these pertinent words? Sin is sin and we should call it what it is, Satan is real; he is the evil one who is out to destroy, and people need to be aware of his evil tactics. And it is important that people understand that a vision is not an illusion; it is what God gives us to walk in His ways and to follow His commands and His will for our life; and he gives people visions of impending danger.

There are so many today that want to change important words in the bible so that it might fall easier on the ears of those listening. It is God's light and His Holy Spirit that enlightens people. It is His words that illuminate ones spirit—not the watered down words of others. God's word is true, and if we are not willing to speak in truth, then we might as well not speak at all. If others think that changing the words that Jesus himself used to attract people can make a difference,

I believe they are wrong; it is the Spirit that makes the difference in whether or not others understand.

# July 2

# A DAY OF RECKONING

*(Ezekiel 14:12 The word of the Lord came to me: "Son of man, if a country sins against me by being unfaithful and I stretch out my hand against it to cut off its food supply and send famine upon it and kill its men and their animals, even if these three men—Noah, Daniel and Job—were in it, they could save only themselves by their righteousness, declares the Sovereign Lord.)*

There are many Christians who believe that we most likely are living in the final days and I am one of them. Everything we hear and see on the TV these days are strong indications of that fact. The bible tells us that no man knows the exact day of Christ's return; however we will be able to know the season. There will be a day of reckoning. It is a very disturbing thing to face the last days if one is not ready to go. It troubles me to think that there might be some of my friends and relatives who have not prepared themselves for eternity.

No body can get to heaven through other's righteousness. There is only one way to God and that is through His Son. Those who do not acknowledge Jesus and accept Him as their personal Savior will be lost for eternity. God is a righteous God. Some may say that God is cruel—not so; to the contrary, he is a just and fair God—punishing only those who disobey Him, dishonor Him and blaspheme His name. He is a loving God—He sent His only Son to die on the cross for my sins and your sins. Everyone has a choice to make. They can choose to come to Him and accept His mercy and His grace, or they can turn their backs on Him. I am comforted by the fact that because I belong to The Father through Jesus Christ, I will never face eternity in Hell but will live forever in Heaven. Do you have that assurance? *("You also must be ready, because the Son of Man will come at an hour when you do not expect him." Luke 12:40)*

# July 3

## SEEDS OF DISCONTENT

*(Ephesians 5:31-33 For this reason a man will leave his father and mother and be united to his wife, and the two will become one flesh. This is a profound mystery—but I am talking about Christ and the Church. However, each one of you also must love his wife as he loves himself, and the wife must respect her husband.)*

I just finished reading about a couple whose marriage was torn apart because the wife did not respect her husband. She talked about how much in love they were the first two years of marriage. She had loved and respected her husband, not only because of his looks but because he had a successful job and was a good Christian man. But her husband decided (with her in agreement) that he would go into business for himself: Four years into their marriage, they found themselves with a son, and a failing business that depleted their savings The wife was angry at the fact that she had to leave her home to enter the work force so that they could make ends meet.

She began to ridicule her husband, calling him a failure and blaming him for everything that had gone wrong. After another child and the death of her mother she slipped in to clinical depression. She began to neglect her husband, her children and herself.

Her husband changed jobs several times although he was providing their needs. She would lie in bed, eat, and nurse her anger for her husband. Little by little, as her ridicule increased, their marriage decreased. One day he told her he could take no more and said he wanted a divorce. She didn't' care, she had gotten beyond that. And he acted on his threats.

She began to see herself in truth. She found herself one hundred pounds over- weight and a broken marriage that she had destroyed. She began to pray, asking God to heal her on every level. She started reading her bible and praying daily that God would help her restore herself and her marriage. She lost all of her excess weight; and God began to show her how she had run her husband off with her lack of respect.

When her husband would come after the children she would tell him about how God was changing her but after what he had been through he was hesitant to believe her. There came a day when through God's Holy Spirit, her husband believed that she really had changed. They were able to allow God to restore their love and respect for one another. Today they are remarried and happy.

Girls are you respecting your husband? Husbands are you showing your wife that you love her? We marry for better or for worse. We need to show love and respect for one another. I have read that women must be shown that their husbands love them; and that husbands must be shown that their wives respect them.

I am so glad that we serve a God who is in the restoration business, aren't you? Even if you think you have a marriage that is beyond restoration, don't give up. Ask God to show you where you have gone wrong and allow Him to turn your heart and life around. Allow Him to replace those ugly seeds of discontent with the beautiful fragrance of your sweet love.

# July 4

# A HUMBLE SPIRIT

(Psalms 149:4 For the Lord takes delight in His people; he crowns the humble with salvation.)

In the study of Ruth, this question was presented to us—'In what way does the media contradict God's desire for us to be humble people.' As I gave it consideration, I concluded that almost everything we see in the programs that we watch and most especially in the commercials; everything is geared to self.

We live in a self-oriented society. What will make me happy? What will make me feel good about myself? What can I do to improve my looks? What can I do to improve my position? Every time I go to find a graduation card, they all give a message that if we believe in ourselves we can do anything. I get so exasperated that I usually end up designing my own cards. Even in greeting cards, the underlying message is usually self.

It would be refreshing to hear—if you want to feel good about yourself help someone in need. If you want to improve your looks, let the light of Jesus shine through. If you want to improve your position, humble yourself and God will honor you. If you want to be successful let God be in control of your life, not you.

God has told us to be humble people. When we put ourselves before God we will fall short of His glory. Do we put self before God? Or are we allowing Him to be in control of our life? God's word says; (*Humble yourselves before the Lord and He will lift you up. James 4:10*)

# July 5

# COINCIDENT OR ORDAINED?

*(Ruth 2:3 So she went out and began to glean in the fields behind the harvesters. As it turned out, she found herself working in a field belonging to Boaz, who was from the clan of Elimelech.)*

As I started reading today's study in Ruth, the Scripture above stopped me right in my tracks. I thought to myself—wait a minute 'as it turned out' really hit me. This was not a coincidence, it was providential. And then as I went further in the study, it was obvious that the author was also stopped at this particular verse.

Circumstances just don't happen with God's people. They are orchestrated by Him. He has every day planned out for us. I know that is difficult for us to understand sometimes, when we are going through struggles. There are times when we wonder where God is in all of it. Can you identify? We don't always know why we are where we are, or why we must go through some of the things that we see only as negatives. But the truth of the matter is, God has allowed it to happen and there must be something that he has planned for us. Maybe it is just simply to bring us closer to Him: Maybe there is a lesson that we need to learn: No matter the reason, we can be assured that God is in it and will use it all for our benefit and for His glory. *(1 Peter 4:15 If you suffer, it should not be as a murderer or thief or any other kind of criminal, or even as a meddler. However, if you suffer as a Christian, do not be ashamed, but praise God that you bear that name.)* Suffering because of Christ and suffering because of sin is two different stories. So let's not confuse the two.

Ruth found herself gleaning in a strange place and was eager to work as hard as she could to provide for Naomi. She had no idea the plan that God had set before her. It is obvious to me that from the time that Elimelech took his family to Moab, even if he made the wrong decision, God was in control and was going to use it all for His glory. So we can see that 'as it turned out' does not mean it was a coincident but rather it was ordained by God.

# July 6

# FRINGE BENEFITS

*(Ruth 2:8-9 So Boaz said to Ruth, "My daughter, listen to me. Don't go and glean in another field and don't go away from here. Stay here with my servant girls. Watch the field where the men are harvesting, and follow along after the girls. I have told the men not to touch you. And whenever you are thirsty, go and get a drink from the water jars the men have filled.")*

Can you imagine the conversation that Ruth must have had with Naomi when she got home that night? I think it must have gone something like this: "Naomi, guess what happened today—not only did Boaz give his permission for me to work in his field, he said for me not to go anywhere else to glean and he told me just how and where. He also said that I could have all of the water that I could drink so that I wouldn't be thirsty. And he said he would protect me. He is the most gracious man I have ever met."

Does this sound sort of familiar to you? It does to me. Doesn't it remind you of what Jesus done for us? When we came to Him for help, he provided all of our needs. He gives us food to eat and water to drink; He gives us protection and direction for our life. Now I did not say that He gives us all we want, but rather all that we need. Boaz did not say, "Ruth go home and I will give you whatever you want". He told her to stay in his field and work with the other servant girls and all of her needs would be met.

In all the times I have read this story of Ruth, this particular passage has not spoken to me as it has today. God does supply all of our needs but he tells us to stay and work in his field. He also says to drink from His well. I don't know about you, but I want to glean from His word and drink from His living water; then take it out in to the world to tell others about our wonderful Savior's love and grace.

# July 7

# SHARING FROM THE HEART

*(Ruth 2:17-18 So Ruth gleaned in the field until evening. Then she threshed the barley she had gathered, and it amounted to about an ephah. She carried it back to town, and her mother-in-law saw how much she had gathered. Ruth also brought out and gave her what she had left over after she had eaten enough.)*

Well here I am again, gleaning from the book of Ruth. Almost every word in this wonderful book has a treasure of information to challenge and encourage us to live as Christians should.

As I was reading this passage of Scripture I could not help but think about my wonderful parents. These two versus precisely describes them. They had very little if judged by the worlds standards, but what they had they shared generously with others, especially their family. They grew the most magnificent garden. Every year it seemed as though they had an abundance of everything. They planted the seed, and nurtured it every day—pulling weeds and watering when necessary. And when it was the proper time for harvesting they gathered it in. They canned everything they could. And then they gave most of it away. They were the kind of people who loved to share also from their own table. I couldn't count the times that we had company for dinner. Many times they would send the left-overs home with their guests. All of this was hard work, but they didn't mind, they seemed to thrive on it. What a blessing my parents were to many people.

The book of Ruth certainly presents a picture of our Lord Jesus and His love and care for us. I am blessed every time I read a verse in it. It inspires me to be more like Ruth and Boaz, but most especially like my Lord.

# July 8

# A FRETFUL PERSON

*(Psalms 37:7-8 Be still before the Lord and wait patiently for him; do not fret when men succeed in their ways, when they carry out their wicked schemes. Refrain from anger and turn from Wrath; do not fret—it leads only to evil.)*

Webster's dictionary describes fret as to eat or gnaw into: <u>corrode, fray</u>, <u>rub</u>, <u>chafe</u>, to make by wearing away a substance.

Wow! Think about that for a while. Fretting eats, gnaws and corrodes. Now we all know that is not a good thing. It wears away a substance. If we are Christians, we have a relationship with God. We certainly don't want fretting to corrode that relationship, do we?

Have you ever fretted about circumstances or hurtful people? Has it ever done any good? Of course not: I don't know anyone who has changed a thing or a person by setting around and fretting. I think if we were honest about it, we could all say that we have committed that sin, I know I have. I say sin, because God's word says not to fret. Why?—because it leads to evil.

Undoubtedly when we sit around fretting about things, we will become frustrated and sometimes angry and anger leads to sin. We must turn all things over to God and wait on Him to solve all problems in our life. We must rest in Him, trust in Him and have faith that everything will work out according to His will. Oswald Chambers wrote— 'Resting in the Lord does not depend on external circumstances at all, but on your relationship to God Himself.' If we have the right kind of relationship with the Lord, we can rest in Him, knowing most assuredly that He will handle all things in His time and in His way. Summation: Let go and let God.

# July 9

# GREAT EXPECTION

*(Psalms 5:3 In the morning, O Lord, you hear my voice; in the morning I lay my requests before you and wait in expectation.)*

So many times I find myself worrying and fretting over things that I cannot control. I have found that it does me no good whatsoever. In fact God's word tells us not to worry. Ref. Matthew 6:34) Have you been there?

What if we got up each morning and laid all of our concerns at the feet of Jesus and then left them there, believing that God is in control and we have nothing to worry about. Don't you imagine that our day would be full of joy as we waited in great expectation for God to work all things out in HIs time and in His way? It makes me happy just writing this.

God's Spirit is telling me that I truly can trust in The One who is in control: For God is the one who gives us the peace that is beyond all understanding. God's Word tells us: *(You will keep in perfect peace him whose mind is steadfast because he trusts in you. Isaiah 26:3)*

I don't know about you but I want to live each day believing that God will take care of all things in my life. I want to have that peace that comes when I put my complete faith in Him. He is the only one who can change any and every circumstance. I am waiting with great expectation knowing that by His magnificent grace God heard my voice and will answer my prayer.

# July 10

# HOPEFUL PLANS

*(Jeremiah 29:11 For I know the plans I have for you, declares the Lord, plans to prosper you and not to harm you, plans to give you hope and a future.)*

I have a niece who has been in Nicaragua for almost 6 months awaiting the final papers to be signed for the two sisters that she and her husband have been trying to adopt for some time. There has been one delay after another. All of those who love her have been praying that the time would be short so that they would be able to come home soon. And truthfully it is difficult to understand why God has allowed this delay.

In my book, 'Help, I'm Dying of Thirst' there is a poem written by William Cowper and the last verse of the poem I used for February 19 is:

Wait for His seasonable aid,
And though it tarry, wait:
The promise may be long delayed,
But cannot come too late.

I am confident that God has His reasons for this delay in Missy's return home with her two girls. We may never know what that reason is, but we can rest in His word; *(Jeremiah 29:1 For I know the plans I have for you, declares the Lord, plans to prosper you and not to harm you, plans to give you hope and a future.)* This delay is without a doubt in His plan. We can trust Him, knowing that he has something in mind for their future.

I must tell you that Missy understands the Scripture that this devotional is based on better that most anyone I know. Her faith and trust never wavers. She signs every email with her name followed by *(Hebrews 11:1 Now faith is being sure of what we hope for and certain of what we do not see.)* We would all be so much better off if we pasted this Scripture in our minds and recalled it daily.

## July 11

# WHERE WILL YOU SPEND ETERNITY?

*(Romans 8:11 If the Spirit of him who raised Jesus from the dead dwells in you, he who raised Christ Jesus from the dead will also give life to your mortal bodies through his Spirit who dwells in you. ESV)*

While on vacation last week, I received four phone calls and one email that announced the death of five people. It seemed as though every time my phone rang, I was going to hear something bad.

It is always sad to hear that someone has passed away, but it isn't always a bad thing. It makes a huge difference when you know that the person leaving this world was ready to go. The knowledge that they had prepared their hearts through their acceptance of Christ, takes away the pain of never seeing them again—that is, of course, if you yourself are a Christian.

I am under the impression that each one of these people knew Jesus as their personal Savior. And so the pain of death lost its sting. ("O death, where is your victory? O death, where is your sting?" ESV)

We never know when we will take our last breath. The most important decision that we will ever make in this life is the choice to accept Jesus as our personal Savior. The choice we make will dictate where we will spend eternity. Have you made that choice? Do you know where you will spend eternity? If you do not know the answer for sure, I urge you to ask Jesus to come in to your heart. He is the only way to the Father. He is the only way to eternal life.

# July 12

# THE GUIDING LIGHT

*(Psalm 43:3-4 Send out your light and your truth; let them lead me; let them bring me to your holy hill and to your dwelling! Then I will go to the altar of God, to God my exceeding joy, and I will praise you with the lyre, O God, my God.)*

When I am searching for the truth in God's word, I have yet to be denied. The Holy Spirit enlightens us to His truth. His word will lead us in the paths of righteousness. He is our light, our strength, our redeemer, our comfort, and our peace. How many times have you been in a place where you think you are alone--a place where you think there is no hope for your circumstances?

Before Jesus came, people went to the altar of sacrifice to worship. Praise God, we do not have to travel to find God. We could be stranded on an island with no other person in sight, yet we would not be alone. For His dwelling place is in our hearts. Because of Jesus sacrifice on the cross, we have the assurance that He is ever abiding in us.

I have read so many stories of people who have been in a lonely, solitary place without the bible by their side, yet the Spirit has reminded them of the promises of God because His word has been written on their hearts and He abides within. I don't know about you, but that makes my soul rejoice.

The only place we will find the truth is in God's word. When we search for Him and His word, He will be found. When we accept Jesus as our personal Savior, He lives in our hearts and we will never walk alone again and His word will abide in us. He fills us with joy, even in times of trouble and we can rejoice in His abiding love.

# July 13

# A VIGILANT HEART

*(Proverbs 4:23 Keep your heart with all vigilance, for from it flow the springs of life.)*

It seems as though we spend most of our life concerning ourselves with our physical needs and those of our family. We strive for success and the goal to reach our personal selfish desires. And because of it, we set our hearts on worldly gain that will not matter at the end of our life here on earth

According to Webster, the meaning of vigilant means—'to be keenly alert to or heedful of trouble or danger, while others are sleeping or unsuspicious.'

What kind of things are you seeking with vigilance? Are you aware of the dangers that could be in store if you are not protecting your heart from the evils of this world? What we allow to take over in our hearts and minds will surely show in our life.

This message in Proverbs was written by a very wise man. What comes from our heart will overflow in our life. Our reputation will become what our life demonstrates. Does your life show your love for the Lord and His influence in your life? If we are vigilant in seeking God and His ways, others will see it. How can we do that? The answer is in *(Psalm 119:9-11 How can a young man keep his way pure? By living according to your word. I seek you with all my heart; do not let me stray from your commands. I have hidden your word in my heart that I might not sin against you.)*

# July 14

# OBEDIENCE IN ADVERSITY

*(2 Corinthians 2:9 The reason I wrote you was to see if you would stand the test and be obedient in everything.)*

A synonym for obedience is submission. Sometimes we have to be submissive to those in authority—and so in that case it is necessary and we have no choice. And sometimes we are submissive to those we love—in which case it is a choice. Are we choosing to be obedient to God? - And if so, why? I believe when we love someone we desire to be obedient and yet at times we rebel against that.

When things are going well and we are having no struggles, we are inclined to be content to follow where God leads. But what about the times when we think God has called us to do some particular thing and it doesn't turn out the way we planned. Oswald Chambers says and I quote 'we should never put our dreams of success as God's purpose.' End quote. There are times when our dreams just don't pan out the way that we expect. What then—will we base our obedience on the fact that all things will turn out the way we want them to; or is our obedience based on our love and faith in our Heavenly Father?

We show our love for the Lord by being obedient to Him in all things. No matter what comes our way. It is a fact that He never promises that everything will go well at all times. And He never promises that everything that we have dreamed will come true. His Word tells us—*(Consider it pure joy, my brothers, whenever you face trials of many kinds, because you know that the testing of your faith develops perseverance. James 1:3)* When we put our complete trust and faith in Him, even in adversity, we can be the obedient servants that He desires us to be. Will our faith and obedience withstand the test of time and adversity?

## July 15

# FREE TO RUN

*(Galatians 5:7 "You were running a good race. Who cut in on you and kept you from obeying the truth? That kind of persuasion does not come from the one who calls you. A little yeast works through the whole batch of dough.")*

When runners' race, they put on their running attire; light clothing, so that they will not be bogged down with excess weight that would keep them from running with ease. They run the race to win. Why do we Christians run the race that Paul speaks about? We run to finish the task set before us-- that of testifying to the gospel of God's grace.

In order to run our race to the finish line, we cannot carry around a lot of excess baggage: Baggage that will slow us down. That kind of baggage can come from those discouragers who try to take our eyes off of the race that we are running. If we are allowing anyone to get in the way of our race and cause us to get off on the wrong path—we must push them aside and get on the right track in which God called us to.

It is true that others will try to discourage us from the task set before us. Do not let that happen. Those who get in our way are prompted by the evil one. Sometimes they will do and say anything to get in our way. God however, makes the path straight when we keep our eyes on the path that He has set before us. Let's throw off all things that hinder us and finish the race.

I read something a minister wrote awhile back—"Life is not a 50-yard dash; it is a marathon. I want you to make it to the finish line; the only way to do that is to focus on Jesus, not your circumstances."

Let's lead the way in witnessing to the love and grace of our Father. Let's win that race.

# July 16

# BELIEVING THE TRUTH

*(Ephesians 4:14 Then we will no longer be infants, tossed back and forth by the waves, and blown here and there by every wind of teaching and by the cunning and craftiness of men in their deceitful scheming.)*

I do not want to offend anyone by using the following statement. It is meant to be funny—believe me when I say it is far from being funny. When I read it, I immediately knew that it was a statement on which God wanted me to address in a devotional. This is the statement that I am talking about--.'A diplomat is someone who can tell you to go to hell in such a way that you will look forward to the trip.'

Satan is cunning and he uses people in his cunning ways to entice others to sin. There is no denying that there are things in life that are fun, but many times that fun leads to sin and destruction. So many in the world today, look to men for their advice instead of looking to God. They allow their influence to mold their future. Unfortunately if they are not seeking answers from God and His people, their influence could lead them straight to Hell.

There are those in this world that do not believe there is a Hell. Well there is: And if you doubt it, you had better get into The Word of God and see what it has to say on that subject. People sin because of their lack of knowledge. God provides that knowledge through His Word. We can choose whom we believe. We can believe God or we can believe in the lies that Satan has so cunningly told through his advocates. Truth comes through the Holy Spirit; not from the father of lies.

If you are influenced by those who you think are funny, extraordinarily brilliant, extremely beautiful, eloquent speakers, enticing in all ways, ask yourself if they represent God in the way they live. If they don't, do not believe their lies. *(Proverbs 14:12 There is a way that seems right to a man, but in the end it leads to death.)*

# July 17

# WHY ARE YOU HERE?

*(Ezekiel 40:4 The man said to me "Son of man, look with your eyes and hear with your ears and pay attention to everything I am going to show you, for that is why you have been brought here. Tell the house of Israel everything you see.")*

There are some things in the bible that puzzle me as to why they are in there; such as the precise measurement of the temple, etc. And I must admit that I still wonder why. But when I read this verse in Ezekiel this morning it suddenly became clear to me that I don't necessarily have to know the reasons why God has chosen to put things in His Book: But I know for sure that there is a reason why it is there. And one day God might reveal the answer to those questions to me. One thing I know; I will not be bothered by the fact that I don't have the answer yet, for I know that if and when He wants me to understand those things that I ponder over—He will at that time reveal them to me.

God tells Ezekiel in the above scripture that he was brought there for a particular reason. I believe that God has brought all of us here for a reason. God reveals things to us in His time and in His way. They may not be as dramatic as Ezekiel's vision was but He will tell us and show us what He wants us to do: However, we must open our eyes to see and our ears to hear and then pay attention so that we can tell others what we have learned from Him and about Him.

For years I wondered what God's purpose for my life was. Looking back I don't believe that I really asked God to show me His purpose. When I started asking Him to show me that purpose— He did. That purpose is to tell others about Him. That is precisely why I am here. My life has not been the same since God revealed His purpose to me.

God uses us all in different ways to testify of His amazing love and grace. How about you? Have you found God's purpose for your life? Have you found a way to testify about Him? Ask Him to show you where, when and how He wants you to do that—I guarantee you that He will honor your prayer.

# July 18

# STORMS OF LIFE

*(Luke 8:24 The disciples went and woke him, saying, "Master, Master, we're going to drown!" He got up and rebuked the wind and the raging waters; the storm subsided, and all was calm).*

Most of us are familiar with this story of how Jesus was asleep in the boat when a raging wind blew in. The disciples were fearful that the boat would capsize. They cried out to Jesus and He immediately calmed the storm. Have you ever wondered who caused that storm? God is blamed for most everything that happens, but could it be that Satan was the cause of that storm? I don't have a concrete answer for that, but I do believe that Satan is the cause of many storms in our life. And I know for certain that if God allowed the storms it is for a very good reason.

As long as we are on the mountaintop, everything is great; but the minute we find ourselves in the valleys, we tend to fall in to the pit of despair. It is a matter of fact that we are going to have storms in our life. To think otherwise is nothing but fallacy. Life deals severe blows, and many times it is because of things that we have done. And sometimes it is because of what others have done to us. Sometimes God allows storms in our life to show us how much we need Him. Other times it is Satan that causes them to try and destroy us. It is how we handle the storms that determine the outcome. Do we put our faith and trust in God when the storms come along, or do we rant and rail because they have come—which is what the evil one wants us to do.

Those who put their trust and faith in God will survive the storm and grow as a result of it. I was listening to a minister the other day and he made the statement that fruit does not grow on mountain tops, it grows in the valleys. I truly believe that he is right. As we walk in the valleys and put our faith in God we will come out bearing fruit. Like the disciples, we have nothing to fear when we call out to Jesus— He will calm the storms and He will walk with us through the valleys where we grow and prune us as we go.

# July 19

# RIGHT OR LEFT

*(Isaiah 30:19-21 O people of Zion, who live in Jerusalem, you will weep no more. How gracious he will be when you cry for help! As soon as he hears he will answer you. Although the Lord gives you the bread of adversity and the water of affliction, your teachers will be hidden no more; with your own eyes you will see them. Whether you turn to the right or to the left, your ears will hear a voice behind you saying; this is the way; walk in it.)*

We hear a lot in the political language lately pertaining to the right and the left. If you lean to the right you are conservative; and if you lean to the left you are liberal. If you are honest about which way you lean, it says a lot about your character and what you believe. Most liberals have totally different views about the issues of the day than the conservatives do. For instance, those on the left will argue in favor of abortion and same sex marriage—in total opposition to those on the right.

Generally speaking those who lean to the right are many times Christians and take their instructions directly from God. If we claim to be Christians shouldn't we base our beliefs on the word of God? Shouldn't we vote our conscience? How can we possibly vote for someone who does not seek the truth in God's word? I believe as Christians we had better be finding out just what God says is right. If we listen to anyone other than the Lord, we will make wrong decisions and sin against God.

The wonderful thing about God is that even when we have been wrong, even if we have been leaning toward the left, He is ready to show us the truth and reveal the lies that we have allowed others to tell us. He will show us in His Word which way to lean—to the left or to the right.

Who do you listen to—false teachers or God? We must seek the will of God and lean on Him for our wisdom. When we cry out to Him, He hears our prayers and forgives us our sins. When all is said and done will we stand for the right of God's word to? Will we walk in His way?

Listen to the voice of God. Lean not in our own understanding, in all our ways acknowledge Him, love Him, and accept Him. It is imperative to know who will lead us to victory in the end. Let's be right so we won't be left when Christ returns,

# July 20

# PRAYER AND COUNTRY

*(2 Chronicles 7:14 If my people who are called by my name, will humble themselves and pray and seek my face and turn from their wicked ways, then will I hear from heaven and will forgive their sin and will heal their land.)*

This has become one of the most quoted Scriptures in the bible in the last few years. With everything going on right now in our country, people have become fearful and discouraged that America is about to fall. We have more problems than we have ever had before. And why do you think that is? I believe it is because we have allowed those people who have ignored the Lord to take control. But we, the people are the ones who have put them in that position of power. I wonder how many have prayed for God's guidance in the selection before we cast our votes. And how many have sought out His wisdom in His Word. How many have weighed the consequences of casting their vote for the wrong person? God's Word instructs us on who and how to vote. If we vote for those who ignore God's Word, what can we expect?

This past week we had one of the most wonderful times in a prayer meeting at church. Our focus in prayer that night was on our country and its problems. The above Scripture is very clear about the 'if' of God's people. It does very little good to just complain about all of our problems. It does not help to place the blame—the only thing that will make the difference is 'if' we Christians listen and obey the Word that God has spoken to us. Look at the words that God emphasizes above—'if' my people will humble themselves and pray and seek my face and turn from their wicked ways then I will hear from heaven and will forgive their sin and heal their land. Will all people who call themselves Christians heed His Word and do what He says for us to do? It is a tall order and the results of what happens to our country hangs in the balance of how we respond to His call.

It is not too late to save our country—but we must take this Scripture to heart. Let's start a revival in our country and pray with fervency that God will restore our land.

# July 21

# ALIVE IN CHRIST

*(Galatians 2:20 I have been crucified with Christ and I no longer live, but Christ lives in me. The life I live in the body, I live by faith in the Son of God, who loved me and gave himself for me.)*

I received an email from a friend who was searching for ways to explain death to her precious 3 year old son. I searched as I prayed that God would give me the Scriptures to try and help her, because I knew it was imperative. I was overwhelmed with the fact that this little one wanted the answer to such a question. There are not many 3 year olds who would be seeking answers for that particular issue. I was touched by this young mother's desire to search out the truth of God's Word on this matter. She didn't just slough it off and try to ignore it. She wanted to be able to answer him in the correct way—God's way. She had said that death frightened him.

As I was thinking about it I remembered how fearful I was of even the thought of death until I became a Christian at the age of 42. I could hardly stand to go to funerals because of that fear. Suddenly I understood that once we know Christ as our personal Savior, we no longer have to fear death because we have eternal life through His Son. When we give our hearts to Him, Christ lives in us and He is our hope of glory. The death of our body has no sting for those who live in Christ Jesus. We will be more alive than ever before when we are in the presence of Jesus.

The life we live in our body is temporary, but the life we live in Christ is for eternity. What about you? Do you know where you will spend eternity? This little 3 year old is searching for his salvation already, are you? If you still fear death, then I dare say, you have not given your whole heart and life to Christ. I plead with you to make that choice today while you still have time. If you die before you make that choice then death is terrible for you, you will have to spend eternity in Hell and will be separated from God and his saints.

# July 22

# FIGHT FOR THE RIGHT

*(Ephesians 6:10-11 Finally, be strong in the Lord and in his mighty power. Put on the full armor of God so that you can take your stand against the devil's schemes)*

A while back my husband attended an annual convention of antique gun dealers. They always have a banquet on Saturday night that many of the dealers attend. We chose not to go this particular year and so were not aware of the events of the evening until we got to the show room the next morning. I had barely entered the room before one on my sisters-in-Christ rushed over to me with the story of what had transpired during the banquet ceremonies. An opening invocation had always been a part of the proceedings with all in attendance agreeing that it was not only proper but welcome. It was assumed that it would be the same on this particular night—until time for the invocation when the President of the club sidled up to the man ready to give it and told him that there had been one or two who had taken offense to the idea of praying and asked that it not be done. Hence, there was no prayer.

By the time I got to the showroom floor the next morning, some of God's people had already put on there armor and were ready to fight the battle. We sat there discussing the proper way to confront this horrendous offense against our Lord. We decided that a petition should be written and signed by all of those who agreed that prayer should continue to be included in the ceremonies. As one of the women walked up to another to ask her to sign the petition, she ignored it and said, "Oh don't worry about it, they are going to discuss that in the board meeting and they will get it straightened out". We later found out that she was lying about it and it was her way of getting out of writing her name on the petition. Many of the board members weren't even aware of what had happened during the banquet.

I must say that I was blessed as I saw the indignation of what had happened on so many faces. There was not a problem in getting enough names on the petition to put a stop to taking prayer out of the equation. It did my heart good to know that God's people were ready at the drop of a hat to fight for Him. Before the morning was over even the President had signed the petition.

We must be on guard against the evil schemes of Satan and his advocates. We must be ready to fight at a moment's notice. If these people of God had not been ready and willing to fight, we may have fallen in to the trap that Satan had laid to stop prayer being offered at the annual convention. Let's remember to keep our armor on and fight for our rights as Christians.

# July 23

# NEVER ENDING CHANGE

*(Hebrews 13:8 Jesus Christ is the same yesterday and today and forever.)*

We live in a world where nothing ever stays the same. It seems as though change is something that we have learned to accept. Sometimes change is difficult and sometimes it is welcome. There are times when it takes us out or our comfort zone and leads us into territory where we do not want to go.

I heard a minister say; "One thing for certain, change reminds us that we are not in control." That is so true. It seems as though we just get used to one way of life, and then things happen that changes our entire direction. We live in very uncertain times when change is taking place every day in this world. Most of us are wondering what in the world tomorrow will bring. If we relied on the fact that things would always stay the same, we would be deluded for certain. In our own country today, we are concerned about whether or not we can meet the debts that we owe. We worry and fret about what we will face tomorrow.

Through all of the changes in our lives, we can be sure of one thing—God never changes. He tells us that His love for us never changes, His word never changes and His plan for us never changes. In this constantly changing world, we know that our Lord remains the same. We can always depend on Him. No matter where we are and no matter what changes life forces on us,—He will walk with us through it all. He promises that He will never leave us or forsake us. Praise God that He is the same yesterday, today and tomorrow.

# July 24

# AMAZING GRACE

*(1 John 1:7- But if we walk in the light, as he is in the light, we have fellowship with one another and the blood of Jesus his Son, purifies us from all sin.)*

I have a friend who is going through very difficult circumstances as a result of her past sin. There is no doubt that sin has far reaching fingers and it many times affects the lives of others. But the beautiful thing about God is His grace that forgives all sin when we confess it. *(1 John 1:9 If we confess our sins, he is faithful and just and will forgive us our sins and purify us from all unrighteousness.)* Wow! What a Savior—just think about that—He purifies us from all unrighteousness.

When we read the story of David—a man after God's own heart—we can't help but see the grace of God. David was an adulterer and a murderer and yet God not only forgave him, he used him in a mighty and powerful way. We have all sinned and fallen short of the glory of God as the Scripture says. But the minute we repent, God forgives us. We are all unworthy of His grace and forgiveness: But because of Jesus death and resurrection, we are made alive in Christ. We no longer have to carry our sin around. Jesus paid the price and we are forgiven if we accept His wonderful gift.

If you are suffering as a result of your past sin, let go of it and let God take control. Come to Jesus and repent and turn your life around. He will forgive you and make you a new person. You won't even recognize yourself as you once were when you were a sinner. God will put new life in you—a life of joy, peace, and a future that you cannot imagine. Be renewed in Christ and experience the beauty of His forgiveness and His amazing grace.

## July 25

# GREENER PASTURES

*(Hebrews 13:5 Keep your lives free from the love of money and be content with what you have, because God has said "Never will I leave you; never will I forsake you.")*

I am sure that you have all heard the idiom 'The grass always looks greener on the other side of the fence.' Have you ever observed cows trying their best to reach through or under a fence to the pasture on the other side? It is pretty comical when you watch the antics they go through in trying to reach that green pasture that is just a little out of their reach. Sometimes they somehow break through and many times get into trouble and cannot find their way back to their own pasture.

Cows are not the only ones that yearn for 'greener pastures.' We humans have a tendency to do that. We sometimes try to reach beyond our limits for things that we think we must have. That is a pretty dangerous thing to do. We can get ourselves in deep trouble going after things that we want instead of being satisfied with what we have. Why is it we so many times do not value what God has given us? Why do we covet those things that others have?

How many times have you witnessed someone who has gotten in to financial problems because they just had to have what others had? And how many times have you seen those who have destroyed their marriage because someone else looked better; only to find out that they ruined their life? The effects of these sins not only hurt those who cause it, but it also has a tremendous effect on many others.

God knows just exactly what we need and sometimes it is not exactly what we want. Let's think about it—do we really want to force ourselves into a place where we don't belong. Only God knows what is best for us. Can't we just be content where we are? Do we always have to seek greener pastures? God will never lead us to dead pastures—He leads us in green pastures. Why look for greener pastures when we have all that we need. He tells us that He will never leave us nor forsake us when we walk with Him. Read the 23rd Psalm again and be reminded of the green pastures where God leads us. How could we ever be in a better place than where God wants us to be?

# JULY 26

# A MIRACLE REVEALED

*(2:1-5 On the third day a wedding took place at Cana in Galilee. Jesus mother was there, and Jesus and his disciples had also been invited to the wedding. When the wine was gone, Jesus' mother said to him, "They have no more wine." "Dear woman, why do you involve me?" Jesus replied, "My time has not yet come.")*

The first miracle that Jesus ever performed was at a wedding. Mary seemed to be one of those who were responsible for the refreshments. And when she discovered that the wine was gone, she told Jesus about it. Up to this point Mary had never seen Jesus perform a miracle. Have you ever wondered why she went to Jesus and told Him about her concern? He answered her with the question of why she would involve Him because His time had not yet come. Yet she turned to the servants and told them to do whatever He told them to do. Mary seemed to be confident that Jesus would handle the situation.

Why did Mary ask for Jesus' help? And how did she know that He would respond to her with the help that she needed. I believe that even though Mary had never seen Jesus perform a miracle. She knew He was special. She knew from the fact that He was born through Immaculate Conception—a miracle in itself—that He was Holy and capable of anything. She would know that nothing would be impossible for Him.

Some people may think that Mary was being very audacious when she went to Jesus about her problem—but I think she was consulting the one person that she knew had the power to change things. She had never once seen a miracle from Him, yet she had faith in Him because she knew Him and His character.

Do we know Jesus well enough that we boldly ask Him to help us with impossible things? He is capable of all things and He cares about every problem that we face in this life. When we are down to our last hope, He is there to meet all of our needs.

Are you in a place where you need help? Do you have an answer? Is there anyone or anything that can help you outside of a miracle? There is one person who can and will come to your aid. He will help you with your problem—all you have to do is ask Him. He may not change your situation, but He will definitely help you through it. He will answer any call according to His will.

# July 27

# ARE YOU A GRASSHOPPER?

*(Numbers 13:31-33 But the men who had gone up with him said, "We can't attack those people; they are stronger than we are." And they spread among the Israelites a bad report about the land they had explored. They said, "The land we explored devours those living in it. All the people we saw there are of great size. We saw the Nephilim there (descendants of Anak come from the Nephilim), we seemed like grasshoppers in our own eyes, and we looked the same to them")*

The Lord told Moses to send one man from each ancestral tribe to explore the land of Canaan, which He was going to give to the Israelites. Moses obeyed and when they returned only two of them gave favorable reports and encouraged all to go in, But the other ten discouraged them and said that they seemed like grasshoppers compared to the powerful looking men they saw. We all know the rest of that story—the Israelites chose to listen to the ten discouragers rather than Joshua and Caleb the two encouragers. They were afraid to enter the land that God had promised them.

I wonder how many times God has asked us to enter into territory that He wants to give us; but we won't go because we are afraid. How many blessings have we missed because we have not listened to the Lord? How many times have we passed up the opportunity to cross over in to a fruitful land? And how many times have we listened to discouragers instead of those encouragers who tell us to enter the place that God has chosen for us?

I don't know about you but I don't want to be a grasshopper, I want to be brave and enter into the place where God wants me to go. I don't want to stay behind in the wilderness wandering about without a purpose. I want to enter the Promised Land. I want to feed on the fruit that God has for me. God doesn't call us to a place and then destroy us like grasshoppers. I want to follow wherever He leads me—don't you?

# July 28

# THE DEFINING GOD

*(1 Corinthians 1:27 But God chose the foolish things of the world to shame the wise; God chose the weak things of the world to shame the strong. He chose the lowly things of this world and the despised things—and the things that are not—to nullify the things that are. So that no one may boast before him? It is because of him that you are in Christ Jesus, who has become for us wisdom from God—that is, our righteousness, holiness, and redemption. Therefore, as it is written: "Let him who boasts boast in the Lord.)*

There was a time that I was the most inferior person in the world—or at least that's what I thought. Those were the days when I let Satan tell me lies. Even after I became a child of the King, I compared myself with my Christian sisters who seemed to be so much more capable than me. They had far better educations; they had much more self-confidence, and far more gregarious personalities than me. I felt like I was pretty insignificant in comparison.

When God spoke to my heart about stepping out of my shy and inferior personality in to the person that He wanted me to be; I argued with Him about my lack of abilities. But He told me that I could do all things through Him and that His grace was sufficient. Praise God, He got through to me and I started to believe Him. I began to pray that He would show me what He wanted me to do. He answered my prayers and opened the doors that He wanted me to enter and gave me the courage to go through them.

It took me years to realize that God sometimes does not call those who are equipped—but He definitely equips the called—otherwise I would be worthless. I could do nothing without Him. He also showed me that every one of us is different and we should never compare ourselves to others. He has a plan for each one of us—a different plan according to His purpose.

Don't ever make the mistake of comparing yourself to others. Don't ever feel inferior to anyone. I have come to understand that that mentality is an insult to our Lord. It is God who defines us. He is the one who shapes us in to the person that He wants us to be. Our part is to believe Him and obey His call on our life. It is then that we can boast, not in ourselves but In The Lord.

# July 29

# DO YOU HEAR HIS VOICE?

*(Isaiah 51:7-8 "Hear me, you who know what is right, you people who have my law in your hearts: Do not fear the reproach of men or be terrified by their insults. For the moth will eat them up like a garment; the worm will devour them like wool. But my righteousness will last forever, my salvation through all generations.")*

I was angry and appalled as I listened to a well know atheist make fun of a Christian woman who is a candidate for president. He had heard this woman talking about hearing from God and he was insulting her by insinuating that she was delusional. But then I read the above Scripture this morning and it very plainly tells us what will happen to those who insult Christians. I would certainly hate to face their future.

Why is it so difficult for people to believe that God speaks to those who know Him? What about all of the men and women that we read about in God's Word who heard God and responded to His call on their life? The bible is God's history book, and everything in it is true. The accounts of all of the wonderful people who God used (because they heard from Him) to carry out His plan are incredible. But of course if you don't believe, you are going to think those who do are out of their minds.

Can you imagine what this world would be like if those who heard from God would ignore Him and go their own way? It would be a very miserable existence and there would be little purpose for anyone. It is the Holy Spirit who calls to those who seek after God. It is through those who seek, hear and respond that God will use to carry out His mission for their life. And every one of them has a specific purpose. God uses all who care to hear and respond to Him to work in His fields.

It is horrifying to think that this world would be ruled by all who do not know the Lord. I am so thankful that God has put some of His people in governmental positions to fight for those things that are right. They are persecuted almost every day for the fact that they stand on God's Word. They have to be brave souls to step in to the political arena and fight in a world that has chosen to take things out of God's hands. The enemy is there to attack them and try to destroy them. Let's remember to pray daily for them as they fight for the Lord and His direction for our country. Let's pray that God would put a shield around them against the arrows of Satan and bind those who are persecuting them. And let's thank God for speaking to them and that they have responded to His call.

# July 30

# THE FLAWLESS WORD

*(2 Samuel 22:31 As for God, his way is perfect; the word of the Lord is flawless. He is a shield for all who take refuge in him.)*

I sat in a bible study one day led by the minister of the church we attended at that time. I don't even remember now what it was we were studying, but I do remember one thing this minister said: "You can't take Scripture literally." I thought I was going to choke. I knew right then that I was definitely in the wrong place. It was the proverbial 'straw that broke the camels back' for me, as I did not ever feel the Spirit under his preaching. It didn't take us long to find another church where the minister believed every word in the bible and preached it.

I wonder why people read the bible at all if they don't believe its literal content. What good will it do us if we take some of the word of God and believe it and then disregard the rest. How on earth can you ever learn from it if you are looking for things to disagree with?

I believe that it is a dangerous thing to tell others that you cannot take the word of God literally, especially a minister—a man who is to preach in Spirit and in Truth. To be honest with you, it was at that time that I began to pray that God would purge the churches of those who are false prophets. It almost makes me ill when I consider all of those who are sitting in churches where the Word is distorted. There are many who love those kinds of ministers—you know the kind that tickle people's ears—the kind that make them feel comfortable in their flesh. Wouldn't you say that those ministers would be feeding the flesh and starving the Spirit?

It's frightening to me to think that there are so many of those kinds of ministers, and even more frightening to think that their denominations sanction them. I am so thankful to be in a church where the Word is preached in Spirit and in Truth. Looking back I see that we were starving to death for the true Word in the church we were in.

Are you in a church where God's Word is distorted? Do you check out for yourself to see if what the minister is preaching is true? If you don't, you should: Otherwise you might be miss-led. *(2 Timothy 2:15 Do*

258

*your best to present yourself to God as one approved, a workman who does not need to be ashamed and who correctly handles the word of truth.)*

Believe me when I say that ignorance is not bliss. God's Word is true and don't let anybody tell you any different.

# July 31

# FEEDING THE SOUL

*(Ephesians 2:3 All of us also lived among them at one time, gratifying the cravings of our flesh and following its desires and thoughts. Like the rest, we were by nature deserving of wrath.)*

One day last winter I was just headed out to the grocery store in spite of the fact that it was only 3 degrees outside; and there were piles and piles of snow where shovels and motorized equipment have provided paths to get around after a 20" snowfall. It seemed like it would be worth it because of my enormous craving for a Rueben sandwich and I did not have the ingredients that I needed to make them.

Throughout the bible it talks about people's cravings and their pursuit to feed their hunger. It is interesting to see that when they were hungry they would turn to God asking Him to feed them. But when they were full they seemed to always turn their backs on Him. There are many today who are constantly looking for something that will satisfy their hungry souls. They are starving to death for God's Word. If they satisfied their hunger for the Lord, they would find that the cravings would cease. We can feed the cravings of our flesh but it will never satisfy until we meet Jesus. Then and only then will are souls be fed. *(Matthew 5:6 Blessed are those who hunger and thirst for righteousness for they will be filled.)*

As soon as I returned home that day, I made those Reuben sandwiches. They were delicious and I probably won't crave another one for a long time; there will be those days when I will crave a certain food. But I praise God because He satisfied the hunger that I once had in my spirit the minute I accepted Him as my personal Savior. He gives me spiritual food every day that keeps my soul satisfied.

# August 1

# WATER OF LIFE

*(Psalms 1:2-3 But his delight is in the law of the Lord, and on his law he meditates day and night. He is like a tree planted by streams of water which yields its fruit in season. And whose leaf does not wither. Whatever he does prospers.)*

I had two beautiful flowers planted in pots, and when I came back from a 7 day trip, I was heart sick to see that they were dry as a bone and withered. I was so sad because I thought that they were beyond reviving. But I decided with a doubtful mind to water them anyway: And wonder of wonders the next day I looked out to find those leaves had perked up overnight. Within another two days the flowers were blooming again.

I could not help but think about how our spirits suffer when we are lacking from spiritual nourishment. Without our water from God's well, we begin to wither and die. Every living thing needs water. The above Scripture tells us that when we meditate day and night in God's law we are like trees planted by streams of water. We never lack spiritual nourishment if we are feeding on His Word and drinking from His well.

Do you find yourself in a place where you are withering from lack of water? Have you been to the well lately? If we don't keep ourselves spiritually healthy, we are not likely to prosper in the spiritual realm. Our life will not produce much fruit without nourishment. It is the water that keeps us strong, healthy, and alive. Our bodies would die without water, likewise so will our spirits.

## August 2

# ENTER WITH THE SWORD

*(Joshua 1:2, 5, 7 Moses my servant is dead. Now then, you and all these people, get ready to cross the Jordan River into the land I am about to give to them—to the Israelites. No one will be able to stand up against you all the days of your life. As I was with Moses so I will be with you; I will never leave you nor forsake you. Be strong and very courageous. Be careful to obey all the law my servant Moses gave you; do not turn from it to the right or to the left, that you may be successful wherever you go.)*

As a young man Joshua served in the Tabernacle and had proved himself to be an obedient, trustworthy and dependable servant. He was, you might say, Moses' right hand man. Is it any wonder that God used him to be the one to lead the Israelites into the Promised Land?

Joshua had seen the miracles that God performed during the period in the wilderness. He also had witnessed the rebellion of the people along the way. No wonder God told him several times to be strong and courageous. God knew that it could be an overwhelming request, so He reiterated the encouragement to be strong. He also reminded him to obey the law that Moses gave him more than once. *(Do not let this Book of the Law depart from your mouth; meditate on it day and night, so that you may be careful to do everything written in it. Then you will be prosperous and successful.)*

I wonder if God is calling you to enter into the Promised Land. Are you afraid that you might face too many obstacles? Are you afraid of failure? We have God's Word to instruct us. I believe that if we truly seek His Word and His will for our life, he will be with us and give us success in all that we do. If He calls us to enter a new place, He will tell us more than once, just like He did Joshua, not to be afraid.

There have been times that I have been afraid to go to the place where God has asked me to go. But I have found that in one way or another He validates and confirms His call so that I might be confident that it is His will for me. Then He gives me the courage to enter in to the place where He wants me to go. He has never failed me.

# August 3

# THE PASSOVER SIGN

*(Joshua 2:12-13 Now then, please swear to me by the LORD that you will show kindness to my family, because I have shown kindness to you. Give me a sure sign that you will spare the lives of my father and mother, my brothers and sisters, and all who belong to them, and that you will save us from death.")*

Rahab was bargaining for her life and that of her family with the two spies that Joshua had sent to Jericho to spy out the land. She went into great detail about how she knew all about the miracles that God had performed for the Israelites in parting the Red Sea, etc. She confessed to them that she knew that their God was the God in heaven above and on the earth below. She was well aware of the fact that God would do what He wanted to do.

Have you ever wondered why the spies went to Rehab's house in the first place, and how she was so readily willing to help them escape from the people of Jericho who was out to destroy them? I believe God led them to the very place that He knew they would find protection. And I believe that God had prepared the heart of Rahab to welcome them. I think she had already decided in her heart that she wanted to serve the one and only true God. She was putting her faith in the one that she believed. She seemed to know that she could trust God to save her and her family from certain destruction through these spies. The spies met her request and told her to tie a scarlet cord in the window of her home and to bring all of her family in for protection. Does that bring back memories of the 'Passover' to you?

Do you ever think that there are people who seem to be so deep in sin that there is surely no hope for them? This story of Rahab should be a great encouragement to you. God can change the heart of any person, no matter what they are involved in and no matter where they are. His Holy Spirit can penetrate any heart. Rahab had heard the stories concerning God and she became a believer. I don't believe that Rahab had come across anybody in life who had explained the character of God. His Holy Spirit was the reason that she made the decision to believe in Him; —and He saved her life and that of her family.

I don't know about you: But I am going to tie a scarlet cord in my window.

What an awesome God——He does not care about our past—— He cares about those who believe that He is who He shows Himself to be. He enlightens those who want to be enlightened. And He gives them a future that is far and above anything that we could ever imagine. He will save the lives of all who are covered by the blood of Jesus.

## August 4

# A CONSECRATED LEADER

(Joshua 3:5 Joshua told the people, "Consecrate yourselves, for tomorrow the Lord will do amazing things among you.")

This wonderful chapter in the book of Joshua is truly reminiscent of what God did when Moses led the Israelites out of Egypt and God parted the sea. When the people broke camp to cross the Jordan, the priests carrying the Ark of the Covenant went ahead of them. Even though the river was at flood stage, as soon as the priests who carried the ark reached it and their feet touched the water's edge, the water stopped flowing and piled up in a heap for a great distance and the people crossed over opposite Jericho. Now that is an amazing thing.

The definition of consecrate means dedicated to a sacred purpose. I believe that Joshua was one of those people who consecrated himself daily. Leaders like Moses and Joshua hear from the Lord and respond and then encourage those whom they lead to consecrate themselves also. God can and will do amazing things in the lives of those who consecrate themselves to Him.

God had told Joshua that he would be exalted in the eyes of all Israel, so that they would know that He was with him, just as he was with Moses. Wow! Don't you wish every man that God has put in a leadership position today would be exalted in the eyes of their people because of their consecrated lives? I wonder how different this world would be if we had more Christian leaders like Joshua. There is no doubt in my mind that if all people who are led by those consecrated leaders, and then consecrate themselves for God's purpose— they could absolutely move mountains.

(Joshua said to the Israelites, "Come here and listen to the words of the Lord your God. This is how you will know that the living God is among you and that he will certainly drive out before you the Canaanites, Hittites, Hivites, Perizzites, Girgashites, Amorites, and Jebusites.)

The most important thing we can do for our country is to pray that our leaders would consecrate themselves and encourage their people to do the same. God would do amazing things for us, if we would all consecrate ourselves for His purpose.

## August 5

# WORLDLY TROUBLES

*(John 16:33 "I have told you these things so that in me you may have peace. In this world you will have trouble. But take heart! I have overcome the world.)*

I am fairly certain that many of you have grieved for all of the victims that lost their lives; and for those who have lost family and friends through all of the natural disasters that have been happening throughout the world. In a town in my own state alone, there has thus far been 132 counted dead and more than that reported missing as a result of a tornado that destroyed most of the town of Joplin, MO. As I turn the news on each day I hear different heart-wrenching stories: Some of them sad beyond measure and some of them miraculous accounts.

There is no way that we will escape the troubles that we have in this world. We are going to have them, Jesus told us that. But there is hope for those who know Him because He has overcome the world, and in that knowledge we find our peace: But what about those who do not know Him? There is no hope for them. They do not have the assurance of eternal life. They do not have the comfort of knowing that they will be reunited with those loved ones who belonged to Jesus.

The only way we can have peace in this world of uncertainty is to walk with the Lord. We can never be destroyed when we put our faith, hope and trust in Him. There is no disaster that can keep us from being victors, even in the face of the storms in this life. Even if through those storms, we would die—we would only step into the presence of Jesus to an eternal life where there is no pain or suffering; and where our loved ones will be there to welcome us.

Do you have the assurance that your eternal life will be spent in Heaven?

# August 6

# DOCTRINE OF GRACE

*(Galatians 2:11-13 When Peter came to Antioch, I opposed him to his face, because he was clearly in the wrong. Before certain men came from James he used to eat with the Gentiles. But when they arrived, he began to draw back and separate himself from the Gentiles because he was afraid of those who belonged to the circumcision group. The other Jews joined him in his hypocrisy, so that by their hypocrisy even Barnabas was led astray.)*

I have the privilege of being a part of a women's ministry that speaks where ever they are called. The denomination does not matter. The Holy Spirit moves and works in the hearts of many, in spite of the fact that they are of different denominations. It is a wonderful thing to see the camaraderie between people when God's grace is free to minister to them.

Sometimes barriers are built when we put church doctrine before the grace of God and His doctrine. Christ came to demolish the law. Most of us understand that; however we must ask the question: Are we judging others on our church doctrines? Are we forcing our laws on others instead of focusing on the grace of God? (*"I do not set aside the grace of God, for if righteousness could be gained through the law, Christ died for nothing." Galatians 2:21*)

Do we minister to those in our own churches because they share our same doctrine? Do we have the attitude that ours is the only way? Or do we mix with others, accepting them in the love of Christ, allowing God's Word to penetrate each heart as they search out their own salvation through the leading of the Holy Spirit?

God's grace is sufficient for all those who seek Him. It is not the laws of the church we attend that make us who we are. No, it is the law that is put on our hearts when we surrender our life to Him that shapes us in to the people that He wants us to be: His people.

There are Christians in all denominations. Let's accept it and respect them as people of God. Let's not take on a 'holier that thou' attitude because they don't go to the same church we do.

## August 7

# DON'T WORRY—BE HAPPY

*(Proverbs 17:22 A cheerful heart is good medicine, but a crushed spirit dries up the bones.)*

There was a popular song out a few years ago called 'Don't Worry—Be Happy'. It was a rather funny song but the title was something to truly consider. And the above Scripture is a wise proverb written for our benefit. Think about it and ponder it in your heart. As I was reading it this morning it surely spoke to me.

How many times are we in a place where things are going badly in our life and all we want to do is curl up and retreat in to a shell? I don't know about you, but I have certainly been there on occasion. I know that it did me absolutely no good. As a matter of fact, it made me feel worse: And when I finally realized that I needed to quit worrying about my circumstance and allow my spirit to be fed by looking up to The One who could cheer me, I regained my joy.

Depression can bring on both spiritual and physical illness. We can't control some of the circumstances in our life, but we can control how we handle them. We can choose to be brought down in to a pit of depression—or we can choose to turn those circumstances over to God and live in peace and joy. God is our peace and He wants to take our crushed spirit and give us a cheerful heart.

# August 8

# ACCENTUATE THE POSITIVE

*(Philippians 4:8 Finally, brothers, whatever is true, whatever is noble, whatever is right, whatever is pure, whatever is lovely, whatever is admirable—if anything is excellent or praiseworthy—think about such things.)*

During the young years of my life there was a song that was popular: The words said to 'accentuate the positive; eliminate the negative; and don't mess with mister in between.' At that time I really thought it was a rather catchy tune and I sang it quite a lot. I never really related it to God's Word. Of course it was not written with His Word in mind and I was not concerned with His Word at that time in my life. However, this song came to my mind this morning and all of a sudden I thought about what a powerful message this chorus could bring to everyone, if they correlated it to what God tells us in Philippians.

How many times do we dwell on negative things? I can honestly say that there are far too many times that I have a tendency to do that. Yet God's Word tells us to think on good and lovely things. Why can't we make our minds up to do just that and not waver? The answer to that question is the 'mister in between'—his name is Satan. He does not want us to focus on the positive—we would be far too peaceful for his liking. And we cannot be effective in our witness if we think negatively. So he tries to discourage us with all of the negative thoughts that he brings to mind. He wants to hold us captive by our negativity.

Let's put off our propensity to allow those negative thoughts to invade our peace. Let's put on that armor once again that Ephesian 6 talks about so that we will be able to fight for our peace of mind and the ability to think only on the positive. When we dwell on Christ and His Word, we will be able to throw off the negative thoughts that come our way. Let's accentuate the positive things in our life.

# August 9

# REJECT TEMPTATION

*(Joshua 7:20-21 Achan replied, "It is true! I have sinned against the Lord, the God of Israel. This is what I have done: When I saw in the plunder a beautiful robe from Babylonia, two hundred shekels of silver and a wedge of gold weighing fifty shekels, I coveted them and took them. They are hidden in the ground inside my tent, with the silver underneath.")*

The Israelites had just torn down the walls of a fortified city. Joshua and the people at that time must have felt like they would be able to defeat any nation because they were in the Lord's favor. And I feel quite certain that what they thought would have been true; but they were not aware of the fact that Achan, one of their own had disobeyed God and sinned against Him.

Joshua sent two spies in to Ai to spy out the region so that he would know how many men it would take to be successful in their pursuit of the land. It seemed small compared to Jericho and so they came back to Joshua and told him that he would need only to send about 3,000 men to take over the land. But they were greatly surprised when they were routed out by the men of Ai. They lost thirty-six men that day.

Joshua questioned the Lord as to why He had not given them favor. The Lord revealed Achan's sin to Joshua. He told Joshua that He would not be with him anymore unless he destroyed the guilty one that had violated His covenant.

Because of Achan's coveting those things that he was not to take—it not only cost the lives of the thirty-six men that had gone out in good faith to fight for the Israelites; but it cost him and his entire family their lives: All because Achan could not resist the temptation to sin against the Lord.

Wow! What a price to pay for disobeying God. We will never get by with sinning against God: There is always a penalty for our sins. It is so easy to see the sins of others, but what about our own? Do we always recognize our sins? Do we give in to our temptations that ultimately lead us to sin? *(But each one is tempted when, by his own evil desire, he is dragged away and enticed. Then, after desire has conceived, it gives birth to sin;*

*and sin, when it is full-grown, gives birth to death. James 1:14-15)* Covetousness leads to temptation. All of us are tempted at times; but we must learn to reject the temptation. Our sins affect others' lives. Let's stop and think about the consequences of giving in to the temptation to sin and reject it.

## August 10

# BELIEVE THE IMPOSSIBLE

*(Joshua 10:12-13a On the day the Lord gave the Israelites victory over the Amorites, Joshua prayed to the Lord in front of all the people of Israel. He said, "Let the sun stand still over Gibeon, and the moon over the valley of Aijalon." So the sun stood still and the moon stayed in place until the nation of Israel had defeated its enemies.)*

This wonderful book of Joshua is such a study on what God will do for the man or woman who puts their complete faith and trust in Him. Joshua was devoted to God and sought His audience in all and every circumstance. It seems like he had major battles facing him continuously, but God constantly told him not to fear or be discouraged because He was going to be successful in his battles. The day that the Israelites fought against the Amorites, Joshua asked the Lord to prolong the light of day in order to complete the battle in victory. And God did the unimaginable— the super unnatural—He made the sun stand still to show His power. Wow! What a God we serve.

We live in fear sometimes because we are in battles that we think we can't possibly win. If God can and will part rivers and cause the sun to stand still, why would we think that He is unable to save us from our enemies? Our problem is—we do not put our complete faith and trust in God. We, in our finite minds, limit the power and strength of our God. God is the same today as He was in Joshua's time. He hears and answers our prayers according to His will when we believe Him and when we trust Him. He will definitely save us from our enemies.

Do we hesitate to ask God for unimaginable circumstances to change the direction of our lives? He tells us to come boldly to His throne of grace and yet we hesitate at times to do just that. We would do well to remember the days of old and the miracles that God performed in the lives of others. In fact we would do well to remember (as Joshua did) what He has done in our own lives in the past. We can trust God for our future no matter how many battles we face. God is our deliverer in all things.

## August 11

# LESSONS LEARNED

*(Joshua 8:30-32 Then Joshua built on Mount Ebal an altar to the Lord, the God of Israel, as Moses the servant of the Lord had commanded the Israelites. He built it according to what is written in the Book of the Law of Moses—an altar of uncut stones, on which no iron tool had been used. On it they offered to the Lord burnt offerings and sacrificed fellowship offerings. There, in the presence of the Israelites, Joshua copied on stones the law of Moses, which he had written.)*

Scripture tells us that Joshua read every word of the law-both the blessings and the curses to the whole assembly of Israelites. Why do you suppose Joshua did all of that? As the saying goes—'A lesson studied is a lesson learned.' I think Moses was reminding the people of the power of God, His sovereignty, His deliverance from their enemies, the blessings given because of obedience and those withheld because of disobedience. He was teaching them to remember everything that they had learned from the past generations to the events of the day.

I think we would do well if we reviewed the sovereignty of God. There is so much to learn from the past and the present. It helps prepare us for our future. If we don't study, how will we ever learn? If we don't commit to memory everything we have learned about God, we will not completely appreciate who He is—The One and Only Holy God: The One who holds our future in His hands. Much depends on our obedience to Him. As we read His word and remember those times when men and women of past generations were either blessed or cursed, we can plainly see that God will deal with us according to our obedience to Him.

Joshua was an obedient servant and he led the people well. He taught them the Law and honored God when He led them to victory. He was a man who gave God all of the glory for the victories in their pursuit of the Promised Land.

Do we remember the blessings that God has given us and do we give Him the glory for the things that He has done? Have we learned valuable lessons from remembering the past generations? And do we read His Word to show us the way? Do we seek His favor by obeying His commands? Joshua did all of these things. I don't know about you but I want to be like Joshua.

## August 12

# WHAT DOES AGE HAVE TO DO WITH IT?

*(Joshua 14:10b-11 "So here I am today, eighty-five years old! I am still as strong today as the day Moses sent me out; I'm just as vigorous to go out to battle now as I was then.")*

I just love this passage of scripture. For someone like me, who is on the downhill side of life (at least according to age), this is most encouraging. If you remember, Caleb and Joshua were the ones who had spied out the Promised Land for Moses when they were young men.

Caleb apparently had fought alongside Joshua in every battle that they encountered. Caleb reminded Joshua that he was eighty-five years old and still going strong. He was still full of vim and vigor. But he asked that he fulfill the Lord's promise to give him his portion of the Promised Land. It had been forty-five years since that promise. And Joshua fulfilled it that very day. What a team! Can't you just imagine that those two had many prayer meetings together during all of the years they served God?

I don't believe that Joshua and Caleb felt confident in their own ability, for I feel certain that they realized the worldly odds were against them; but they knew that God was in control and they had confidence in Him. I don't think they ever even considered that they might fail in these campaigns. Their faith and trust was far too strong for negative thoughts. And they were never intimidated by their age.

We are never too young or too old to do the job that God has called us to do: And we are never too old or feeble to fight the battles that face us. When we walk with the Lord and put our faith and trust in Him, we are victorious in all things. What an amazing thought. Why then should we feel inferior because of our age, our stature, or our inabilities? God is concerned only with our desire and obedience to serve Him. He will give us the strength and ability to carry out His commands. And He will always fulfill His promise to us.

I have been so blessed while writing about the things that transpired in the book of Joshua. It is such an example for us all: An example of what a Godly man or woman looks like. Joshua spent his entire life serving God and trusting in Him. Age has nothing to do with who we are in Christ. Joshua and Caleb did not let their age deter them in the least. Nor did they let the battles they faced discourage them. They just kept on trusting God and winning the battles they fought with confidence.

## August 13

# FAITH THAT DOES NOT WAVER

*(Hebrews 11:3 By faith we understand that the universe was formed at God's command, so that what is seen was not made out of what was visible.)*

We Christians have no problem believing that the world was created by God. We know through the Scriptures that Jesus enabled the lame to walk and to give sight to the blind. We believe that He was able to turn water in to wine, to heal the sick and to even raise people from death to life: Why then do we have doubts that God will answer our prayers?

Have there been times when you doubted that your prayers for someone would never come to fruition? I am sorry to say that there have been many times that I have prayed with doubt. Not because I doubted God but because of my lack of faith in people. But however I paint the picture it is still showing a lack of faith in God; for God is able to change any heart—I know because He changed mine. Think about what Paul was before he met the Lord on the road to Damascus. He was a persecutor to those who were followers of Christ. Yet God opened his eyes to see the truth of who Jesus was. He not only turned from his sin, but he became one of the most influential followers and teachers of Jesus in history.

*(Hebrews 11:1 Now faith is being sure of what we hope for and certain of what we do not see.)* So no matter what we see or don't see, we must keep our faith in Jesus. (*Hebrew 12:2 Let us fix our eyes on Jesus, the author and perfector of our faith, who for the joy set before him endured the cross, scorning its shame and sat down at the right hand of the throne of God.)* God is able to change any situation and any heart. God is not pleased with us when we lack faith—so have faith in God, keep your eyes on Him and pray that your faith will not waver.

## August 14

# HEARING BUT NOT UNDERSTANDING

*(Daniel 2:47 The king said to Daniel, "Surely your God is the God of gods and the Lord of kings and a revealer of mysteries, for you were able to reveal this mystery.")*

After Nebuchadnezzar had consulted everyone else for an answer to a dream that he had without results; Daniel, after seeking God was able to explain the dream to the king. The king fell down at Daniels feet and paid him honor and ordered that an offering and incense be presented to him.

In Chapter 3 we read that the king then made an image of gold and instructed everyone to bow down to it. And if they didn't they would be thrown into a blazing furnace. Wouldn't you think that after Daniel told the king everything God had revealed to him, that the king would turn to the Lord and worship Him? Well he didn't—he heard the story but he just didn't get it.

I wonder how many people hear the story of Jesus time and time again but still don't get it. Many people sit in church Sunday after Sunday; they hear the word preached and may even compliment the minister on a good sermon; and yet walk away unchanged. They may even see that God does exist, but they just don't get the real picture. The rest of their week is spent worshipping other gods in their life. I would venture to say that they could read the entire book of Daniel and be incensed at the fact that the king still worshipped other gods. But they would not understand that what they are doing when they reject Jesus is the very same thing that Nebuchadnezzar did; they hear but they just don't get it.

I know this is true first hand; I was one of those people. I heard the story of Jesus my entire life but it was forty two years before I got it. I knew that God was real but I chose to walk in ignorance. Why, you might ask did I do that? I believe that I was afraid of what might be required of me if I surrendered my heart to Jesus. I wanted to be free to control my own life. In reality it was when I finally got it and allowed God to be in control that I was set free from the chains that had me bound.

## August 15

# HEARING AND UNDERSTANDING

*(Daniel 4:14 At the end of that time, I, Nebuchadnezzar, raised my eyes toward heaven and my sanity was restored. Then I praised the Most High; I honored and glorified him who lives forever.)*

I get so excited when I read this part in Daniel: When King Nebuchadnezzar finally got it. He did not understand who God really was however, until he fell to the bottom. His royal authority was taken from him; he was driven away from people and lived like a wild animal; he ate grass like cattle. And after seven years living like this; then he acknowledged who God was.

This all came about after King Nebuchadnezzar had another dream that Daniel explained to him, after he had consulted everyone else first. The grace of God is amazing. It took this king a long time to finally get the message, but God continued to speak to him through Daniel until the day that He must have saw that Nebuchadnezzar was ready to hear from Him directly. He had prepared the king's heart and showed Him through his humbled circumstances that He is God and in control of all things.

I am certainly glad that God continued to pursue me for forty – two years. He led me to the point where I knew that I needed to turn my eyes and my heart to him. My husband was facing bypass surgery and I knew I had no control over the situation. I was totally aware of my need for a Savior—I finally understood who God really was, is and always will be. I can truly identify with what Nebuchadnezzar said *(Now I, Nebuchadnezzar, praise and exalt and glorify the King of heaven, because everything he does is right and all his ways are just. And those who walk in pride he is able to humble. Daniel 4:37)*

## August 16

# TRUST DURING TRIALS

*(James 1:2-4 Consider it pure joy, my brothers, whenever you face trials of many kinds, because you know that the testing of your faith develops perseverance. Perseverance must finish its work that you may be mature and complete, not lacking anything.)*

Are there times in your life that you feel as though you just can't take anymore trials and disappointments? I don't know about you, but there sure has been for me. When those times come along in our life, and they most likely will, we have a choice to make. We can allow those things to discourage us to the point of giving up; or we can put our faith in God and allow Him to use them to grow us up. The Scripture says that the testing of our faith develops perseverance so that we will be mature and complete, not lacking anything. Wow! Now that is an encouragement in itself.

I believe that if we never had trials in our life, we would never learn to be dependent on the Lord. He is the only one who can pave the way for us to become the people that He wants us to be. Sometimes it takes storms in our life to see our need for the sheltering wings of God. He shows us that no matter what comes our way, we find our strength in Him. And through Him we can face any trial. And as we weather the storm, our faith becomes stronger. We could not come through those trials victoriously without God. When we put our complete trust and faith in Him, we will be able to say that we lack nothing.

So then, we can consider it pure joy when we face those trials, knowing that He is maturing us. Isn't that what we want? I want God to mature me so that I will be ready to do anything that he asks me to do. We can be assured that our faith will be stronger when we persevere. So don't give up when you are going through those trials. Persevere and God will make you stronger as your faith increases.

# August 17

# REWARDED FAITH

*(Hebrews 11:6 And without faith it is impossible to please God, because anyone who comes to him must believe that he exists and that he rewards those who earnestly seek him.)*

The kind of faith that this Scripture is talking about is not to be compared with a ho-hum attitude. It is a faith that comes through passion for our Lord: A passion that gives us cause and the desire to seek Him in all of His fullness. I believe the reward that is talked about here, is finding the relationship that God desires from us. We are rewarded with His revelation to our understanding of who He is. Without a passionate desire to seek Him, we will never please Him. We will never be completely satisfied without the reward that is talked about in this Scripture. Brother Lawrence said once—"There is no sweeter manner of living in the world than continuous communion with God: Only those who have experienced it can understand."

I have been a Christian since 1982, but I have not always been passionate about seeking the reward of truly embracing all that He has for me. I think maybe there was a part of me that feared that kind of a relationship. Can you identify with that? I will tell you honestly that I was never satisfied when I was withholding that passionate desire to have the kind of faith that He wanted from me. The day I surrendered my total will to Him, was the day that He began to speak to my heart and give me the desire to be all that He wanted me to be—not that I have attained that yet, but I am seeking His wisdom to walk in His ways. I missed out on a lot of years wasted as I walked in that ho-hum faith.

*(Hebrews 11:1 Now faith is being sure of what we hope for and certain of what we do not see.)* Hope in this Scripture is not speaking of a worldly hope that maybe something might possibly happen. This hope is the assurance that it is going to happen. It is a hope that we put in Christ for His promises that are always true—not sometimes, but always. Our faith will never waver with this spiritual hope that comes through loving our Lord.

## August 18

# ACKNOWLEDGING GOD'S AMAZING GRACE

*(Lamentations 3:22-24 Because of the Lord's great love we are not consumed, for his compassions never fail; great is your faithfulness. I say to myself, "The Lord is my portion; therefore I will wait for him.)*

O the beautiful thought and knowledge of God's mercy and grace. How could I ever live without it? I have accepted it and I experience it every day; yet it is still difficult for me to comprehend. It is beyond anything ever known to the human mind. The grace of God far exceeds anything else one could ever imagine. It is because of His grace that I was chosen from the very beginning. It was by His grace that I have been redeemed. It is by His grace that He leads me to places that I would never have thought possible. And it is by His grace that I can withstand anything that comes my way. I am humbled by His mercy and His grace that is new every morning.

Have you considered the magnificent grace and mercy that God's love bestows on you? I believe that if you are a Christian, the answer to that question would be yes. I don't know about you, but I know that I would be lost, I would be defeated, I would be helpless to do anything worthwhile without His amazing grace. When I think about all of the times that He has shown me His grace, it is overwhelming. How could anyone have the kind of merciful love and grace that our Heavenly Father has for us?

There are those who have chosen to turn their backs on the grace that He offers them. They will not accept His merciful love. How sad to think that I was once one of those people. Yet God's grace convicted me of my sins and by His grace He drew me to Him. And now I experience His mercy and His grace each day. I pray that if you haven't experienced God's grace, that you would open up your heart to accept His love and mercy. It is by His grace that we are saved. *(But because of his great love for us, God, who is rich in mercy, made us alive with Christ even when we were dead in transgressions—it is by grace you have been saved. Ephesians 2:4-5)*

# August 19

# MORE OF GOD'S GRACE

*(Ephesians 2:8-10 For it is by grace you have been saved, through faith and this not from yourselves, it is the gift of God—not by works, so that no one can boast. For we are God's workmanship, created in Christ Jesus to do good works which God prepared in advance for us to do.)*

Wow! Here is another picture of God's amazing grace. We are who we are in Christ because of His grace. We are His children only because of His sacrifice on the cross. There is absolutely nothing we can do to deserve it. The grace that He bestows on us is unmerited. We can do nothing, we can say nothing, nor can we bribe our way to earning it. And it is an awesome knowledge that God prepared the work that He wanted us to do before we even accepted His grace of redemption. Now that is omniscience.

The Scripture is clear—we are all God's workmanship, created in Christ to do good works which He prepared in advance for us to do. Not just me and not just you—but to all who have been saved by His grace. None of us can ever boast about anything that we do for the Lord. He is the reason that we can carry out His plan for our lives.

I don't know about you, but I know that I could never do anything in my own power; but because of God's grace I can do anything and everything that He created me to do. *(I can do everything through Him, who gives me strength. Philippians 4:13)* That my friend is exciting, don't you agree? Before Christ, I suffered greatly from low self-esteem, but when God took control of my life, He gave me a purpose that I would never have dreamed possible. I truly became a new person in Him. And now I am who I am because of His grace and only because of His grace.

## August 20

# THE DESTRUCTION OF LIARS

*(Psalms 5:6 You destroy those who tell lies; bloodthirsty and deceitful men the Lord abhors.)*

I have been following the trial of a mother accused of killing her little girl. I have watched witness after witness get up and swear to God that they will tell the truth: Yet there are so many conflicting stories that reveal the fact that someone is lying— So many that it will make it difficult for the jury to discern just who is telling the truth. It makes you wonder if they are unconscious of the fact that they are lying to God and that they are misusing His Name by swearing on it.

As I have listened to the story of the lives involved in this particular family, I am sickened by how Satan has used all of these people in one way or another to tear their lives and relationships apart. But most of all it is sad and disturbing to see how their lives have been destroyed by the fact that some have led a life of lies.

We may get by with the lies we tell to others, but we will never escape the fact that God knows every lie that has ever been told, and that He will destroy those who tell them. God's word says, *(You have not lied to men but to God. Acts 5:4)* Think about the seriousness of lying—it is not to be taken lightly. Lying destroys lives and relationships.

We learn how to lie when we are little to try and escape the punishment of the wrong that we have done and are trying to hide. We should teach our children from the time that they learn to sin in this way; that there will be consequences for what they do. We need to let them know that it comes from the evil one. *(John 8:44 You belong to your father, the devil, and you want to carry out your father's desire., He was a murderer from the beginning, not holding to the truth for there is no truth in him. When he lies, he speaks his native language, for he is a liar and the father of lies.)*

We tell lies to either hide our sin or that of someone else's, in which case it then becomes our sin also. I believe at one time or another we have all lied in one way or another and then we justify it with telling ourselves that it is just a little white lie. Is it? I don't think so. One lie leads to another until it destroys. Let's not let the father of lies lead us into sin. Let's remember that when we lie, we are lying to our Father, and he won't let it go unpunished.

## August 21

# FEAR OF DEATH

*(Hebrews 2:14-15 Since the children have flesh and blood, he too shared in their humanity so that by his death he might destroy him who holds the power of death—that is, the devil—and free those who all their lives were held in slavery by their fear of death.)*

The first 42 years of my life, I was frightened by even the thought of death. I hated to go to funerals because it made me think about my own death. Then one day all of that changed. I surrendered my heart to the Lord. I was free from that gripping fear of death. I suddenly understood that because of Christ's death on The Cross, I received eternal life. I finally knew that my life would never end. I would just step out of this body and this world into a new body and into a perfect world.

Are you afraid to die? You shouldn't be. There is a way to be sure that you will never die. The only way to eternal life is through Jesus Christ. He paid the penalty for your sin just as He did for mine. He gave His life so that we may live. If you live in fear of dying, stop right now and eliminate that fear by giving your heart to the one who paid the price for your sin—Jesus Christ. It is that simple. *(1 Corinthians 15:54-55 When the perishable has been clothed with the imperishable and the mortal with immortality, then the saying that is written will come true: "Death has been swallowed up in victory." "Where, O death is your sting?")*

# August 22

# RENEWED FORGIVENESS

*(Judges 5:7 When the Israelites cried to the Lord because of Midian, he sent them a prophet who said, "This is what the Lord, the God of Israel, says: I brought you up out of Egypt, out of the land of slavery, I snatched you from the power of Egypt and from the hand of all your oppressors. I drove them from before you and gave you their land. I said to you, 'I am the Lord your God; do not worship the gods of the Amorites, in whose land you live.' But you have not listened to me.")*

Once again we see the Israelites crying out to God for help. How many times have we read in the Old Testament how the Israelites followed the Lord's commands for a while, and then became enslaved again to things that threatened to destroy them? When we read about these obstinate people, we become incensed at their rebellion.

God had told them not to worship the gods of the Amorites. Are we like the Israelites? Do we take our eyes off of the Lord in favor of the God's set before us? We also can be led astray by those who do not know the Lord. It is easy to get involved with people who will encourage us to turn away from the Lord and go our own way. Satan likes nothing more than for us to become involved with sinful people. He will cloud our minds and our hearts to the point of turning away from the very One who has given us freedom from the sin that had us entangled in the first place. How is it that we can so quickly forget from whence we came?

When we leave the teaching of those who know the Lord; when we turn our backs on what we have learned; when we choose to have our own will; we can expect disaster. There will come a day that we will know that we have made the wrong choice. And we will pay the consequences. I am always overwhelmed that because of God's grace, He is always willing to hear our cry for help, even after we have rebelled against Him: He will forgive us once again. O, but for the grace of God.

## August 23

# WHEN DOUBTS ASSAIL

*(Judges 6:14-16 The Lord turned to him and said, "Go in the strength you have and save Israel out of Midian's hand. Am I not sending you?" "But Lord, Gideon asked, "how can I save Israel? My clan is the weakest in Manasseh, and I am the least in my family." The Lord answered, "I will be with you, and you will strike down all the Midianites together.")*

When Gideon was told to go and save Israel out of the Midian's hands, Gideon's response was to tell the Lord how weak he was. Instead of focusing on God's strength, he was focusing on his own weakness. He asked the Lord for signs that would show him that he was really hearing right from God.

Can you identify with Gideon in his doubt about himself? I sure can. I think it is a pretty human response. I am overwhelmed when God asks me to do anything. My first response is, I can't—I am not qualified—I am the least person to be able to do what you have asked me to do. But God inevitably informs me that I can do all things through Him. He is the one who gives me strength.

Notice that Gideon asked God that he not go away until he brought an offering to Him. God's response was, "I will wait until you return." Don't you just love it? It certainly shows that Gideon wanted to show his love and respect to God by worshipping Him. And the fact that God would wait on him, shows how patient God is with us when we doubt ourselves. Gideon brought his offering to Him, and the Lord told him to go in peace and not to be afraid because he was not going to die. Have you ever been there? The Lord will always meet us at the altar of worship. He will always give us peace and strength to do what He has asked us to do. He will not walk away and leave us helpless when we seek His face.

Are you having doubts about what God has asked you to do? Remember Gideon.

# August 24

# ASKING FOR AFFIRMATION

*(Judges 6:36-37 Gideon said to God, "If you will save Israel by my hand as you have promised—look, I will place a wool fleece on the threshing floor. If there is dew only on the fleece and all the ground is dry, then I will know that you will save Israel by my hand as you said")*

Have you ever asked God to give you a sign or affirmation for something that you believe He has called you to do? I have, more than once. As a matter of fact, just about everything He asks me to do, I implore Him to reaffirm it. He has never failed to do that for me.

We already know that Gideon felt like he was the less likely person to save the Israelites from the Medians, so why wouldn't he want to be certain that it truly was a call from God. He did not have confidence in his own abilities, but he did have confidence in God. He just wanted to make certain that he was hearing correctly and directly from God and for no other reason.

I never have confidence in myself, so I need affirmation that God is with me at all times, through all things. Don't you? It terrifies me to think that I would get involved in something that God did not want me to do. That is a scary position. For if God is not in it, it will surely fail. I think Gideon felt the same way. On the other hand, I believe he had already determined in his heart that he would certainly follow through when he got affirmation that it was truly a message from God.

I can certainly identify with Gideon: I just recently have gone through the exact same situation—is what I think I heard really from God. I also have asked him to reaffirm His call—and He has. I will go ahead and do the thing that God has put on my heart with the assurance and affirmation that it is from Him. Are you going through a similar situation? Are you wondering if you heard God right? Ask Him to reaffirm it and He will.

## August 25

# FROM RAGS TO RICHES

*(Isaiah 64:6 All of us have become like one who is unclean, and all our righteous acts are like filthy rags; we all shrivel up like a leaf, and like the wind our sins sweep us away.)*

What makes us righteous? I will tell you one thing—it is not what we do; it is not what we say; and it is not what we think. There are those who believe that because they do good works, they are righteous. But God's word says that those righteous acts are like filthy rags.

There are a lot of good people in this world who do good things, but it will never make them righteous: Being righteous means that we have a right relationship with God. Christ is the only way to righteousness. His death on the cross paved the way for our righteousness—but we must accept Him as our personal Savior. There is no other way to enter the gate to Heaven except through God's Son. No matter how hard we work, we will never enter into His righteousness without His cleansing blood.

But because of God's grace we have become righteous people. Our filthy rags have become riches. (But because of his great love for us, God, who is rich in mercy, made us alive with Christ even when we were dead in transgressions—it is by grace you have been saved. And God raised us up with Christ and seated us with him in the heavenly realms in Christ Jesus, in order that in the coming ages he might show the incomparable riches of his grace, expressed in his kindness to us in Christ Jesus. For it is by grace you have been saved through faith—and this not from yourselves, it is the gift of God—not by works, so that no one can boast.)

And there you have it in a nut shell—we are righteous only through the blood of Jesus.

# August 26

# YESTERDAY, TODAY & TOMORROW

*(James 4:13-14 Now listen, you who say, "Today or tomorrow we will go to this or that city, spend a year there, carry on business and make money." Why, you do not even know what will happen tomorrow. What is your life? You are a mist that appears for a little while and then vanishes.)*

What is time? Time is the measure of life. Our time on this earth is ordained by God. Only He knows what lies ahead. Even today is not promised to us. We could wake up in the morning and be but a vapor by the end of the day. We have no control over our time on this earth.

Why then do we worry so much about our yesterdays, todays, and tomorrows? God tells us not to worry about our life. He will supply our needs day by day, and moment by moment. Our tomorrows are gone; we cannot take them back and change a thing. Today is here and we should embrace it with joy and gladness, and not worry about those things that we have no control over. Tomorrow may never come for us, so why should we sit around and worry about the things that may or may not happen. If it is in God's will that we wake up tomorrow, He is able to lead us through it.

We get so wrapped up in our ideas of what we should or should not do. We make plans for those things that we want to do tomorrow. Who knows whether we will get them all accomplished or not. If God wants us to—we will. It is the eagerness to be obedient to Him that he desires. When we say, "Yes Lord", that is enough for Him. He will take care of the way, how, who, when, and where according to His perfect will. His plan will be carried out, you can depend on that. If His desire is for us to live another day to accomplish His will, we will. I believe that we should take each hour as is comes, seeking His will for our lives, but we should never worry about it. Submission is what He wants, regardless of what day it is, or how old we are. Our life should never be measured by our own stick. Let's rejoice each day in the Lord. *(This is the day the Lord has made, let us be glad and rejoice in it. Psalm 118:24)* Let's take one day at a time and make the most of it as we allow Him to lead us.

## August 27

# FLEE FROM YOUR ENEMIES

*(Psalms 6:8-10 Away from me, all you who do evil, for the Lord has heard my weeping. The Lord has heard my cry for mercy; the Lord accepts my prayer. All my enemies will be ashamed and dismayed; they will turn back in sudden disgrace.)*

J. Edwin Orr describes some of the work among new converts in Halifax during the Second Great Awakening in Britain: "Among them was a boxer who had just won a money-prize and a belt. A crowd of his erstwhile companions stood outside the hall in order to ridicule him, and they hailed the converted boxer with a shout: 'He's gettin' converted! What about that belt? You either have to fight for it or give it up!' The boxer retorted: 'I'll both give it up and you up! If you won't go with me to heaven, I won't go with you to hell!' He gave them the belt, but persuaded some of them to accompany him to the services, where another was converted and set busily working."

When we ask God for his mercy and forgiveness, He is quick to accept our plea of repentance. He embraces us with His love. The enemy cannot stand it and he uses our so called friends to try and destroy what God has done in our lives. It is imperative that we give up the acquaintances that suddenly have become our enemies: Those who want to pull us back into sin. If they are not willing to accept who we are in Christ, we must separate ourselves from them.

If they are influenced by our new found life, they will not try to pull us down; rather we might just be the catalyst that causes them to come to Jesus. Once we accept Jesus as our Savior, we have a responsibility to live up to the name of Christian. We are to set an example to the world. We cannot live the way that we did before Christ. If we do not want to change our life style, we need to ask ourselves if we truly accepted Christ, or did we just mouth the words and go through the motions?

When we come to Christ, we are a new creation, the old person is gone and the new one steps up to be identified with Christ. (Ref. 2 Corinthians 5:17). In the above Scripture, David was telling all of those who were his enemies to get entirely away from him. Let's have the courage to turn back our enemies and embrace all that God has for us as we seek His will for our life.

## August 28

# A JOYFUL REUNION

*(Psalms 119:74 May those who fear you rejoice when they see me, for I have put my hope in your word.)*

I recently spent two days with four other women who love the Lord with all their hearts. Every time we meet together it is sheer joy. We spend our entire time together praying, singing, laughing, sharing His word and planning for the ministry that we share together. It is like a party with God as our special invited guest. He is the center of attention as we seek His presence and His authoritarian wisdom and advice.

We listen to each other's concerns and praises and lift one another up in prayer. It is difficult to put into words just how magnificent our time together is. Charles Spurgeon says it this way—quote— "We do not only meet to share each other's burdens, but to partake in each other's joys, gracious men contribute largely to the stock of mutual gladness. Hopeful men bring gladness with them". — Unquote. The reason we have such a great time is because we put our hope in God and His Word.

People miss so much by not sharing their love and excitement for the Lord with each other. Maybe it is because they feel uncomfortable doing so. Maybe they think they would be considered weird or fanatical. Are you one who hesitates to be vocal and demonstrative of your love for the Lord? Don't be; if you would let go of your reserve I believe you would know the joy that I am talking about.

# August 29

# A HISTORY LESSON

*(Psalm 40:5 Many, O Lord my God, are the wonders you have done. The things you planned for us no one can recount to you; were I to speak and tell of them, they would be too many to declare.)*

God does amazing things in the lives of those who are surrendered to Him. He can take the vilest sinner who has fought against Him, and turn them in to a dynamic soldier in His army. He can change the hearts and the lives of those perishing in their hopelessness; and He can break the chains that keep them in bondage. There is no way to count the marvelous things that He does for those who love Him.

As I ponder my past; as I recall my short comings; as I remember my life before Christ—I am totally amazed by the difference He made in my life. I am no longer who I used to be. God turned my life around—He turned it upside down—He gave me hope and a future that I could never have imagined. I truly found a new life in Christ. My history became His Story. I became a new creation the minute I accepted His love and His grace. I was no longer the same. He wrote the ending to the story of a life that would have been hopeless, and gave me a new beginning and a new ending. I would have died in my sins if not for His grace. Some Christians use the term that they were born again, and others take offense at that. Yet that is exactly what happens when we come to Christ. He truly creates us anew—He gives us a new birth. *(2 Corinthians 5:17 Therefore, if anyone is in Christ, he is a new creation; the old has gone, the new has come!)*

I know if you are a Christian, you can identify with what I am saying. I am so thankful that my past history has become His Story— aren't you? There is no way to convey the wonderful things that God has done. It is something that one has to experience through their own choice to let Jesus rewrite their history. If you think that your life is out of control and you have no future—think again. God is ready to give you a new beginning. All you have to do is ask.

## August 30

# CRACKED VESSELS

*(2 Corinthians 4:7 But we have this treasure in jars of clay to show that this all surpassing power is from God and not from us.)*

Have you ever felt the discouragement of having made a mistake in your quest to be all that God wants you to be? Have you felt like you have disgraced yourself because of it? Or even worse, that you have disgraced God and therefore are not worthy of your calling? I have, and it is a most disparaging place to be. But when we have thoughts like that, we are letting the evil one do the talking, not God.

We are who we are in Christ, not of ourselves. We have been given treasures that come with knowing Christ as our personal Savior. Those treasures are the knowledge that God has given to us; not because we are perfect, we are not, nor will we ever be. Jesus was the only perfect man to ever walk this earth. We are vessels made of clay. And we all know that clay cracks once in a while. I believe that God allows that to happen to show us and the world that He is the all surpassing power behind the clay vessel. We can do nothing outside of Him.

Don't be discouraged when your vessel shows a crack, it only means that you are not perfect. God has chosen to use those vessels of clay to be a light to the world. Why didn't Paul choose to describe us as a harder substance, such as a diamond? Could it be that clay is pliable? Do others need to see that we are only a vessel to be used by God? When people understand that God can use the ordinary to do extraordinary things, it shows that we are weak but He is strong. He is the power behind all things.

Others should not compare these clay vessels with Jesus. When all is said and done, people need to realize that we are human but God has chosen to use us, in our imperfections to spread His word.

# August 31

# A SHORT LEGACY

*(Judges 10:1-2 After the time of Abimelech a man of Issachar, Tola son of Puah, the son of Dodo, rose to save Israel. He lived in Shamir, in the hill country of Ephraim. He led Israel twenty-three years; then he died, and was buried in Shamir.)*

The only thing we know about Tola is that he was the son of Puah and the grandson of Dodo from the tribe of Issachar and that he judged Israel for twenty-three years after Abimelech died and lived at Shamir in Mount Ephraim, where he was also buried. Of all the Biblical judges, the least is written about Tola. None of his deeds are recorded. The entire account of his life is written in two short verses. But what a story those two versus tell.

This is one of those 'WOW' places in the bible that hit me like a bolt of lightning. I wonder how many times I have read it, but it never resonated with me. What a powerful message in these two short versus—so few words, but such a powerful story of the life of a man surrendered to His Lord. The little that we read here tells an entire life story about this man of God—He lived, He rose to save Israel—He led them for twenty-three years—He died and was buried in Shamir. This man named Tola was born for this specific purpose. He did the job that God called him to do with little fan-fare.

Do you know any Tolas? I do—they are those people who live to serve the Lord. They are not well known but their ministry is powerful. They work quietly behind the scenes serving the Lord and carrying out His will for their life. They may never receive any accolades of accomplishment in this life, but oh what a quiet and powerful legacy they will leave.

I want to be like Tola, don't you? I would like for people to say when I am gone—I didn't know her but I understand that she loved and served the Lord. I want my legacy to be that I was a woman who accomplished what God wanted me to do. I do not desire any accolades from the world but I desire to enter into Heaven and hear God say—"Well done my good and faithful servant."

# September 1

# NEEDLESS WORRY

*(John 14:27 "Peace I leave with you, my peace I give you. I do not give to you as the world gives: Do not let your hearts be troubled and do not be afraid.)*

If we put our focus on all that is going in this evil world, we would be prostrate with worry. Let's face it; there is not much to look forward to in this world by all indications. Every time we turn on the news, open a paper, or listen to the problems all over the world, we are leaving ourselves open for despair and fear. There does not seem to be a very happy and secure future. But we cannot and should not let the troubles in this life rob us from the peace that God wants us to have. *(Proverbs 13:12 Hope deferred makes the heart sick, but a longing fulfilled is a tree of life.)*

In spite of all the bad news and doubt of a confident future here on earth, we have a hope that does not come from anybody or anything on this earth. It comes by way of a personal relationship with our Lord. Our hope is in Him. It matters not what happens in this life for the Christian because they know their future. Their future is secure in the knowledge that one day our troubles will be over and we will live in the presence of God without the worries and concerns of the old life here on earth.

Don't let your hearts be troubled. When Satan tries to destroy your peace, remember that the Holy Spirit resides within you and He is more powerful than the one who is in the world trying to rob you of your peace. Don't dwell on the negative things around you, but rather think of all of the good things that God has done for you and is doing for you. *(Philippians 4:8 Finally, brothers, whatever is true, whatever is noble, whatever is right, whatever is pure whatever is lovely, whatever is admirable—if anything is excellent or praiseworthy—think about such things.)*

When you give way to worry and fear, it does not come from the Lord: It comes from the evil one. He does not want you to live in the peace that God gives you—the peace that passes all understanding. Let go of your fear and receive God's peace.

# September 2

# GIVING WAY TO TEMPTATION

*(James 1:14 But each one is tempted when, by his own evil desire, he is dragged away and enticed. Then, after desire has conceived, it gives birth to sin; and sin, when it is full-grown, gives birth to death.)*

I was so sad to find out just last week that a couple had ended their marriage because the wife in the relationship was tempted by the life-style of friends. Now this was a Christian woman (at least she claimed to be) who thought she was missing out on all the fun in life. She felt as if life was passing her by. She gave way to her temptation.

I am astounded and dismayed by the fact that there are so many marriages breaking up these days. What in the world has happened? How come people can't seem to stay in a committed relationship? The answer is sin.

Satan loves to destroy families—and one way he does it, is to make one feel like they deserve to be free from the obligation of a commitment to their spouse. They forget about the love that they once had for their mate because they allow their temptations to take over their life. There are many marriages destroyed because of adultery. Adultery usually starts with a look—a word—a touch—that leads to the full act of adultery. In other words instead of turning away from their own evil desire, they are dragged away and enticed and that enticement ends in sin.

Sin can be fun, which is the enticement tool that Satan uses: And many fall for his lies and deception. But think about the destruction. I believe that everyone who gives in to that enticement will one day regret the choice they made. I wonder how many out there who have destroyed a home, can say that they are truly happy. There is always a consequence to sin. When we sin, we not only hurt ourselves, but those close to us. We usually end up hurting those we love most of all. And once one gives in to the enticement to sin—they can never go back to the place where they were. Things will never be the same again.

Before we give in to temptation, one should consider the conse-quences. Are you being tempted by someone or by something that seems good, but you know is sin? Stop; quit dwelling on it: Turn your back on it or it will destroy you. Don't give in to the temptation to sin for it gives birth to death.

## September 3

# THE PURSUIT OF HAPPINESS

*(Ephesians 3:7-8 I became a servant of this gospel by the gift of God's grace given me through the working of his power. Although I am less than the least of all God's people, this grace was given me: to preach to the Gentiles the unsearchable riches of Christ.)*

For 42 years I ran from the Lord. I thought I had to be perfect to be a Christian. I never saw God as a gracious God; I pictured Him as a strict disciplinarian. I feared God, not with awesome fear, but fear that I couldn't measure up to what He expected of me. I never pictured Him as a loving God, just one who was ready to punish me if I didn't do things right. But then through the Holy Spirit, He got my attention when my husband was facing bypass surgery in 1982. They hadn't done much of that in those days and it was a terribly frightening thing to think about. I wanted to pray for his healing, but God spoke to my heart and said that I needed healing first. I knew what He meant and I gave my heart to the Lord at that precise time.

I started reading my bible and a wonderful friend led me through a very elementary bible study. I had been in church as a child, but ran from God after I was married because of the reasons I have already explained. Suddenly I was seeing how much God loved me and that it was by His grace that I was saved. It had nothing to do about what I did or didn't do. I learned that I could do nothing to earn His love. He already loved me and had paid the price for my sins on The Cross. It was such an exciting time and I learned to love Him and His Word tremendously.

I can certainly identify with what Paul is saying in the above scripture. I am the least likely to be used of God and yet He has given me a purpose and a great desire to spread His word. I give God all the glory for all that He has done in my life: It is all because of His love, His grace, and the working of His power. I am so grateful that He pursued me when I could have continued to run from Him. Because of His pursuit of me, I have complete happiness and peace. I want to serve Him the rest of my life.

# September 4

# THE WINGS OF REFUGE

*(Psalm 91:4-5, 14 He will cover you with his feathers, and under his wings you will find refuge; his faithfulness will be your shield and rampart. You will not fear the terror of night, nor the arrow that flies by day, nor the pestilence that stalks in the darkness, nor the plague that destroys at midday. "Because he loves me," says the Lord, "I will rescue him; I will protect him, for he acknowledges my name.)*

We all have a propensity to worry: And why wouldn't we, when we live in such uncertain times? All one has to do is listen to the news to see that evil does exist and it seems to be the prevailing force in the world today. Not only do we worry about what goes on in the world around us, we also worry about our own personal circumstances. In one way or another, we all walk in deep valleys at times, not knowing where the path will lead.

The above verse tells us that God will cover us with His wings of refuge. He says because we love Him he will protect us. What a comforting thought! Can we take that all in and believe what God is telling us? If you are worried and fearful about your circumstances, close your eyes and think about the promises of God, let your spirit feel the arms of God wrapped around you. Give your worry and fear to Him and let Him still your heart and your mind and give you peace. Yes there is evil in this world but we don't have to give in to our fears for the Scripture tells us (*You, dear children, are from God and have overcome them, because the one who is in you is greater that the one who is in the world. 1 John 4:4)*

# September 5

# TIME WITH GOD

*(Psalm 119:147 I rise before dawn and cry for help; I have put my hope in your word.)*

This Scripture in psalms really speaks to my heart. For those of you, who know me well; know that I am an early riser: Most days, I am awake somewhere between 3:30-5:00. I don't make the choice to get up that early, but it seems to be when God speaks to me with a clear voice. That is not to say that I hear him audibly, but within my spirit. It is a time of day when He has my undivided attention. Most of the world around me is still asleep and there is nothing to distract me from my time with God. It is when I speak to Him and Him to me. I have a special place in my home that I call my sanctuary. The Lord never fails to meet me there. I share my praises and my concerns with Him and He never lets me down. When I am discouraged, He lifts me up and gives me peace. When I am weak, He gives me strength, when I am troubled He calms my fears. When I am happy, He hears my songs of joy and praise.

God doesn't care what time of day we meet with Him. There are some who just are not morning people; and there is nothing wrong with that. I have a friend who has her special time with the Lord late at night. The important thing is; that we find the time to be with the Lord. We live in a fast paced world. It seems most of us are rushing here and there doing all sorts of things. Many of them are good things, but if we are ignoring our private time with the Lord, we need to rethink our plans for the day. I find that when I take the time to be with the Lord, everything in my life goes smoother. That doesn't mean that we don't have problems; but when we meet with our Savior, we can have peace and find direction for each day.

God wants our companionship. How can we establish an intimate relationship with anyone without spending time with them? If you are finding it difficult to spend quiet time with God, ask Him to eliminate those unnecessary things that are robbing you of your daily bread.

# September 6

# A TRAGIC VOW

*(Judges 11:30, 31, 34, 35 And Jephthah made a vow to the Lord: "If you give the Ammonites into my hands, whatever comes out of the door of my house to meet me when I return in triumph from the Ammonites will be the Lord's, and I will sacrifice it as a burnt offering." When Jephthah returned to his home in Mizpah, who should come out to meet him but his daughter, dancing to the sound of tambourines. She was an only child. Except for her he had neither son nor daughter!)*

Are you familiar with this account of Jephthah and his daughter? The first time I read about Jephthah's tragic vow, I was very confused. I wondered why God would allow something like this to happen. I have sense realized that the vow was made by Jephthah, God did not have anything to do with it. Jephthah must have thought that God would not help him if he did not offer him something in return. God does not expect anything in return for His favors except our obedience to Him. He would never want us to sacrifice a life of an innocent person. Jephthah was greatly disturbed when his daughter came out of that door and he tore his clothes and cried, thinking that he had to follow up on his vow. But I think he made another foolish mistake, he did not recognize the fact that God had not bargained with him, so he was not bound to his one sided vow.

Have you ever bargained with God—promising Him certain things in order to bribe him in to doing what you want Him to do? He must shake His head in sorrow for our endeavor to bring Him down to less than sovereign. God does not bargain with us. He does not put conditions to our prayers except to pray according to His will. He is a merciful God. All He wants from us is obedience. I think the story of Jepthah is one of the most tragic stories in the bible. It is pure fallacy to think that God would make a vow with us to attain what we want; especially when it would harm someone else.

# September 7

# AN ENCOURAGING TEACHER

*(Philippians 2:1-2 If you have any encouragement from being united with Christ, if any comfort from his love, if any fellowship with the Spirit, if any tenderness and compassion, then make my joy complete by being like-minded, having the same love, being one in spirit and purpose.)*

The excitement of school starting is upon us. It has caused me to remember a time in my very distant past, when I was in the fourth grade. My teacher's name was Miss Kennedy. I shall never forget her. I thought she was beautiful. She had one blue eye and one brown eye. I think though it was her inner beauty that shown through. She was the most wonderful teacher I had in all of my school years. I have since thought that she surely must have been a Christian. She treated every child the same—as if they were special. She had no favorites and she encouraged every one to do their best, without putting constrained pressure on them.

Teachers are in a position to encourage young students to be all that God wants them to be. Unfortunately in this evil world we live in, they are not always allowed to speak about God, as it has become politically incorrect. But if they are Christians themselves they can demonstrate the love and encouragement through the Holy Spirit that their students will remember for the rest of their life. They can make a huge impact on the lives of their students by being the encourager that God wants them to be. I believe that there have been many people who have stepped up to excellence in their life as a result of a teacher who encouraged them. Teaching is a gift from God, and His gift to them should be exemplified by encouraging their students.

We need to pray that God will protect our schools and our students from being taught by those who are not gifted teachers. Teachers can make or break the confidence of the young hearts that are under their influence. Those who discourage instead of encouraging their young students should have no place in our education system. Our schools should be aware of the character of those who are shaping the lives of our youth. Every teacher should encourage their students to be all that they can be. I am thankful that my grandchildren are blessed by having a Christian school available in our town where the teachers are allowed to teach them that—through Christ they can do all things.

# September 8

# O SWEET HOPE

*(Micah 7:7 But as for me, I watch in hope for the Lord, I wait for God my Savior; my God will hear me.)*

Every one I talk to these days is concerned about the world situation. It is a frightening thing to hear about all of the conflict and strife, not only in our own country but in the entire world. Our future is far less than optimistic. Everywhere we turn, we see what seem to be, insurmountable obstacles. Will we ever be at peace again in this world? My personal opinion is no, we won't.

We have more problems than we can count. Unanswered questions assail us. There are questions about our financial situation, not just nationally but in our own personal life. Many are asking themselves if their job is secure. Alas, there are many who have lost their jobs and wonder if there is anything out there for them.

We live under the threat of war constantly. We are already in battles that have been going on for some time and face the possibility of more almost every day. Many are concerned about their loved ones who are fighting in foreign lands.

Natural disasters seem to be occurring with unprecedented frequency and manner; adding to the problem of an already shortage of food. These disasters have taken many lives and homes, leaving people with a hopeless feeling.

All of these problems are very real. If we focus on them, we could all suffer from a feeling of hopelessness. But our hope is in the Lord. He is the only one who can calm our fears and give us peace in the midst of all of the calamities that surround us. There are no answers for the problems that we face each day. But there is an answer as to how we can handle them. The answer is found in our God: He is our hope and our strength. *(Psalm 46:1-7 God is our refuge and strength, an ever present help in trouble. Therefore we will not fear, though the earth gives way and the mountains fall into the heart of the sea, though its waters roar and foam and the mountains quake with their surging. There is a river whose streams make glad the city of God the holy place where the Most High dwells. God is within her, she will not fall; God will help her at break of day. Nations are in uproar, kingdoms fall; he lifts his voice the earth melts. The Lord Almighty is with us; the God of Jacob is our fortress.)*

## September 9

# A GROANING PRAYER

*(Romans 8:26-27 In the same way, the Spirit helps us in our weakness. We do not know what we ought to pray for, but the Spirit himself intercedes for us with groans that words cannot express. And he who searches our hearts knows the mind of the Spirit, because the Spirit intercedes for the saints in accordance with God's will.)*

This Scripture just amazes me. There have been so many times in my life when I was so disturbed about situations that were out of my control—times when I did not know how to pray any more: All I could do is just moan and cry. Can you identify?

Well the truth is, we do not have to know how to pray in situations like this. The Holy Spirit knows our hearts, our thoughts, and our heartaches. And He will intercede on our behalf. What a comforting thought that we do not have to be articulate in our prayers, we just have to open our heart to Jesus; give everything to Him; lay our troubles at the foot of the cross and allow Him to take over—even on those days that we cannot pray.

God is our Peace; our Redeemer; our Friend. He never leaves us helpless. He is there through every battle in our life and He is always ready to intercede on our behalf.

God knows our heart and He hears our painful cries without even having to put them into words. What an amazing God!

# September 10

# WAIT AND SEE

*(Genesis 15:2-4 But Abram said,"O Sovereign Lord, what can you give me since I remain childless and the one who will inherit my estate is Eliezer of Damascus?" And Abram said, "You have given me no children; so a servant in my household will be my heir," Then the word of the Lord came to him: "This man will not be your heir, but a son coming from your own body will be your heir.")*

God had promised Abram that he would give him a son of his own. Scripture tells us that when he and Sari didn't have that son in the time frame that they thought was reasonable; they took control of the situation and made their own plans to have an heir. We all know the disastrous results of that. Read all about it in Genesis 16 & 17. The results of that are being felt today.

Are we like Abram and Sarai? Do we take things in our own hands when we can't see God at work? Just because we can't see God's plan doesn't mean that He isn't working in our lives. We must allow God to bring about those things that He has planned on His time frame, not ours. If we run ahead of God and take control of our own lives, it could be a disaster. We need to trust and wait on the Lord. *(I am still confident of this: I will see the goodness of the Lord in the land of the living. Wait for the Lord; be strong and take heart and wait for the Lord. Psalms 27:13-14.)* Let's just wait and see what marvelous things God has for us.

# September 11

# BLESSED HOPE

*(Romans 8:24-25 For in this hope we were saved. But hope that is seen is no hope at all. But if we hope for what we do not yet have, we wait for it patiently.)*

We are not mind readers, and we cannot see the future. But one thing is certain; when we give our lives to Christ we have the assurance that we have everlasting hope. We cannot see it but we know that it is true.

Sometimes life deals us severe blows—blows that knock the wind right out of our sails. There are things that happen that we have no control over and we groan with anguish as we wait on the Lord. But we can and must put our hope in the Lord for the things we cannot see. The Scripture says that hope that is seen is no hope at all. Hope is waiting on the Lord with full assurance that He will make good His promises.

Are you going through trials that have you paralyzed with fear, anxiety, feelings of failure, and hopelessness? Release them to the Lord. Do not let the evil one destroy your peace. Remember the hope that comes from knowing Jesus. Focus on that and not on your circumstances.

I don't know about you, but I expect to receive what God has promised me—hope for the future.

## September 12

# VICTORY IN THE LORD

*(Proverbs 21:31 The horse is made ready for the day of battle, but victory rests with the Lord).*

The wise words of Solomon give us much to ponder. As I was reading in Proverbs this morning, this particular verse stood out in a large way. I wonder how many of us line up every defensive tool we can possibly use, thinking we will surely win the battle that we are in. I don't know about you, but when I am attacked my first reaction is to plan a counterattack. At one time in my life, I would have been dogmatic in my plan to fight my own battle in my own way. Can you identify?

We waste a tremendous amount of time, trying to gain victory on our own steam but we will never win without the Lord's help. We might even think that we have won a battle, but believe me, without depending on God; we will never win the war. I have learned that victory lies in my trust, faith and dependence on my Lord. Are you in a battle right now? Do you feel like you have everything under control? Are you trusting in your own defenses, or are you giving it to God, and letting Him fight the battle for you? He is the way to victory.

# September 13

# PRAYING FOR OUR ENEMIES

*(Matthew 5:44-45 But I tell you, love your enemies and pray for those who perse-cute you, that you may be children of your Father in heaven. He causes his sun to rise on the evil and the good, and sends rain on the righteous and the unrighteous.)*

The kind of love that Jesus is talking about here is beyond anything that we could conjure up in our human efforts. But if we are children of God we must be willing to look beyond the frailties of our enemies and pray for them. After all, we Christians can call ourselves by that name only because we have been saved by God's grace.

God loves everyone, even those who deny Him. He died for their salvation, just as He died for yours and mine. Just because they have turned their backs on Him, it does not keep Him from loving them. I believe that He still prays for them to come to Him. They have the freedom to reject Him but it does not alter the fact that He still loves them.

Have you ever wondered why some people who do not give God a thought seem to have a charmed life? You know, those who never seem to have problems like some Christians do. I must admit, I have wondered about that at times. But the truth is told in the above verse; He causes his sun to rise on the evil and the good, and sends rain on the righteous and the unrighteous. If that is not unconditional love, I don't know what is.

Can we possibly show that kind of love to our enemies? Yes, but only by the grace of God. I must admit that it is sometimes difficult to pray for those who have persecuted me. Can you identify? But God has instructed us to love them and pray for them; and He will help us to overcome that human tendency to hate them.

## September 14

# RENEWED STRENGTH

*(Judges 16:22 But the hair on his head began to grow again after it had been shaved.)*

Samson went through a lot because of his weakness for women. You must be familiar with his story. He lost his strength when his hair was cut because he gave in to Delila"s pleading. Today I want to talk about the rest of the story: Starting with the fact that his hair started to grow back immediately.

The Philistines were celebrating the fact that their god Dagon had delivered Samson in to their hands. They brought Samson out to perform for them—He performed—oh how he performed: Certainly not in the way that they expected. Samson asked that he be put where he could feel the pillars for support. He prayed that God would remember him and strengthen him once more. He also prayed that he would die along with the Philistines. God answered his prayers. *(Then Samson reached toward the two central pillars on which the temple stood. Bracing himself against them, his right hand on the one and his left hand on the other, Samson said, "Let me die with the Philistines! Then he pushed with all his might, and down came the temple on the rulers and all the people in it. Judges 16:29, 30a).*

Isn't it encouraging knowing that even though we may suffer because of our weaknesses, God is still willing to allow us to repent and go on with His plan for our life? Our story I am pretty certain is not as dramatic as Samson's, but there are many times that we fall in to the traps of our own weakness; those traps that take our eyes off of the purpose that God has for us. But that does not have to be the end of the story. God still wants to renew our strength in Him, so that we can finish the race that He has called us to run.

# September 15

# A BLESSED BURDEN

*(Galatians 6:2 Carry each other's burdens, and in this way you will fulfill the law of Christ.)*

An American was walking down the streets of a Chinese city. He was intrigued by the children, many of whom were carrying smaller brothers and sisters on their backs, but still they managed to play their games. He told one boy that it was too bad that he had to carry the heavy burden. The boy quickly replied "He's no burden, he's my brother."

There are so many hurting people in this world: There are those who would not be able to function physically if not for the aid of another. And there are many who need help in their spiritual weakness. There is no doubt about it, there are people everywhere who are going through storms in their life and they need help.

I was visiting with a friend the other day who was sharing an experience that he and his wife had. They had a tire that went totally flat and he had pulled over on the side of the road to change it. As they were sitting there a man pulled up in front of them. He got out of his car dressed in a mechanic's uniform and said, "Do you have a problem" to which he replied yes. The man asked if he could help and my friend said "No I can fix it." But the man insisted that since he already had his dirty mechanics clothing on, that he could fix it in no time. And he did. When he was finished they offered him money for his time. He said "Oh no, I was helping the Lord. It was a blessing".

In both cases of the two stories in the above text—the helpers did not consider their aid a burden—but a blessing. What kind of attitude do we have when we help those in need? Do we consider it a blessing or a burden? I will be the first to admit that there have been times I have helped someone and felt the burden instead of the blessing. But God's Word says that we should carry each other's burdens; and that by doing so we will fulfill the law of Christ. Now that is a blessing.

# September 16

# THE SIN OF ELI

*(1 Samuel 3:12-14) At that time I will carry out against Eli everything I spoke against his family—from beginning to end. For I told him that I would judge his family forever because of the sin he knew about; his sons made themselves contemptible and he failed to restrain them. Therefore, I swore to the house of Eli, The guilt of Eli's house will never be atoned for by sacrifice or offering.")*

Eli was not only a father, he was a priest and a priest is responsible for those who are under his direction. Eli rebuked his sons for the sins that they were committing but as priests under his direction he should have done more than rebuke them—he should have removed them from their positions. They were not worthy of calling themselves priests. It was quite evident that his sons did not know the Lord, yet they had been appointed priests. Eli's family suffered the consequences of their sin forever because Eli knew about their sins and failed to constrain them.

This is a pretty direct warning to ministers and priests. Yet the news is full of sins that men in the pulpit have done—vile sins against innocent victims. Yet some of those who are in leadership roles have chosen to hide the sin from the world and allow those who are guilty to remain in their positions. What a devastating thing: How do families come to terms with the abuse their loved ones have suffered at the hands of these so-called men of God? For that matter what does the world think, when they discover that the church has hid the sin?

My feeling is that those who are ministers and priests who hide the sin of those serving under them are as guilty as the ones who commit the sin. If God punished Eli for what he did—he will surely punish those today who are doing the same thing. Those who serve the Lord in the pulpit will be held accountable for allowing others under them to get away with conduct unbecoming to God.

*(Ecclesiastes 12:13-14 Now all has been heard; here is the conclusion of the matter: Fear God and keep his commandments, for this is the whole duty of man. For God will bring every deed into judgment, including every hidden thing, whether it is good or evil.)*

# September 17

# VICTORY IN WEAKNESS

*(Matthew 26:41 Watch and pray so that you will not fall into temptation. The spirit is willing, but the body is weak.)*

How many times have you promised yourself that you were going to make a positive change in your life, but then within a matter of a short time, you failed to carry it through? Most people have at some time or another. Why can't we keep those resolutions? I think it is because we are trying to do it in our own strength, don't you?

*Do* you have a weakness? I would be willing to bet that each one of you answered that question with a capital yes. I know that I do. One of mine is worry. I keep falling back in to the old habit of worrying. We don't have the same weakness, but there are two things that we all have in common: The first one is Satan will try and tell you that you might as well give up and give in because you will never overcome the temptation. The second one is we are over comers in Christ. *(Philippians 4:13 I can do everything through him who gives me strength.)*

If you have made a resolution in your heart to change things in your life for the better, don't listen to Satan's lies; he is the tempter and the father of lies. Listen to the voice of God who tells you that you can do all things through Him. You can overcome anything that hinders your ability to change if you let God do it for you. So today get on track with God and let Him give you the strength that you need to overcome.

# September 18

# FLIRTING WITH TEMPTATION

*(James 1:14-15 Then, after desire has conceived, it gives birth to sin; and sin when it is full-grown, gives birth to death. But each one is tempted when, by his own evil desire, he is dragged away and enticed. Then, after desire has conceived, it gives birth to sin, and sin, when it is full-grown, gives birth to death.)*

Have you ever tried to kill a fly? If you are like me, I always miss a couple of times before I actually kill one. What amazes me is that it just keeps coming back again and again—so intent he is in getting to the thing that has attracted him.

Isn't that the way we are sometimes when we want something badly. We don't seem to realize that if it is a sinful thing, it could possibly kill us if we keep going back to the temptation. Sometimes when we get the first taste of the thing that has tempted us, it just makes our craving for it that much stronger.

I have a friend who is going through treatment right now for a drug habit that has had a hold on him for some time. Instead of putting his faith and trust in God, he is angry. Why do you suppose he is angry? Could it be that Satan has him so entangled in the desire for his craving that it has clouded his mind about the things that are really important to him, even his very life?

It is alarming to see the destruction that comes from sin: Sin that we have allowed to enter our life by not turning away from the temptation that led us to it in the first place. It is sometimes so hard to turn our life around when we have become slaves to the sin. In fact, most of the time, it is next to impossible if we do not allow God to take control. We cannot fight sin alone. We must allow Jesus to fight our battles for us.

There are so many people who are entangled in sin. We must realize but for the grace of God we could be one of them. Instead of looking down our noses at the plight that they have gotten into, let's do our part to lift them up in prayer, and ask that God will give them strength in His power to overcome the sin that has them chained.

# September 19

# CLOTHED WITH KINDNESS

*(Colossians 3:12 Therefore, as God's chosen people, holy and dearly loved, clothe yourselves with compassion, kindness, humility, gentleness and patience.)*

The grade school I attended was two blocks from an orphanage, so all of the orphans of that age attended the same school that I did. I truly don't remember any of them except one boy. He was an albino and he had bulging eyes. I always felt sorry for him because the kids teased him unmercifully by calling him unkind names.

One day the teacher called him up to her desk and asked him if he would take something in to the principal's office. When he left the classroom she closed the door and began to speak to the rest of us about Alan. She told us that he could not help the fact that he looked a little different than the rest of us; and she said it was cruel to tease him because it hurt his feelings terribly. She explained that he was left at the doorstep of the orphanage as a baby and nobody knew who he belonged to. She told us in no uncertain terms that if she heard anybody teasing him again, they would be punished.

I have thought about Alan many times through the years and wondered what ever happened to him. I also think about the compassionate teacher who came to his defense and stilled the tongues of those who continually tortured him by their hateful remarks. It was because of her compassion for him that the teasing stopped.

I read about a person who was physically handicapped and she said that people had a tendency to ignore her as if they did not see her, and it hurt. Sometimes we feel uncomfortable and don't know what to say or how to react to someone who is handicapped. Let's remember that they want to be treated as if they are no different than we are.

Have you ever considered that those people who don't know Christ as their Savior could be classified as handicapped. I think they are severely handicapped—we need to remember that we were just like them at one time, and would still be today if not for God's compassionate mercy.

The above Scripture tells us to clothe our self with compassion, kindness, humility, gentleness and patience. Every human being deserves to be treated with compassion, no matter who they are. Are we always compassionate—even to those who are sinners?

# September 20

# THE UNSEEN HOPE

*(2nd Corinthians 4:18: "We set our eyes not on what we see but on what we cannot see. What we see will only last a short time, but what we cannot see will last forever.")*

I am reminded that we can thank God for the things we cannot see. We have a tendency to focus on the things in this life that quite often bring us down. There is so much going on around us that is (let's just call it what it is) evil. We try to take our minds off of it but the worry of it all just won't seem to let go: So we forget the knowledge and the truth that God is in control—that is if we allow Him to be.

Why are we such creatures of habit? Why is it so easy for us to dwell on the negative things rather than the positive? If we are Christians we should not even allow the negatives to enter our mind, but we do. It's that human frailty that plagues us and keeps us in turmoil. *(Philippians 4:8 Finally, brothers and sisters, whatever is true, whatever is noble, whatever is right, whatever is pure, whatever is lovely, whatever is admirable—if anything is excellent or praiseworthy—think about such things.)*

I have been thanking God each day for the things I cannot see. It keeps me from focusing on the negatives. None of us can see the future, but those of us who know Jesus can be sure that He is working out the things that we cannot see. Those prayers that we have prayed and are still waiting to be answered—they will be in God's time and in His way and according to His will.

# September 21

# TAKE TIME TO SEE

*(Exodus 3:2-5 There the angel of the Lord appeared to him in flames of fire from within a bush. Moses saw that though the bush was on fire it did not burn up, so Moses thought, "I will go over and see this strange sight—why the bush does not burn up." When the Lord saw that he had gone over to look, God called to him from within the bush, "Moses! Moses." And Moses said, "Here I am.")*

One of the most famous stories of the bible is about Moses and the burning bush. When I was reading it again this morning, I was suddenly struck by the fact that Moses took the time to go over to see why this bush was burning but not burning up, When God saw that he was curious enough to investigate this unusual sight, God called out his name and Moses said, "Here I am." Then God told him not to come any closer, but to take off his shoes because the place where he was standing was holy ground.

Now we all know that God used him to lead the Israelites out of their bondage in Egypt. I wonder what would have happened if Moses had not taken the time to find out what was happening. It makes one ponder on times when God has put a burning bush in our lives, but we did not bother to find out if it was a sign or message from God directed right to us. I wonder how many blessings we and others have missed because of our negligent and unresponsive action to God's call.

God knew right away that Moses was the man for the job. First of all he took the time to see what was going on. And his immediate response when God called his name was "Here I am." Moses did not doubt that it was God who was talking to him. He hid his face because he was afraid to look at God. He was in awe of Him. Wow! Doesn't it excite you to think that God would talk to you? Well He does—when we acknowledge the things that He puts on our heart and in our path; He will talk to us; and just like He did with Moses—He will tell us what He wants us to do. Have you taken the time to investigate those burning bushes?

## September 22

# ALLOWING GOD TO BE LORD OF ALL

*(1 Samuel 13:13-14 "You acted foolishly," Samuel said. "You have not kept the command the Lord your God gave you; if you had, he would have established your kingdom over Israel for all time. But now your kingdom will not endure; the Lord has sought out a man after his own heart and appointed him leader of his people, because you have not kept the Lord's command.")*

The Israelites had just been told by Samuel that if they and the king feared the Lord and served and obeyed him all would be good, but if they didn't God's hand would be against them. (1 Samuel 12:14-15) When Saul saw his men scattering out of fear, instead of waiting for Samuel to administer the sacrifice, he became impatient and decided to do it himself—an act that he knew was wrong. This act of foolishness is what ultimately caused Saul's downfall. He and his men took their eyes off of the Lord, and out of fear, the men scattered and Saul took matters in to his own hands.

God knew what would happen when the people insisted on appointing a king to rule over them. They already had the perfect King, God himself, but they did not trust Him, they wanted one that they could see. Remember what God told Samuel when the people asked for a king? *(But when they said, "Give us a king to lead us," this displeased Samuel; so he prayed to the LORD. And the LORD told him: "Listen to all that the people are saying to you; it is not you they have rejected, but they have rejected me as their king. As they have done from the day I brought them up out of Egypt until this day, forsaking me and serving other gods, so they are doing to you. Now listen to them; but warn them solemnly and let them know what the king who will reign over them will claim as his rights." 1 Samuel 8 6-9)*

How quickly we forget the admonitions of the Lord. How many times have we taken things into our own hands when we think the Lord is too slow to answer our prayers? How often does fear cause us to do foolish things?

When we don't allow God to be Lord in our life, we are surely going to make mistakes of all kinds. We may know Christ as our Savior, but do we really allow Him to be Lord in our life? It is a question we should all ponder—the answer will make the difference as to whether or not we have success in what we do.

# September 23

# NEVER LOOK BACK

*(Luke 9:62 Jesus replied, "No one who puts his hand to the plow and looks back is fit for service to the kingdom of God.")*

Has God ever called you to do something that you were not ready to do? Have you put Him off by trying to fit His request in to your time schedule? Have you ever answered His call by saying you will do it later? Has your excuse been that your job will not allow you the time—you still have demanding children at home who need your attention—you have elderly parents that you need to care for—you are waiting until you retire—you still have things that you need to take care of before you take on the task that He has asked you to do? What has been your excuse?

I believe all of the above excuses are weak and they are exactly what they are; excuses putting God off. I would venture to guess that most of us at one time or another has done that very thing. But Jesus said, when we look back we are not fit for service in the kingdom of God. It frightens me now, to think that I have done that in the past. I have learned (and I hope that I will never forget) that the only way I can please God is to answer His call with "Yes, Lord lead me on". No matter what God asks us to do; He will smooth the way and take care of all the things that we concern ourselves with.

Surely we can trust God when He calls us to serve Him. We don't serve a God that is heartless—He would never ask us to do something that would be harmful to us or our family. He cares about all of our circumstances and He is willing and able to take care of them all. I truly believe that we will be blessed by serving God when and where He leads us. We will never regret serving God when and where He calls us.

## September 24

# WHO IS JESUS?

*(1 Timothy 2:1-7 I urge, then, first of all, that petitions, prayers, intercession and thanksgiving be made for everyone— for kings and all those in authority, that we may live peaceful and quiet lives in all godliness and holiness. This is good, and pleases God our Savior, who wants all people to be saved and to come to knowledge of the truth. For there is one God and one mediator between God and men, the man Christ Jesus, who gave himself as a ransom for all men—the testimony given in its proper time.)*

A few weeks ago my youngest granddaughter asked me a very pertinent question: She said, "Grandma, when did Jesus grow up?" I was astounded that a little girl not quite 5 yet could ask such an intelligent question.

Sometimes I wonder if adults don't see Jesus still as a babe in a manger. Have they really considered that He was sent to earth as a baby, to be raised in man's world, so that He would be able to experience all that earthly men go through? Do some not realize that He grew up to be the Savior of the world? He was and is the mediator between God and men.

We must understand the truth of the Trinity. God, Jesus and The Holy Spirit—THE THREE IN ONE. I don't believe that we can totally grasp the truth until we have accepted Jesus: The baby who came to earth as a man for one purpose—to be the Savior for all those who accept Him. He rose again and sent His Holy Spirit to live in us. It is that Holy Spirit who gives us wisdom to understand who He really is. The above Scripture says it all. *"This is good, and pleases God our Savior, who wants all people to be saved and come to knowledge of the truth."* It is when we are saved that we can gain the knowledge of the truth.

Do you know and understand when Jesus grew up? If not, why not? Come to the Cross of Jesus, give your heart to Him and seek His truth.

# September 25

# SEEKING MORE

*(Exodus 33:13, 18-20 If you are pleased with me, teach me your ways so I may know you and continue to find favor with you. Then Moses said, "Now show me your glory."javascript:void(0); And the LORD said, "I will cause all my goodness to pass in front of you, and I will proclaim my name, the LORD, in your presence. I will have mercy on whom I will have mercy, and I will have compassion on whom I will have compassion. But," he said, "You cannot see my face, for no one may see me and live.")*

Moses had sought the Lord through the entire journey from Egypt. After the people's great sin of making an idol, He asked the Lord not to destroy all of them and God honored his request. Wouldn't you say that he had a very good relationship with the Lord? But notice in the Scripture above, he was not satisfied with the status quo—he wanted to gain more knowledge. He wanted to know God better. God recognized his sincerity and he agreed to allow him to see more of his goodness.

Are we satisfied with our knowledge of God, or are we constantly seeking for more and more? I believe that the more we fall in love with God and His Word, the more we will want to know. The more we search— the more we will find, the more we ask—the more He will reveal His true character. God is not a figment of imagination—He is real; and He desires for us to gain more knowledge of Him and His character. He loves us and wants us to spend quality time with Him. And that means spending time talking with Him and reading His Word. The more we get to know Him the more we are in His favor—because he wants to bless us for our efforts in seeking a closer walk with Him. I am not saying that He loves those who seek Him any more than He loves others, but He delights in those who spend time with Him-developing a closer relationship.

Going to church is a wonderful thing to do—bible studies are great—spending time with our Christian family is a blessing—but nothing can take the place of that personal pursuit of gaining more knowledge as we sequester ourselves in a quiet place and seek the knowledge of the Lord on a one to one basis with Him.

## September 26

# PROTECTION

*(Matthew 7:15 "Watch out for false prophets. They come to you in sheep's clothing, but inwardly they are ferocious wolves.)*

I was extremely shy when I was a small child and when we were surrounded by strangers or anybody that I did not know well or was not used to being around, I made sure that my mother was close at hand. I recall a time when we were at a family reunion: I realized all of a sudden that mother was not standing next to me and I looked around the room to spot the dress that she was wearing; when I spotted it I ran to her and threw my arms around her legs. Suddenly the woman that I thought was my mother began to speak; I looked up in horror as I took in the fact that it was not my mother at all, it was someone who had a dress on similar to hers. Everyone laughed at the surprised and panicked look on my face—everyone that is except me.

This particular remembrance has caused me to think about all of the children who have been kidnapped and led astray by strangers who want to harm them. I am so disturbed every time I hear about a missing child, because I know that whoever took them is out to harm them. Children are often lured away by strangers who promise them something or entice them with anything that will make it easy for the abductor to carry out their evil plan.

As I was considering the scenarios of the evil plots that could lure these innocent children, I could not help but think about us adults. How many times are we tempted and lured away from the protection of our Heavenly Father?—and all because the world looks enticing. Far too many times we are led astray by the false promises that the world offers us.

Some people are led astray by false prophets who promise that they will receive everything they want if they follow Jesus. God never promises us that we will receive all that we desire—He promises us that He will provide all of our needs. So often those things that we desire are detrimental to us in many ways. We should be very careful about who we trust when it comes to seeking wisdom. If we do not check out the truth in God's Word, we can be ill informed and carried away by someone else's lies. Watch out for false prophets—they may look good and they may sound good, but they are nothing but ferocious wolves luring you in to their den of deceit.

## September 27

# OUR ALL IN ALL

*(Psalm 91:1-2 He who dwells in the shelter of the Most High will rest in the shadow of the Almighty. I will say of the Lord, "He is my refuge and my fortress, my God, in whom I trust.")*

Do you know anyone who does not have problems of one kind or another? I don't know one person who can say that everything in their life runs smoothly. There may be some great pretenders who say that their life is perfect, but I would have to question their honesty. In this life we are going to have troubles and strife.

I honestly don't know how people handle all of the problems that come their way unless they know the Lord. I don't know about you; but there have been times when I have been overwhelmed by problems. But I am never defeated because God is my all in all. He is there to deliver me through every storm.

Are you having difficulties in your life? I can tell you where you can find the answer to overcoming them: Through Jesus Christ, the one and only Savior: The one who died on the cross and won the victory for those who believe and receive Him. He walks with us down every rugged path and leads us to a restful place. He never promised us that we would not have problems; but He did promise us that He would be beside us all the way to lead us on.

Dear Heavenly Father,

When I am discouraged—you give me hope. Galatians 6:9
When I am restless in spirit—you give me peace. Psalm 119:165
When I am weak—you give me strength. Isaiah 3:15
When I am lonely—you are near to me. Deuteronomy 31:6
When I am fearful—you give me courage. John 14:27
When I am in confusion—you enlighten me. Proverbs 3:5-6
When I am down—you lift me up.2 Thessalonians 2:16-17
Thank you Lord; for being my all in all.

# September 28

# TEACH THE CHILDREN

*(Deuteronomy 4:10 "Remember the day you stood before the Lord your God at Horeb, when he said to me, "Assemble the people before me to hear my words so that they may learn to revere me as long as they live in the land and may teach them to their children.")*

I was reading a story about a little boy who was traveling along in the back seat of his daddy's car. When out of nowhere he said "Daddy, know what? Nothing is too hard for God!" he proclaimed with enthusiasm. His father responds, "Son you are absolutely right! How did you know that?" He replied, "Cause that's what you tell me all the time, Daddy." Apparently the Father did not even recall telling his little boy that—but the child remembered.

The father in the above story apparently had such a habit of telling his little one of God's greatness, that if just came naturally to him. That story touched my heart and made me wonder how many parents are teaching their children such wisdom without even thinking about it. It should be so engrained in our minds to teach our children the ways of God, that it becomes natural for us.

I wish I could tell you that I taught my children well when they were little, but alas I cannot. Oh I talked about Jesus to them once in a while, but I didn't have a personal relationship with Him at that time, so it certainly wasn't second nature to me. It is the biggest regret of my life. I pray always that parents would teach their children the ways of God while they are a tender age. They will always remember what you have taught them. My mother taught me the ways of God early on, and even though I went my own way for many years, I one day heard His call and responded. I cannot go back and change the things that I did wrong; but I can share with you the regret I have in not bringing my children up in the admonition of the Lord: And pray that you will not make the same mistake that I did. We will one day have to give an account to God as to whether or not we taught our children about Him.

Children learn from what we say and what we do. What are you teaching your children? Are you teaching them to put God first in their lives? Are you teaching them the Word of God? Are you pointing them to Jesus? Are you teaching them to revere God? What does your life say to them as they watch the choices that you make each day?

# September 29

# DOUBTING GOD

*(Genesis 18:10-12 Then the Lord said, "I will surely return to you about this time next year, and Sarah your wife will have a son." Now Sarah was listening at the entrance to the tent, which was behind him. Abraham and Sarah were already old and well advanced in years and Sarah was past the age of child bearing. So Sarah laughed to herself as she thought, "After I am worn out and my master is old, will I now have this pleasure?")*

Let's be honest with our self, do you think you might have doubted God under Sarah's circumstances? She was well past her child bearing years, and now she overhears this man tell her husband that she would have a child the very next year. Obviously she did not understand that it was God Himself who was telling Abraham this. Honestly, I think I would have doubted it also.

I can certainly identify with Sarah. When God asked me to serve Him in the form of writing, in my own way I laughed because at first I doubted that it was the Lord telling me that. I was not a writer or a bible scholar. All I could see was the impossibility of what I heard. After all I was 68 years old when I had this encounter with God. Wasn't I too old to do this thing? And why me when there were others far younger and more qualified? I still don't have the answers to the why, but I do know that it was definitely God's voice; otherwise it could not and would not have happened. I don't know why God chose me, but He did and I have learned never to scoff at God's voice.

Are you doubting—maybe even laughing at what God is saying to you? Don't laugh at God—What He says He will do. You may think you are not qualified; you may think you are too young or too old; but God is an amazing God. He uses and qualifies the most unlikely people to carry out His plan for their lives. Believe Him:

And don't ever doubt what God tells you. He has a plan for you no matter what you might think. He can and will do the impossible. He is Almighty God.

# September 30

# FROM FEAR TO FREEDOM

*(Acts 16:23, 25, 29, 30, and 31 After they had been severely flogged, they were thrown into prison, and the jailer was commanded to guard them carefully. About midnight Paul and Silas were praying and singing hymns to God, and the other prisoners were listening to them. Suddenly there was such a violent earthquake that the foundations of the prison were shaken. At once all the prison doors flew open, and everybody's chains came loose. The jailer called for lights, rushed in and fell trembling before Paul and Silas. He then brought them out and asked "Sirs, what must I do to be saved?" They replied, "Believe in the Lord Jesus, and you will be saved—you and your household.")*

Scripture records that the jailer awoke from sleeping and saw that the prison doors were open. He assumed the prisoners had escaped, and he was so frightened that he was going to kill himself. Then Paul and Silas cried out "Don't harm yourself! We are all here." He must have been dumbfounded to see that they had not walked out when they could have escaped, after the severe flogging that they had taken. I can only imagine that the jailer was remembering the singing and praying that was going on just before he fell asleep. He surely was impressed by what he heard and saw—that they were men who knew who this Jesus was: So impressed in fact, that he wanted to know this man who had performed a miracle right in that jail cell.

I wonder what kind of countenance we Christians show when we are going through difficult circumstances. Do we moan and groan and complain about the troubles we are having? Do we walk around with sad and dejected looks? Do we blame God for our circumstances? Or do we do as Paul and Silas, keep on singing and praying. The way we handle ourselves through our trials speaks volumes to those who don't know the Lord. I have heard many people speak of the faith that some Christians have during trial and tribulations. Don't ever think the world is not watching us. They most assuredly are. So let's show the world that we can remain faithful and strong because of the strength and peace we receive through our Lord.

# October 1

# THE POWER OF PRAYER

*(James 5:16b The effectual fervent prayer of a righteous man availeth much.) KJV*

A poorly dressed lady with a look of defeat on her face, walked into a grocery store. She approached the owner of the store in a most humble manner and asked if he would let her charge a few groceries. She softly explained that her husband was very ill and unable to work, they had seven children and they needed food. The grocer scoffed at her and requested that she leave his store.

Visualizing the family needs, she said: 'Please, sir! I will bring you the money just as soon as I can." He told her he could not give her credit, as she did not have a charge account at his store.

Standing beside the counter was a customer who overheard the conversation between the two. The customer walked forward and told the grocer man that he would stand good for whatever she needed for her family.

The grocer man said in a very reluctant voice, "Do you have a grocery list?

The woman replied "Yes sir" "O.K." he said, put your grocery list on the scales and whatever your grocery list weighs, I will give you that amount in groceries."

Louise, hesitated a moment with a bowed head, then she reached into her purse and took out a piece of paper and scribbled something on it. She then laid the piece of paper on the scale carefully with her head still bowed. The eyes of the grocer man and the customer showed amazement as the scales went down and stayed down.

The grocer man staring at the scales turned slowly to the customer and said begrudgingly, "I can't believe it." The customer smiled and the grocer man started putting the groceries on the other side of the scales. The scale did not balance so he continued to put more and more groceries on them until the scales would hold no more. The grocer man stood there in utter disgust.

Finally, he grabbed the piece of paper from the scales and looked at it with greater amazement. It was not a grocery list; it was a prayer that said: "Dear Lord, you know my needs and I am leaving this in your hands."

The grocer man gave her the groceries that he had gathered and placed on the scales and stood in stunned silence. Louise thanked him and left the store. The customer handed a fifty-dollar bill to John as he said, "It was worth every penny of it."

It was sometime later that the grocer discovered the scales were broken; therefore, only God knows how much a prayer weighs.

Author Unknown

I have no idea whether this story is true or not. I do know that it is a wonderful example of what God can and will do for those who pray. I have heard actual stories from many people who have experienced answered prayer. I myself have had so many prayers answered that I could not count them. I think sometimes if the stories of answered prayer aren't extremely dramatic, we don't acknowledge them; we tend to forget all of the prayers that are answered on a daily basis. Such as protecting our children—having our needs met—healing our physical ailments, giving us peace in the midst of a storm—hearts that have been changed—broken relationships that have been restored, etc.

Prayer is not only a privilege; God's Word tells us that—*(The prayer of a righteous man is powerful and effective. James 5:16b)*: So don't ever underestimate the power of prayer. God hears and answers our call for help in every circumstance according to His will.

# October 2

# IS LIFE A STAGE?

*(Colossians 1:10 And we pray this in order that you may live a life worthy of the Lord and may please him in every way; bearing fruit in every good work, growing in the knowledge of God.)*

Have you ever been in a play? You know the procedure; you start rehearsals well in advance of the real thing. You practice your parts over and over again, with the hopes that when the curtain comes down opening night that your part will have been played perfectly: All the time craving the applause of the audience.

Many people seem to admire actors. They buy magazines to read about their lives. They seem to be so impressed with everything they do. Hey, let's get real—they are just people acting out a part. People should be impressed with those who live their lives worthy of the Lord.

Do we treat life like it is a play, pretending and acting out our parts? Do we seek the approval and the applause of man? Or do we live our life to please God? Life is not a rehearsal, it is the real thing. There will not be another chance to correct the mistakes we have made when the curtain comes down and our life here on earth is over.

Our performance as a human being is in a sense directed by somebody—Satan or God. It is our choice to pick the one that we want to be our director. We can follow the ruler of this world and serve his purpose. We can fool ourselves in to thinking that our actions are worthy to be praised and applauded. But the truth is, unless we let God direct our life, all the acts we have performed in this life, whether good or bad, will be for naught at the end of our days. The Christian's performance in this life should mimic that of Christ—Christ in us—the hope of glory.

## October 3

# REBELLIOUS CHILDREN

*(Jeremiah 31:15 This is what the Lord says: "A voice is heard in Ramah, mourning and great weeping, Rachel weeping for her children and refusing to be comforted, because they are no more.")*

In the past several months I have heard so many stories about how children have rebelled against their parents, not only children who are still in the home, but those who are grown. It is difficult to understand why someone you have loved since their conception could hurt their parents so badly. How can they show such disrespect for them? What happens to them that they would turn against those who have loved and nurtured them more than anyone on this earth? I believe it is because Satan is trying his best to tear families apart. Apparently he is having his way in many homes.

There are not many things that hurt worse than a child who has turned against you. If you are suffering because of a rebellious child keep praying, lay them at the foot of The Cross, and wait for the Lord. *(Jeremiah 31:16-17 This is what the Lord says: "Restrain your voice from weeping and your eyes from tears for your work will be rewarded," declares the Lord. "They will return from the land of the enemy. So there is hope for your descendants," declares the Lord. "Your children will return to their own land.)*

Take heart, God is still in control. Do not try to control the situation, for nothing you say or do will change the heart of another person, only God can do that. Stop crying, pray and wait on the Lord.

## October 4

# A GENTLE WHISPER

*(1 Kings 19:11-12 The LORD said, "Go out and stand on the mountain in the presence of the LORD, for the LORD is about to pass by." Then a great and powerful wind tore the mountains apart and shattered the rocks before the LORD, but the LORD was not in the wind. After the wind there was an earthquake, but the LORD was not in the earthquake. After the earthquake came a fire, but the LORD was not in the fire. And after the fire came a gentle whisper.)*

Sometime we think if God doesn't speak to us in a loud voice, he doesn't speak to us at all. But doesn't it make since that we can hear Him better if there is not a lot of clamor and commotion about us. There have been times when people get caught up in the emotionalism of the moment and make a display of hearing from the Lord, but they never seem to go anywhere: It is easy to do when we are in a setting where others are praising God with total abandonment. But often times it is when we leave that place—when we are totally alone that He will speak to us in a gentle way.

I have found that when God speaks to me, it is when I am alone with Him, usually in the middle of the night, and it is always in a still small voice. I think it is the only time that I can really hear Him—a time when He has my full undivided attention—it is a time when there is nobody or anything that distracts me. It is then that I can hear from Him, it is then that I have my most precious times with Him.

I remember a time when I went to a Women's Conference—I had been praying that God would show me what He wanted me to do. The conference was great. It was loud with praise music and many people were speaking with enthusiasm and I was enjoying every minute of it: But I was disappointed that He had not answered my prayer of what He wanted me to do. It was not until a couple of nights later that I heard from the Lord. And it happened to be at 2:00 am—and it was in a still small voice. To this day, it is usually in the wee hours of the morning that He speaks to me.

Remember how God called to Samuel in the wee hours of the morning? At first he did not recognize His voice—but God kept calling Him until He realized who it was.

When and where does He speak to you?

## October 5

# HIDDEN TREASURES

*(Isaiah 45:3 "I will give you the treasures of darkness, riches stored in secret places so that you may know that I am the LORD, your God.)*

Last week was one of the most stressful weeks I have ever had. It seemed like if it had not been for bad news, I would have had no news at all. It started off with the news that a friend had tried to take her life—then attending a funeral and sharing the grief with a family who was laying a young son/husband/father to rest—hearing of one who had been told that he had terminal cancer—holding a friend who sobbed on my shoulder as she shared the pain of her 20 year marriage breaking up. Not to mention several other attacks on my own family in different areas.

More than a month ago, I was asked to sing a special in my church. I had planned to sing a certain song, but for some reason or another I chose a different one than I had planned for that day. The song I sang was 'Roses Will Bloom Again'. It is a beautiful song, and the day I sang it I realized that God had planned it for that particular time. It was a treasure hidden in the darkness of the hour. I cannot tell you how many people told me that they were blessed by the words of the song: Those who had or are going through pain of one kind or another. Through the song they had been reminded that there was light in the darkness. That one day their roses would bloom again.

We all need to be reminded that even though we have trials and troubles, God will use them for His glory. He does give us treasures in the darkness—riches stored in secret places so that we will know that He is God. There is always light in the darkness of our lives if we are Christians.

God did not promise that we would not have trials. As a matter of fact He says *("I form the light and create darkness, I bring prosperity and create disaster; I, the Lord, do all these things.")* Ref. Isaiah 45:7. But we have salvation in the Lord. He uses each and every thing, both good and bad to shape us into the people that He wants us to be.

He does promise us that He will walk with us through every trial, even though He has allowed them. He tells us He will never leave us nor forsake us. We can and should thank Him for the things that we cannot see: Those things that are hidden in the darkness that surrounds us.

Just like the song says:

'Roses will bloom again

Just wait and see

Don't mourn what might have been,

Only God knows how and when that

Roses will bloom again.'

## October 6

# FORGETTING THE PAST

*(Philippians 3: 13-14 Brothers and sisters, I do not consider myself yet to have taken hold of it. But one thing I do: Forgetting what is behind and straining toward what is ahead, I press on toward the goal to win the prize for which God has called me heavenward in Christ Jesus.)*

I have been a Christian for many years, and like Paul I do not consider myself yet to have taken hold of it. My biggest problem is allowing Satan to bring back the painful memories of my past: The years that I did not have my children in church on a regular basis. I will have days of peace and freedom from the past, and then suddenly once again, I find myself dwelling on those past mistakes. It is then that I am reminded that I must not revisit that time in my life. It is over; God forgave me when I gave my heart to Him.

I would guess that you know exactly what I am talking about. Our past sins come out of nowhere to haunt us. Those thoughts do not come from God and they give leeway for Satan to come in and try to destroy our joy and peace in the Lord. God has forgotten our past sins and remembers them no more. (Ref. Isaiah 43:25) We must remember that and quit beating ourselves up over what God has forgiven and forgotten. It dishonors His grace—the grace that paid the price for our sins.

We must press on toward the goal to win the prize for which God has called us heavenward in Christ Jesus. We are newly created when we come to Jesus. In others words we are born anew. Let's leave the past behind and press forward with our Lord Jesus.

## October 7

# AN ENCOURAGING WITNESS

*(Acts 8:2-3 Godly men buried Stephen and mourned deeply for him. But Saul began to destroy the church. Going from house to house, he dragged off men and women and put them in prison.)*

One day last week a friend of mine was summoned to the hospital to minister to a man who had just been told that he had terminal cancer. He was not a Christian and my friend asked him if he would like to ask Jesus in to his heart. The man replied that he had been a wicked man and that God would not want anything to do with him. My friend shared his testimony of his past of being an alcoholic and the man was totally amazed. He was so impressed in fact, that he said he would like to receive the salvation offered to him. Thus, my friend led him to the Lord.

When Stephen was stoned to death, Saul stood by with approval. And then went on persecuting men and women simply because they were followers of Christ. This story is about the man who met Jesus on the road to Damascus. He was a changed man, even his name was changed. And we all know the rest of Paul's story. He was the least person likely to come to Christ. He had a terrible past and yet God revealed himself to him and totally changed the life of this persecutor.

Paul shared his redemption story with everyone he came in contact with. We all need to be ready to share our testimony with others. They need to know that we have all been sinners. We are saved only by God's grace. There are many people who think their past has been so bad that they do not deserve forgiveness. If Paul could be forgiven, anybody can. There is no sin so big that the love and grace of Christ will not forgive. The only exception is blaspheming the Holy Spirit. (Luke 12:10; Mark 3:29; Matthew 12: 31-32—Words spoken by Jesus, Himself.)

If you are one of the people who think God could never forgive you, think again. He not only will forgive you, He is waiting with open arms for you to come to Him.

# October 8

# SEWING SEED

*(Psalm 126:6 He who goes out weeping carrying seed to sow, will return with songs of joy, carrying sheaves with him.)*

I am so thankful for the things that my mother taught me as I was growing up; but the most wonderful and important of them all was the things of God. Looking back I know that she must have shed many tears as she waited and prayed that the Spiritual seeds she planted would one day bring her joy: And it did. She waited however, for forty two years before I responded and God brought them to fruition.

God has given me the opportunity to witness to people that He brings into my life. Many days I weep as I pray for the seeds to take root and grow. I looked up the meaning of 'seed corn' and it said, 'Seed that is saved from one year's harvest for the subsequent year's planting'. Isn't that the way we should be with sharing the word of God? We should always carry that seed corn with us for another planting.

The above Scripture is so encouraging to me. Just to think that there will be songs of joy because those seeds might produce many sheaves. I never connected this Scripture with the old song 'Bringing in the Sheaves.' until this very morning. Won't it be a wonderful thing to see those to whom we have witnessed in Heaven?

Another thought came to me, if every soul that is saved will plant a seed, and then that one will plant a seed, and then the next, and the next—Just think of the crop that will be produced. We will all sing songs of joy together as we see the sheaves gathered together one day.

## October 9

# DO NOT PURSUE EVIL

*(Proverbs 4:14 Do not set foot on the path of the wicked or walk in the way of evil men.)*

There are many Christians who seem to walk with one foot in the world and one foot with the Lord. I used to be one of them. But God continued to convict me until I made the choice to follow Him and the truth of His word. Now I am not saying that I never sin. We all sin at times because we are human. What I am saying is that I do not blatantly sin against what His word says.

I believe that if we are living a life straddling the fence, we need to ask ourselves some pertinent questions—such as: Why do I continue to indulge in the same sin on a regular basis? Am I allowing sinners to influence me in a negative way? Am I hanging out with the wrong people? Have I become addicted to a habit? Am I serious about walking with the Lord and doing His will or am I determined to continue in my sin in spite of my conviction?

We live in this world but we do not have to become like the world. If you are one of these people who are compromising your Christianity, run away from the people or things that are having a negative influence in your life. *(John 17:15-21 I do not ask you to take them out of the world, but to keep them from the evil one. They are not of the world, even as I am not of the world. Sanctify them in the truth; Your word is truth. As you sent me into the world, I also have sent them into the world. For their sakes I sanctify myself, that they themselves also may be sanctified in truth.)* I can tell you from experience that you will never have complete peace unless you make the decision not to commit those sins that you know are blatantly against God's word. If you are convicted of your sin and ignoring it, you have a problem; because your dishonoring God.

We are called to be witnesses for Christ, and we can't do that unless we give up those sins that send the wrong message to those watching, can we? If you are struggling with this problem, I would like to encourage you to read the entire chapter of Proverbs 4. I think you will glean a lot of wisdom from it.

# October 10

# TEACHING JESUS

*(Acts 4:13 When they saw the courage of Peter and John and realized that they were unschooled, ordinary men, they were astonished and they took note that these men had been with Jesus.)*

I went to a church service one day for the purpose of witnessing the baptism of a young girl. It seemed like the entire service was orchestrated: Men walking down the aisles with their pretty robes on; songs being sung that were not at all familiar to me, and they seemed to have a chanting sound. They made a show of the sacraments that were being offered to their members only. I would venture to say that most (if not all) of these men who had a part in the service had formal educations in theology. But the service was cold.

There are many churches just like the one I have described. The leaders of the church have been schooled in their seminaries, they have degrees in theology, but they stand in the pulpit teaching lies. I have my doubts that they are led by the Holy Spirit. They go through the ceremonies every Sunday, but do not teach the plan of salvation. It makes me wonder if they were called by God or if they just chose to go into the ministry for other reasons.

I once attended a church whose pastor taught from his heart—a heart I feel sure was filled with the Holy Spirit. My husband and I were happy there until that pastor left and the pulpit was then filled with a man who had a glib tongue, but never taught the plan of salvation. We stayed for a while until we realized that we were wasting our time there. We felt a need to move on to where we could hear God's word being taught through the power of the Holy Spirit.

I would rather hear an uneducated person speaking the truth of God's word, than I would someone who has a list of degrees but does not preach through the power of the Holy Spirit, wouldn't you? One can certainly tell whether or not someone has been with Jesus, just as this Scripture says. I don't know about you, but I do not want to waste my time in a church that is orchestrated by man. I want to be in one where the Holy Spirit is prevalent.

# October 11

# OBEY OR REBEL

*(Jeremiah 18:7-10 If at any time I announce that a nation or kingdom is to be uprooted, torn down and destroyed, and if that nation I warned repents of its evil, then I will relent and not inflict on it the disaster I had planned. And if at another time I announce that a nation or kingdom is to be built up and planted, and if it does evil in my sight and does not obey me, then I will reconsider the good I had intended to do for it.)*

A mother was relating a story to me not long ago about her daughter who had asked her permission to attend a certain function; and her mother told her she could; but before the time the event happened, her daughter's attitude became somewhat rebellious. Her mother warned her that if it did not change she would reconsider her decision to let her attend the event that she was greatly looking forward to. Unfortunately her attitude did not change and her mother punished her according to her warning.

The above story was brought to my mind as I read this passage of Scripture. Our Father will take away the blessing that He had planned for us when we are obstinate, and refuse to heed His warning. We bring sorrow on ourselves when we don't listen and obey, and we defiantly go ahead and do things our way.

On the other hand those who have rebelled against God and He has announced that they will be destroyed and then they repent, He will relent and not inflict the punishment He had threatened. God is a fair, just, and gracious God. Just like we expect our children to listen and obey, He expects us to also; and just as we punish our children when they refuse to listen, our Father punishes us.

God will not force us to obey His commands, but if we don't, we will certainly pay the price for our disobedience. Knowing this why do we make the choice to rebel at times? Is it because we just want to take control of our own life?

I think we sometimes believe that God never changes His mind for the plans He has for us—but according to this Scripture—that is not true. We can have a lot to do about His decisions for us, we can obey or we can rebel.

# October 12

# YOUR FIRST LOVE

*(Revelation 2:4 Yet I hold this against you: You have forsaken your first love.)*

I don't know about you, but it makes me extremely sad when I hear that a marriage is breaking up because someone has decided they don't love their spouse anymore. The biggest percentage of them is because someone else has come in to the picture. However, that is not the only reason. Other things start to look more exciting to them than a quiet married life. I can't imagine the devastating blow it must be to the injured spouse. When we marry, we take a vow that our love for each other will last forever. It is a dangerous thing to become disenchanted with the person that we have vowed to love and cherish for the rest of our life.

When we become Christians, we enter into a covenant with Jesus. We make a vow that we will love and serve Him forever. How then do we become so distracted by the world that we forget about the covenant that we made with Christ? We become so consumed by other things or other people that we are led astray, and then before we know it, that passion that we once had for the Lord becomes less and less until it destroys our relationship with Him; and that light that once shined so brightly begins to fade. How He must grieve when we forsake Him for other things.

God prefaces the above Scripture by telling the Ephesians that He knows all of the good things that they have done. And then He tells them that He will hold the fact that they had forsaken Him against them. He tells them that if they don't repent He will remove their lampstand from its place. One commentary says: 'Unless that revival came, then the light would go out and leave the Church in darkness, no longer to be a guide and life giving agency to those around it.'

Remember that we are supposed to be lights in a world of darkness. So how can we be when that light has gone out? If you have forsaken that passionate love that you first had for Christ; repent and return to Him with the love that you had when you first accepted Him as your personal Savior. Remember and return to that joy and passion that you once had. Let His light shine through you once again.

# October 13

# A HARDENED HEART

*(Exodus 11:3, 10 (The Lord made the Egyptians favorably disposed toward the people, and Moses himself was highly regarded in Egypt by Pharaoh's officials and by the people.) Moses and Aaron performed all these wonders before Pharaoh's heart and he would not let the Israelites go out of his country.)*

The last plague that God would bring on Pharaoh and Egypt was the death of the first born son in every Egyptian household from Pharaoh to the slave girl's son and to the cattle as well. Can't you just imagine that all of Pharaoh's officials and people were hoping that he would let the Israelites go? They had lived through all of the plagues that God had brought against Egypt and they knew that God would do what He said He would do. They all had respect for Moses and they were willing to give the Israelites whatever they needed to make the trip to worship God. But Pharaoh's heart was so hardened he would not relent.

Scripture records that Moses became very angry with Pharaoh because he would not listen. Moses knew the destruction that lay ahead for the Egyptian people and I believe he was heart sick that the stubborn Pharaoh would actually let this terrible plague happen. I believe that he had a heart for the people of Egypt and his anger burned for that reason.

Doesn't it make you heart sick and sometimes angry when you try to make people see who God is—and they won't listen? The only way that Pharaoh was going to release the Israelites was through the death of many. I fear that there are many people today who have hardened their hearts. They are too stubborn to listen to God's people. I wonder what it will take to open their eyes. For those who have hardened their hearts against God—there is no hope for them if they don't allow God to soften their heart. They, like Pharaoh will die and they will spend eternity in Hell.

# October 14

# WORK IT OUT WITH GOD

*(Philippians 2:12-13 Therefore, my dear friends, as you have always obeyed—not only in my presence, but now much more in my absence—continue to work out your salvation with fear and trembling, For it is God who works in you to will and to act according to his good purpose.)*

Not long ago a false profit predicted that the world would come to an end. It is amazing to me that so many people believed it; some to the point of giving everything they had away. If they had even bothered to look to see what God's word said, they would have known that the prediction was false. His Word tells us—*("No one knows about that day or hour, not even the angels in heaven, nor the Son, but only the Father." Matthew 24:36)*

It has been a very deep concern with me lately, that there are so many that hang on the words of others for their spiritual knowledge. We all have those people who we admire as Godly people. And there are times when we consult them for advice and wisdom. There is absolutely nothing wrong with that—however, we should never take another's word over God's. When we have a question, we need to check out His word and not take another's as gospel.

It saddens me to see how many people hang on the words of false profits—and there are many. They don't have a clue as to whether they are telling the true facts; because they don't bother to read what God's word has to say. If it makes them feel good, that is all they care about. They can be very convincing in their falsehood, and they are extremely dangerous to those who do not care to find out the truth.

It doesn't matter who we are listening to: it can even be a minister that we admire and respect, but no man or woman is infallible: So we need to check out even what they are telling us. Some take the word of others for granted because they are spiritual giants but only God's Word is infallible.

God's word is true—when we are working out our own salvation—He will never fail us. Let's work it out with the Lord and don't take other's word for the gospel truth because they are human and make mistakes—even the most Godly.

## October 15

# BE READY

*(Exodus 12:11 This is how you are to eat it; with your cloak tucked into your belt, your sandals on your feet and your staff in your hand, Eat it in haste; it is the Lord's Passover.)*

I don't know about you, but every time I read the account of the Israelites fleeing from Egypt, the land of their bondage; I can't help but relate it to the time when Christ will return for His people. The above Scripture is talking about the Israelites, preparing themselves to leave in haste and leave the blood of sacrifice on their doors so that when the Lord saw that they were His people, He would pass by leaving them unaffected by the plague that He was going to bring on the Egyptians.

There have been so many tragic events in the world—natural disasters which suddenly take the lives of many: Automobile and plane crashes take the lives of those unsuspecting people who probably thought that their life on this earth would last a long time. We never know when we get up each morning but what it might be the last day of our life on this earth.

It makes me wonder how many on this earth will have their cloak tucked in and ready to go. There will not be time to prepare in the last minute—because when Christ returns for His people; it will happen in the blink of an eye. God's Word warns us well in advance to be ready.

Some people have the luxury of a lingering death to make their peace with God, but there are many who will never have that last chance because their life will be snuffed out in a second's time.

I spoke with an old cowboy last week who just happened to be a wonderful Christian. He told me that his testimony is that he is thankful for everyday that he wakes up—and he is thankful that he is only one breath away from Heaven. He had prepared himself to meet Jesus. Do you have that same peace and assurance? Is your cloak tucked in for a hasty departure? If not, please ask God to prepare your heart to enter in to your eternal home with Him.

## October 16

# THE GRUMBLERS

*(Exodus 15:13, 22-24 "In your unfailing love you will lead the people you have redeemed. In your strength you will guide them to your holy dwelling.)Then Moses led Israel from the Red Sea and they went into the Desert Of Shur. For three days they traveled in the desert without finding water. When they came to Marah, they could not drink its water because it was bitter. (That is why the place is called Marah.) So the people grumbled against Moses, saying, "What are we to drink?")*

Just look at this: When the Lord delivered them across the Red Sea to safety from the Egyptians and after they saw the miracles that He had done for them, and watching their enemies drown as the water engulfed them; the Israelites were singing praises to God for all that He had done. But 3 days later they were grumbling against Moses because the water was bitter. Think of it; only 3 days did their praise for the Lord last. If you are familiar with Exodus you know that whenever the people were not getting what they wanted, they would begin to grumble—over and over again. They would grumble to Moses not realizing that when they grumbled to him they were grumbling to God

It's easy to see the mistakes of the Israelites, but don't we do the same thing? We grumble when we don't get the things we want when we want them. How ungrateful can we be? God gives us blessings after blessings. And we turn right around and complain about something else.

We need to start counting our blessings instead of grumbling about the things that we don't have. I think we would be much happier people don't you?

# October 17

# ABIDING SPIRIT

*(Psalm 139: 7-10 Where can I go from your Spirit? Where can I flee from your presence? If I go up to the heavens, you are there; if I make my bed in the depths, you are there. If I rise on the wings of the dawn if I settle on the far side of the sea, even there your hand will guide me, your right hand will hold me fast.)*

What a comforting thought, that no matter where I am the Lord is with me. He knows all about me—everything I do, everything I say, everything I think. He knows all of my frustrations. He knows every blessing because He gives them to me. He knows when I am discouraged: He knows when I am sad: He knows all of my victories and all of my failures. I don't know about you, but I am so glad that He is with me at all times; even in those times that I may not look like a Godly woman. There are times when I would rather He didn't hear what I say, or see what I do, or know my thoughts: Yet I am thankful that He sees me through even those times. Without His watch care over me, I might just get lost in my own selfish desires and weaknesses.

Where can I go from His Spirit? Absolutely nowhere; for His Spirit lives in me, giving me peace, wisdom, instruction, direction, protection and when I need it, chastisement. He walks with me down every path I take. He is my security. What would I do without Him? I would surely fall. But because of His grace and His love He holds my hand to guide me daily.

Are there times when you feel like you are alone? If you are a child of God, you are never alone—not even for one second. Let's rejoice together for His guiding and abiding Spirit.

## October 18

# A WOMAN IN A MAN'S WORLD

*(2 Samuel 20:16-17 A wise woman called from the city, "Listen! Listen! Tell Joab to come here so I can speak to him." He went toward her and she asked, "Are you Joab?" "I am," he answered. She said, "Listen to what your servant has to say. "I'm listening," he said.)*

This woman that is referred to in the above Scripture is not even given a name; but because of one troublemaker, and because of her discernment and concern over the destruction of her city, she was brave enough to come forward and speak to save her beloved land.

Joab was bound to destroy the city to get to Sheba, the man who had lifted his hand against, David. But when the woman made a plea to Joab, he agreed that he would not destroy the city if they would turn Sheba over to him. The woman responded that they would throw his head over the wall. It was so and Joab left and went back to the king in Jerusalem. And the city that this woman loved was saved.

What an amazing story. Here is an unknown woman, and I am under the assumption that because she has not been named, she must have been just an ordinary citizen who loved her country. I wonder how many women in this world today would be brave enough to come forward and speak to save their land and the innocent people that live there.

I must admit, I have to identify this woman with the brave Christian women in America today that are willing to step out in a world who is sort of hostile to women (especially Christians) in politics. It seems as though they are under attack much more than the men are. Yet they are willing to withstand the vicious attacks on them. I cannot believe that it is because they want to be in power. I have been aware of the difference that most people make when a Christian woman enters the political arena; and it seems to me that they cover most issues better than the men do; and I ask myself, "Is it a power struggle between the sexes or what?" For I don't think anyone can deny the fact that there is a difference.

Don't go thinking that I am a Women libber—I am anything but that. But I do believe that Christian women have a somewhat more tender heart toward those things and people that they love. And I think that they should have the respect that they deserve. After all God used this unknown woman to save a city, and to end the life of a man that you might term in today's vocabulary, as a terrorist.

## October 19

# THE MIGHTY FORTRESS

*(2 Samuel 22:2-4 The Lord is my rock, my fortress and my deliverer; my God is my rock, in whom I take refuge, my shield and the horn of my salvation. He is my stronghold, my refuge and my savior—from violent men you save me. I call to the Lord, who is worthy of praise, and I am saved from my enemies.)*

I have a friend who has just come through a personal battle that few of us will ever know. Her peace and happiness were threatened by a formidable enemy and there were times when she became very discouraged. But the battle for her has ended and her enemy has been defeated.

Instead of giving in to her fear, she put her trust and faith in God. She realized that she could do nothing about the situation, and she knew that her only hope was divine intervention. So she took refuge in the rock that shielded her from her enemy. And she was ultimately saved from the destruction that Satan had prepared. God was her stronghold and her Savior.

There are times when we all feel defeated by the enemy, but we really have nothing to fear when we know Christ as our personal Savior. He is truly our refuge and strength through all of our troubles. When we are His children and we cry out to Him in our distress, He will most assuredly deliver us from our enemy.

Are you going through a battle that you feel you cannot win? Are you a child of the King? Do you know Him as your personal Savior? If you do, you can put your faith and trust in Him. Give all of your worries over to Him and wait for Him to win the battle for you. He is your stronghold, your refuge and you're Savior and He will save you from your enemy. He is your mighty fortress.

## October 20

# WHAT'S BETTER THAN PERFECTION?

*(2 Samuel 22:31-33 "As for God, his way is perfect; the word of the Lord is flawless. He is a shield for all who take refuge in him. For who is God besides the Lord? And who is the Rock except our God? It is God who arms me with strength and makes my way perfect.)*

I wonder why we spend so much time in worry, frustration, doubt, fear, discouragement, and in general, thinking about all of the things that we cannot control. When we really stop to think about it, it is foolishness to live with that kind of mentality. When we finally realize who God is—when we know that Jesus provided a way for our salvation—and when we grasp on to the fact that the Holy Spirit lives in us from the time we accepted Jesus as our own personal Savior—why would we allow ourselves to live in such turmoil?

Let's take the above scripture a few words at a time to see what it is really saying to us. *God's way is perfect*—so why wouldn't we look to Him and trust Him for His perfect will and direction? *The word of the Lord is flawless*—which means that we can believe every word in the bible; so why don't we search out the truth? *He is a shield for all who take refuge in him*—so why don't we immediately run to His arms for safety? *For who is God besides the Lord?*—*there* is only one God and nobody else can ever take His place. He is omnipotent, omnipresent, and omniscient, and He alone is worthy to be praised. *And who is the Rock except our God?* God is the only one that we can trust—He and only He is the Rock of our firm foundation. *It is God who arms me with strength and makes my way perfect*—He will give us strength to walk the path where He leads us.

Don't you think it is about time we start believing and receiving the truth? Sometimes we have a difficult time comprehending just how great our God is; so we limit His blessings to us because we fail to embrace the truth of who He is and who we are in Him. We spend wasted time in our pit of doubt and fear; let's let go and let God take control of our life. We have nothing to lose and everything to gain.

# October 21

# SHOWERS OF BLESSINGS

*(Ezekiel 34:26 I will make them and the places surrounding my hill a blessing, I will send down showers in season; there will be showers of blessing.)*

I attended a 25 year celebration this past week of the founding of a church that was started by a friend and brother in Christ. Their theme was on rain. In that particular setting they were using the story of Elijah. If you are familiar with the bible, you probably remember that there had been a severe famine in Samaria. God told Elijah to go and present himself to Ahab and He would send rain. I am not going to go into detail except to say that Elijah was obedient to God. I do encourage you to read the entire account In 1Kings:18. There is certainly a lot to the story and if you have not read it, be sure to do so. You will be blessed.

I believe when my brother was called to start this church; it could not have been an easy thing to do. But he recognized God's call and said, "Yes, Lord." There must have been times through the first months and years of this ministry that he felt the drought, wondering when the showers of blessings would fall. But he never gave up—he persevered during the dry times, and there came a day when he saw the sign that the rain was coming to give water and abundant life to this church that God had asked him to plant. It has been twenty-five years since the day that this man of God began this particular ministry. The church has grown as God sent the showers of blessings—and it continues to grow. Probably more than Pastor Gary ever thought possible.

*(Ezekiel 34:23 I will place over them one shepherd my servant David, and he will tend them; he will tend them and be their shepherd. I the Lord will be their God, and my servant David will be prince among them. I the Lord have spoken.)* It seems to me that this Scripture describes this particular minister as if his picture were right next to it.

God calls men, and women, to go where He leads them. I truly believe that when they obey His command—they will receive showers of blessings. Has God called you to step out and go to a place that is outside of your comfort zone? Are you willing to say, "Yes, Lord" in spite of the fact that it does not look at all promising from the mind's eye? It is not an easy decision sometimes, as the evil one will try anything and everything he can to try and discourage those who are called: Even at times using your own biological and/or Christian family to discourage you. But don't give up hope, keep praying and look toward Heaven, because the rain is coming and you will definitely receive showers of blessing if you obey the Master's call.

# October 22

# A WATCHFUL EYE

*(Psalms 121:5-8 The Lord watches over you—the Lord is your shade at your right hand; the sun will not harm you by day, nor the moon by night, The Lord will keep you from all harm—he will watch over your life; the Lord will watch over your coming and going both now and forevermore.)*

I jokingly told my husband one morning that God had saved him from the act of murder. That was a little bit of a stretch, as I know he would never even entertain that idea. But in all honesty he would have been very upset with me if we had embarked on the journey that we had planned to take. I might add, not nearly as upset as I would have been from the embarrassment of such a stupid mistake.

This is the story—I had an appointment for a medical test on Tuesday. We needed to be there by 8:00—since it is about 80 miles away; we decided that we should leave by 6:00 in case we got bogged down by city traffic. I have to tell you that we just got home Monday after-noon from a 5 day trip and we were both extremely exhausted and were definitely not crazy about the idea of having to take that trip the next morning. I decided to go to bed early: I set my alarm and climbed into bed with a sigh that I was ready to rest—when out of the blue, a thought came to me that it was not this Tuesday that I was to have the test, but rather the next Tuesday. I literally ran out to the car to retrieve the papers that I had so thoughtfully placed in the seat in case I would forget the next morning; sure enough the papers said October 25—not October 18.

Now I know that some might think that my subconscious mind reminded me of the correct date—but I know that it was God that brought it to my mind. God cares about everything we do, and He watches over us and saves us many times from our human blunders. I have no doubt but what He saved us from a very disturbing mistake. Oh, the world would not have ended by the mistake, but it would have definitely added stress to our already tired bodies; and it would have robbed us of that time of coveted and needed rest. Never underestimate God's watchful eye. I wonder how many other times He has saved me from making a huge mistake—I will probably never know—probably too many to count.

## October 23

# A RECIPE FOR LIVING

*(Psalms 63:5 My soul will be satisfied as with the richest of foods; with singing lips my mouth will praise you.)*

I made one of my son's favorite dishes the other night—Lasagna. When we began to eat, the first words out of his mouth were, "This is delicious, sometimes Lasagna is so dry, but this is great." Of course my selfish desire for praise raised my self-esteem as a cook. But you know, I really had nothing to do with it. The dish was great because of the recipe I used and the ingredients that were put in to it. You cooks no that it is always a compliment when someone asks for your recipe.

As I was thinking about it this morning and I began to relate it to our testimony for the Lord. I began to wonder if we put so much thought in to the ingredients that might ultimately make our testimony of the Lord's grace so delicious that others might ask for the recipe. I know one thing, when I have tried to make a dish without a good recipe; it seems as if there is always something missing. It is after I tweak it and seek for the secret missing ingredient, that it begins to taste like I want it to.

It is one thing to be a Christian, but there is something wonderful and magnetic about a Christian who is really excited about their relationship with the Lord. There are those who live their life as a quiet sad faced Christian: They seem to have no joy in their salvation. There is just some secret ingredient missing. I don't think those kind of Christians would be that appealing to the world. It takes time with the Lord and seeking His Word to find the right ingredients that will produce a walk that is appealing to others. Does our relationship with the Lord leave a hunger for others to eat and be satisfied?

## October 24

# LIGHT OF LIFE

*(Psalms 56:13 For you have delivered me from death and my feet from stumbling that I may walk before God in the light of life.)*

As I was reading the other day I came across the following information— Artificial lights interfere with an insect's ability to detect the moonlight. They appear brighter, and radiate their light in multiple directions. Once an insect flies close enough to a light bulb, it attempts to navigate by way of the artificial light, rather than the moon. Since the light bulb radiates light on all sides, the insect simply cannot keep the light source at a constant angle, as it does with the moon. It attempts to navigate a straight path, but ends up caught in an endless spiral dance around the bulb.

How many times are we attracted by artificial light? The world has many lights that are alluring to us—and sometimes we foolishly follow that light; and we end up just like the insects—in an endless spiral dance that leads us away from the true light.

The alluring artificial light of this world will end up harming us or killing us. We will not find our pathway to God if we get caught up in it—only through the light of Jesus will we find eternal life—He is our real light source.

Have you ever sat and watched an insect as it flies round and round a light bulb? I have and I have always been mystified as to why. Now that I know the answer, I don't think I will ever see that poor insect's turmoil without thinking about Jesus being the only true light. I could have been just like one of those insects if the Light of Jesus had not led me out of darkness. Let's not get caught up in the artificial lights of the world, but rather follow the real light—the light of life—Jesus.

# October 25

# TESTED AND TRIED

*(James 1:2-3 Consider it pure joy, my brothers, whenever you face trials of many kinds, because you know that the testing of your faith develops perseverance.)*

We all face trials in our life at times. And many times we wonder why God has allowed them to come our way.

God's word says that we should consider it pure joy when we face trials because the testing of our faith develops perseverance. God allows those trials in our lives—if we did not have any, how would our faith develop in to the kind of faith that God desires. We would soon expect everything to be perfect.

There is never a time that God promises us that all will be smooth sailing if we follow Christ. To the contrary, He says that we will have trials of many kinds. But through all of the trials, we grow in our faith and that pleases God. When He sees us through those trials our trust in Him becomes stronger and stronger. I don't know about you but I find myself relying on the Lord more through the trials than I do when all is going well. And when I come through those trials—and I always do— I feel I know a little more about God's grace

*(James 1:12 Blessed is the man who perseveres under trial, because when he has stood the test, he will receive the crown of life that God has promised to those who love him.)* That makes it worth all of the trials that come our way—don't you think?

# October 26

# FEAR OF SPEAKING

*(Jeremiah 1:6-9 "Ah, Sovereign LORD," I said, "I do not know how to speak; I am only a child." But the LORD said to me, "Do not say, 'I am only a child.' You must go to everyone I send you to and say whatever I command you. Do not be afraid of them, for I am with you and will rescue you," declares the LORD. Then the LORD reached out his hand and touched my mouth and said to me, "Now, I have put my words in your mouth.)*

Wow! I can certainly identify with Jeremiah. Several months ago, I felt God's call for me to speak. I have prayed and prayed about what to do. I asked Him if He wanted me to speak, that a door would be open for me to do so. That door has been opened and after much prayer I have agreed. I, like Jeremiah, do not feel qualified to speak, but just as God told Jeremiah, He has also told me that He will put the words in my mouth.

I must admit that I am very excited about the fact that I will be giving my testimony of what God has done in my life. I will share the miracle of how God has chosen me to tell the story of my salvation. My life changed in 1982 when I was 42 years old. But it wasn't until I was 68 that I was willing to surrender everything to God. I took all of the things that I was trying to control and laid them at the feet of Jesus and since then my life has not been the same. God has given me a gift that I would never have thought possible—the gift of writing about His amazing grace. And now He has asked me to speak to give hope to those who have no hope.

I have no doubt but what God will give me the words to speak, because He has given me the words to write. Just think of it; I am the most unlikely person to ever do the things that He has called me to do. But I understand why —for I can never boast about myself, but I can certainly boast in what God has chosen to do through me. What a wonderful amazing God. He has shown me His purpose for my life and given me all that I need to fulfill that purpose. And I am telling the world about it. If I don't, I feel like the stones will cry out (ref. Luke 19:40).

# October 27

# A THIEF

*(John 10:9-10 I am the gate; whoever enters through me will be saved. He will come in and go out, and find pasture. The thief comes only to steal and kill and destroy; I have come that they may have life, and have it to the full.)*

I used to be a smoker. I was raised in a Christian home and I hid my smoking for years from my parents, knowing that they would not approve. But one of my children mentioned it one day to them and it was no longer a secret.

You have no idea how many times I think about how I robbed myself and my parents of fellowship together simply because I would not be free to indulge in my habit whenever I wanted. I know they were aware of that and they even told me to go ahead and smoke, because they did not want it to interfere with time spent with me: But I was too ashamed to smoke in their presence so I committed a greater wrong by staying away.

I cannot describe the sorrow and anguish I feel as I think about the precious time that was stolen from me and my parents; precious time of being in their presence. I grieve and cry thinking about it. I can't go back and undue the past—however I can share my regrets with others and warn them of the things that Satan will do to steal and rob us of those things that are precious.

I am thankful that before they left this world, I did accept Christ and I had a few more years with my parents without the chains of bondage that robbed me of time with my wonderful mother and dad. I am thankful that Jesus is my Shepherd and I can rest in His pasture. I am so glad that He has forgiven me for those times that I robbed my beloved parents of time with their baby.

Are you in some kind of bondage where you feel that you have to hide from others? If you are, run to Jesus and allow Him to break those chains.

## October 28

# A DISOBEDIENT PROPHET

*(1 Kings 13:18-19 The old prophet answered, "I too am a prophet, as you are. And an angel said to me by the word of the Lord: 'Bring him back with you to your house so that he may eat bread and drink water.'" (But he was lying to him.) So the man of God returned with him and ate and drank in his house.)*

This man of God had heard from the Lord, and up to this point in Scripture, he had been obedient. Why in the world would he let someone else convince him that it would be ok to do what God had emphatically instructed him not to do? It is a mystery to those of us reading it, and yet don't we often do the same thing?

Why would anyone who has heard from the Lord, then turn around and listen to someone else—allowing them to coerce them in to disobedience? Do we sometimes think that others know God better than we do, so we allow their voice to be heard over the voice of God? This man of God was a prophet, but when the other one told him he was a prophet also, he believed him over and above what God had instructed him to do.

The decision that the prophet made in the above Scripture led to his destruction: That leads me to think that God is not pleased when we take someone else's word over His. When God gives us a message we should not and cannot take another's word over His. Don't you think that if God changed His mind about something he has told you to do—He would enlighten you himself? I do.

Let's listen to the Lord and obey and honor His command. We can get into trouble if we allow others to sway us away from what God has called us to do.

# October 29

# AN ENCOURAGING WORD

*(Hebrews 10:24 And let us consider how we may spur one another on toward love and good deeds. Let us not give up meeting together, as some are in the habit of doing, but let us encourage one another—and all the more as you see the Day approaching).*

One of the most enjoyable times for me is when I spend time in the company of a friend that I can share my love for The Lord with. Yesterday was one of those days. As Mary and I sat across from each other at lunch discussing the qualities of God, we both became excited about what we had discovered about the grace of God. The more we talked, the more each of us revealed the blessings that God had bestowed on us. We not only nourished our bodies but our spirits were completely full when we got up from that lunch table.

One of the greatest blessings God gives us is our Christian sisters and brothers. I can't imagine not having those people in my life who encourage me to a deeper walk with my Lord. Whoever wrote the above Scripture surely knew what he was talking about. We do need the encouragement of one another. We all know that we can do all things through Christ, but sometimes we just need someone to remind us of that. When we are excited about serving the Lord, we are energized to spread the word to the entire world. The signs say that there is not much time left to do that. So let's keep those fires burning brightly so that those who do not know Jesus as their personal Savior might be ignited by the flames of our passion for Him.

## October 30

# ONE DAY AT A TIME

*(Lamentations 3:22-23 Because of the LORD'S great love we are not con-sumed, for his compassions never fail. They are new every morning; great is your faithfulness.)*

One day last week I was sharing with a brother how God is always so gracious to show me His faithfulness, every time I am threatened with discouragement. He handed me a tract titled 'One Day at a Time': And in this tract was a wonderful poem; the following is a stanza of this particular poem.

Not yesterdays load we are called on to bear.
Not the morrow's uncertain and shadowy care;
Why should we look forward or back with dismay?
Our needs as our mercies, are but for the day.

As I ponder on the above Scripture and this poem, I realize that looking back on past failures is not only useless but destructive. And worrying about the future will do no good at all. In truth both dis-honor our God of all mercies. When we put our faith and trust in Him, we will not be focused on those things of the past that we cannot change or those things of the future that we cannot control. God does not remember our sins of the past, and He is in control of the future. His mercies are new every morning. So we should meet every day as Psalms 118:24 says: (This is the day the Lord has made, let us rejoice and be glad in it.)

## October 31

# INTERCESSORY PRAYER

*(1 Kings 13:6 When King Jeroboam heard what the man of God cried out against the altar at Bethel, he stretched out his hand from the altar and said, "Seize him!" But the hand he stretched out toward the man shriveled up, so that he could not pull it back. Also, the altar was split apart and its ashes poured out according to the sign given by the man of God by the word of the Lord. Then the king said to the man of God, "Intercede with the Lord your God and pray for me that my hand may be restored." So the man of God interceded with the Lord, and the king's hand was restored and became as it was before.)*

I wonder how many of us would pray for healing for one of our enemies. Jeroboam had just threatened the man of God, and yet he prayed for him. Praying for someone we love is one thing—but praying for someone who is out to harm us is quite another.

This account of intercessory prayer is quite an unusual one. I doubt that any of us would ever be faced with this kind of prayer request—but we are asked to pray for our enemies. *(Matthew 5:44 But I tell you: Love your enemies and pray for those who persecute you.)* It is a difficult thing to pray for those who persecute you. However we must do that because God's word is emphatic about it.

Do you have any enemies that you know of? I would guess that you have had what you might term 'sandpaper people' who seem to always rub you the wrong way: people who just seem to want to make digs or insults: I know I have. Do you pray for those people? At one time I would say that it was more than I could do, but God has shown me that when I pray for those 'sandpaper people', I begin to see them in a different light. I heard someone say once that you can't harbor anger against those whom you pray for very long. There is just something about praying for people that tenderizes your heart toward them.

God says to love your enemies and pray for them. I believe that God will bless us for doing that. I would hate to think that someone would refuse to pray for me for any reason, wouldn't you?

# November 1

# HONORING YOUR PARENTS

*(Ephesians 6:2 Children, obey your parents in the Lord, for this is right.)*

I was at my mother's the day she was preparing to make a move in to the local residential care facility. We were going through some of the things that she wanted to take with her, and separating things that she wanted to give to others. All of my life I had admired a coal oil lamp that had been given to her by a relative. The globe of the lamp had small Scottish dogs around the middle. I have never seen another like it.

Before I left that day, mother told me that she wanted me to have that lamp. She went to get a box to put it in, and because I was in a hurry, I just sat the lamp in the box without wrapping it. Mother said, "Hon, you had better wrap that up so it won't get busted." I told her it would be ok because I had separated the globe from the base: But as I was on my way to put it in my car, a gust of wind came up, and you guessed it, it blew that globe out of the box. I watched in horror as the glass smashed into many pieces.

Since that time, I have tried to find a replacement for that lamp, but have never been successful. I had to put just a plain globe on it; and of course, it will never take the place of the beautiful original one.

I have grieved over that fateful day—not only because of the fact that the globe was ruined, but mostly because I had not listened to my mother. She had cherished that lamp for years—and because of my carelessness and lack of respect for my mother's plea to protect it—it was ruined.

Mother has long since gone to be with the Lord and I still live with the regret that I had not honored my mother. If I had obeyed her that day, I would still be enjoying the beauty of that lamp. But most of all I would not be living with the regret of my sin of not only listening to her that day, but all of the other times I did not honor my parents like I should have. I cannot turn back the time and change the decisions I made—but I can warn everyone to honor your parents.

Other than God, there is nobody who loves us more than our parents. Surely we can respect them enough to honor them. Parents want the best for their children. They would never advise them to do something that would harm them. Listen to your parents, respect them, and honor them. You will never regret it.

# November 2

# LOVING DISCIPLINE

*(Hebrews12:5-6 And you have forgotten that word of encouragement that addresses you as sons: "My son, do not make light of the Lord's discipline, and do not lose heart when he rebukes you, because the Lord disciplines those he loves, and he punishes everyone he accepts as a son.)*

Have you ever had to discipline your child and have them then accuse you of not loving them? I remember several times when my children said that to me. It would make me feel sad, and I would try to explain to them that it is because of my love for them that I or their father had to discipline them. Sometimes we would have to discipline them to keep them from being hurt in one way or another. I would always tell them that it hurt me worse than it did them: But they never seemed to believe me. I wondered at the time if they thought I enjoyed it. Can you identify?

Aren't we just like that when our Heavenly Father disciplines us. I believe it hurts Him when He has to discipline us; but He does it for our own good. We do not like discipline any more than our children do, but we must realize that it is necessary to make us grow and to protect us from mistakes that could ultimately destroy us. We must realize also that He disciplines us because He loves us. The scripture says that He punishes those He accepts as sons. Wow! That sheds a bright light in my heart, how about you?

# November 3

# WAITING AND WATCHING

*(Habakkuk 2:1 I will stand at my watch and station myself on the ramparts; I will look to see what he will say to me, and what answer I am to give to this complaint)*

Are there times when you are asking for direction on what to do about a particular problem and when you don't get a quick response from the Lord, you take things in your own hands and plunge in where you shouldn't have gone? I must admit that I have been guilty of that more than once. It is always a mistake. I am always sorry for my speedy decisions. It is complete fallacy to think that we can take control of a situation that we have asked God to handle, and expect everything to be ok.

Habakkuk was not a man to rush in where angels fear to tread. He held fast in his decision to wait and see what God's answer would be. The Lord told him to wait for the appointed time. *(Habakkuk 2:3 For the revelation awaits an appointed time; it speaks of the end and will not prove false. Though it linger, wait for it, it will certainly come and will not delay.)* God's ways are perfect and His timing is perfect. Will we ever learn to wait on the Lord? Let's determine in our hearts to wait on Him from this point on. *(Wait for the Lord; be strong and take heart and wait for the Lord. Psalms 17:14)* Remember, God has promised that He hears and answers the prayers of those who believe. Read 1 John 5:14-15

# November 4

# YOU MAKE THE CHOICE

*(1 Kings 18: 21 Elijah went before the people and said. "How long will you waver between two opinions? If the Lord is God, follow him, but if Baal is God, follow him.")*

There was a time that I walked with one foot in the world and one foot with God. Let me tell you, it is not a happy place to be in. There came a day when I knew that I had to make a choice. I made that choice and my life has never been the same.

(Matthew 6:24 *"No one can serve two masters. Either he will hate the one and love the other, or he will be devoted to the one and despise the other. You cannot serve both God and Money.)* If our heart is not totally dedicated to the Lord, we will never be effective in ministry. If we don't give our lives totally to the Lord—if we don't allow Him to be Lord in our lives, we will never grow into the person that God wants us to be. We will be like leaves in the wind—tossed back and forth. We will never be stable in our walk if we allow the gods of this world to have even part of our thoughts.

Do you waver in your walk? Do you serve God one day and serve the gods of this world the next? (Exodus 20:3 You shall have no other gods before me.)

God's word tells us to make a choice of which one we will follow. What choice have you made? It is a sobering question and one that we must answer.

God wants to give you abundant life and He cannot do that if you aren't wholly following Him. (John 10:10 The thief comes only to steal and kill and destroy; I have come that they may have life, and have it to the full.) Are you living in the fullness of God?

# November 5

# EFFECTED BY AFFLICTION

*(Psalms 119:71 It was good for me to be afflicted so that I might learn your decrees.)*

I can certainly identify and agree with what the Psalmist is saying here. For it was as a result of breaking my femur that brought me to the place that led me to seek God's Word in a way that I never had before. It brought me back to the basics.

I remember how excited I was to study God's Word when I first became a Christian: But through time and circumstances I had lost my enthusiasm for studying His Word. I would still read it every day but there were many times that I would finish reading it only to realize that not a word had penetrated my mind. That all changed at the time of my affliction.

I had a dear friend who died from breast cancer: But she testified to the world before her physical death, that as a result of her affliction, her life had been saved. It was as a result of her affliction that she found the Lord and embraced Him as her personal Savior.

Many times we hear people say the same thing about an affliction bringing them closer to God and His Word: And many times using it to bring them to the Cross where they most likely would not have gone, without being put in a position where they turned to God.

Sometimes people rail at God for allowing afflictions in their lives, but if they would open their hearts to see that sometimes God brings them through unpleasant circumstances to draw them closer to Him, they would gain wisdom and peace in the place that God has allowed. I wonder how many lives have actually been saved by afflictions that the world might see as tragedies. Pity the person who does not understand that God is in control and He would not allow anything to happen to one of His children without a reason.

# November 6

# THE CHOICE TO BELIEVE

*(Luke 8:12 Those along the path are the ones who hear, and then the devil comes and takes away the word from their hearts, so that they may not believe and be saved.)*

I have been witnessing to an atheist for several years, without any effect; At least I don't think so. However I continue to pray that he will open his eyes and his heart to the truth one day. I have such a difficult time understanding how anyone could ignore the fact that God exists. I could never even consider the fact that He doesn't. The proof of His existence is all around us. How anyone could adopt the 'big bang' theory or any other theory other than The Creator, is beyond me.

I agree with the quote below by J. Vernon McGee.

Quote "Today, when people say they cannot believe, it is not a mental problem; it is a matter of the will of the heart—they do not want to believe. Some say they have certain "mental reservations," mental hurdles which they cannot get over. My friend, your mind is not big enough to take even one little hurdle. The problem is never in the mind but in the will. There is sin in the life, and a man does not want to turn to God; he does not want to believe Him." End quote

People don't believe because they want to control their own destiny, the destiny that will lead them to eternal Hell. They just don't realize that Jesus is the way to eternal life. They are afraid to put their lives in the hands of a Savior, because they may have to surrender to the only One who can give them all that they search and hunger for. They are to be pitied above all men.

How sad to think that someone does not want to believe. What kind of sin could be so entangling that it would cause a person to harden their heart to the truth of God's existence. It makes me sad, yet at the same time it energizes me to keep on trying to persuade them. We have such a limited time to win those people over to the Lord. Let's keep trying to show them the way to Jesus. And pray that they will make the right choice—the only choice that will assure them a future for eternity in Heaven.

## November 7

# A WITNESS FOR CHRIST

*(John 1:6-8 There came a man who was sent from God; his name was John. He came as a witness to testify concerning that light, so that through him all men might believe. He himself was not the light; he came only as a witness to the light.)*

I think we all know who John the Baptist was. He was sent by God as the forerunner of Jesus. He was born for the specific purpose of telling the good news of the coming Savior—the Light of the world. The above Scripture says he was sent to testify about the Light so that all men might believe: Notice it says might believe, not that they all would believe.

As God's children we are also here for a purpose: That purpose is to spread the good news of Jesus: The one who came to earth as a man: The one who gave up His life on The Cross so that all who receive Him will have eternal life: The one who died for all men, even the vilest of sinners: The one who rose again and because He lives—we also live. His Holy Spirit comes to reside in our hearts the minute we receive Him as our personal Savior.

Are we testifying to others about this wonderful, marvelous Savior? Are we pointing others to the Cross? Are we telling them about His amazing grace? Who knows but what someone we talk to might believe and receive the gift of salvation through our personal testimony. We can't make the choice for them, but we can certainly point them to the Cross. I am pretty sure that not everyone that John talked to was converted, and I am pretty sure that everyone we talk to won't be either. But it will be worth it all if even one person will come to know Jesus as a result of us spreading the good news. *(Mark 16:15 He said to them, "Go into all the world and preach the good news to all creation.")*

Let's be bold and start telling the world about our Savior.

# November 8

# LIFE ETERNAL

*(1 John 5:10-12 Anyone who believes in the Son of God has this testimony in his heart. Anyone who does not believe God has made him out to be a liar, because he has not believed the testimony God has given about his Son. And this is the testimony: God has given us eternal life, and this life is in his Son. He who has the Son has life; he who does not have the Son of God does not have life.)*

On this Easter Sunday, we are naturally focused on the death and resurrection of Jesus. When we truly ponder the horror of what God's Son went through to carry out His Father's plan, it takes our breath away. As humans we can't imagine that kind of love—a love that was willing to sacrifice one's only son to save sinners: The love of the Son who said, "Father not my will, but yours be done." If we look at this wonderful sacrifice individually and personally, it is amazing. Just think about the fact that Jesus died just for you and just for me, even if we had been the only person on this earth: That's how much He loves us.

I can't imagine how one would not want to accept the salvation offered to us. And yet, there are so many people in this world who are more interested in their lives today than they are of where they will spend eternity. They deny Christ when they turn their backs on Him. There are actually those who believe that everyone will go to Heaven. And there are some who believe that there is no after-life. But the Scripture tells us that those who do not believe God, has made Him out to be a liar. Only those who believe and know Jesus as their personal Lord and Savior will be saved. And the bible is very clear that there is a Heaven and a Hell.

It is very simple to understand. It is a choice that everyone must make. Do you believe? Have you received Christ as your personal Savior? Don't wait—this may be the last day of your life. If that were true—where would you spend eternity?

Go to The Cross and you will have eternal life.

# November 9

## BLESSED LIGHT

*(Genesis 1:14-15 Then God said, "Let there be lights in the expanse of the heavens to separate the day from the night, and let them be for signs and for seasons and for days and years; and let them be for lights in the expanse of the heavens to give light on the earth; and it was so.) NASB*

I purchased a new bible a few months ago, but have been reluctant to use it. Not only is it a different version than what I have always used—it isn't marked, highlighted and written in with all of the things that have spoken to me so significantly through the years. Can you identify? It comes to the place where you just don't think that you can possibly hear the message as loudly in another bible. This morning I took the plunge and opened that new one up. And wonder of wonders, in the very first chapter, God spoke to my heart with a powerful realization. A verse that I had become so familiar with, was speaking to me with new insight.

I suddenly was stopped short at the above verse. Can you imagine a world without light? Without the light that God spoke into being, we could not have functioned in this world. Without light we would not even be able to see our hands in front of us: We could not have lived without light. Ponder on that for awhile.

I have always felt extremely sorry for those who are blind and cannot see the beautiful sights that God has made. They have to see the beauty through other's eyes. But Spiritual light is different, even a blind person can experience all the beauty of that. Jennifer Rothschild is blind, but it has not stopped her from being and seeing God's beauty. He has given her such Spiritual Light that it is almost blinding to look upon. She has far more light than most people. She has the light of Jesus.

The light that God spoke into being was for everyone. But the Light of Jesus is only for those who care to see truth. One cannot have His Light through the eyes of another. It is The Light that is revealed only when we accept Jesus. *(John 8:12 Then Jesus again spoke to them, saying, "I am the Light of the world; he who follows Me will not walk in the darkness but will have the Light of life.")* NASB

We do not have the power to turn light on in the hearts of others: Only Jesus can do that. However, we can point them to the Light by letting His light shine through us. *(Matthew 5:16 "Let your light shine before men in such a way that they may see your good works, and glorify your Father who is in Heaven.)*NASB

# November 10

# LONELY EXILE

*(Jeremiah 29:13-14 Then you will call upon me and come and pray to me, and I will listen to you. You will seek me with all your heart. I will bring you back from captivity. I will gather you from all the nations and places where I have banished you," declares the Lord, and will bring you back to the place from which I carried you into exile.")*

Are there times when you feel as if God has carried you into exile? I sure have had those times. And they are not a very good place to be. It is a lonely place—a place where it seems as if you can't feel the Lord's presence and you can't hear His voice. And you feel as if you are in a slimy pit and can't get out. I don't know about you, but when I don't feel like I can hear the Lord, I am miserable. I wonder if the worries of this world are what sometimes put us there. If we are worried about any issue, we are not putting our faith and trust in God and it can separate us from Him.

God says when we call upon Him and go to Him in prayer and seek Him with all our heart, He will bring us back from our exile. Whether he has put us there for a reason or whether we put ourselves there, He will bring us back. He wants to lift us out of the slimy pit. *(Psalm 40:2-3 He lifted me out of the slimy pit, out of the mud and mire; he set my feet on a rock and gave me a firm place to stand. He put a new song in my mouth, a hymn of praise to our God. Many will see and fear and put their trust in the Lord,)* It is wonderful when the time of being in exile is over and we have a new song in our heart and a hymn of praise to our God.

# November 11

# SINS SUBTLE ATTRACTION

*(Genesis 3:4—6 "You will not surely die," the serpent said to the woman. "For God knows that when you eat of it your eyes will be opened, and you will be like God, knowing good and evil." When the woman saw that the fruit of the tree was good for food and pleasing to the eye, and also desirable for gaining wisdom, she took some and ate it. She also gave some to her husband, who was with her, and he ate it.)*

When God created Adam and Eve, He put them in a beautiful garden where they had everything that they needed. He only asked one thing of them—not to eat the forbidden fruit. But the serpent enticed Eve, by telling her lies. She believed him and ate from the tree. She even succeeded in convincing Adam to eat from it also. Thus—sin entered the world.

Nothing much has changed in the sin department. Sin is enticing. And the one who is doing the enticing is Satan. He lies to people when he says that it will be ok and they believe him. So they go against God and basically allow Satan to put them in chains. So what hope to the people have?

God's ultimate plan for man was to live in that Garden of Eden; but because of Adam and Eve's choice to sin: He had to make a way for the redemption of that sin. Jesus paid the supreme sacrifice for our sins when He died on The Cross taking our sins with Him. He arose on the third day in order that we might have eternal life. However, just like Adam and Eve—we must make the choice. We can recognize and accept what Jesus did on The Cross and receive Him as our personal Savior—or we can turn our backs on Him and have our own way which will lead to eternal damnation.

Have you been to The Cross?

# November 12

# PROTECTION FOR THE RIGHTEOUS

*(Psalms 5:11-12 But let all who take refuge in you be glad; let them ever sing for joy. Spread your protection over them that those who love your name may rejoice in you. For surely, O Lord, you bless the righteous; you surround them with your favor as with a shield.)*

There are so many of God's people who are suffering because of hurt that others have inflicted on them. In the past month I have visited with several different women who shared the battles that Satan has brought to their doorstep: Good Christian women who love and serve the Lord. Every one of them however is finding strength in God. They know that they are not defeated, because they are taking refuge in their Protector.

I don't know any Christian who has not had battles to fight: Even sometimes battles that they themselves have been responsible for. But God never forsakes us when we turn to Him for refuge and strength. When we cry out to God for guidance, forgiveness, peace, understanding, and protection, He is always there. He is not a God to be praised only in the good times: He is to be praised most especially in the bad times. He alone can give us all we need to fight the battles and give us protection from the enemy.

If you are going through a fire right now that threatens to destroy you, run to Jesus and rejoice in the knowledge that He is your refuge. *(Psalms 144:2 He is my loving God and my fortress, my stronghold and my deliverer, my shield, in whom I take refuge, who subdues peoples under me.)*

Let us rejoice and sing for joy to The One we love, because God will surround us with His favor when we take refuge in Him. God has His arms outstretched to those who care to run to Him.

## November 13

# MOLDED BY THE POTTER

*(Jeremiah 18:5 Then the word of the Lord came to me: "O house of Israel, can I not do with you as this potter does?" declares the Lord. "Like clay in the hand of the potter, so are you in my hand, O house of Israel.)*

Looking back on my life, I can clearly see that I allowed Satan to mold me. He had used things in my younger years that made me feel inferior and caused me to turn my back on the Lord. But praise God, He is bigger and more powerful than anything Satan could bring my way. God ultimately used all of those negative things in my past for good. The moment I gave my heart to Jesus, He took me in His hands like a lump of clay and began to remold me into the woman that He wanted me to be. He is still molding me and reshaping me; and I know that He will continue to do that until I reach perfection: And that won't be until I enter into His presence. I used to have a poster that said, 'Please be patient with me—God is not finished with me yet.'

Do you feel like you are simply too ugly, too sinful, too hopeless, or too unworthy for God to take you into His hands? Well He doesn't feel that way. He says to come to Him and He will make you into a new creation. He can take the hardest clay and shape it into whatever He wants it to be. He can make all things beautiful in His time and according to His will. He has a plan for all of us. But we must be willing to submit to His will so that we will be pliable in His hands.

# November 14

# DISCERNING TRUTH

*(Acts 5:38 Therefore, in the present case I advise you: Leave these men alone! Let them go! For if their purpose or activity is of human origin, it will fail. But if it is from God, you will not be able to stop these men; you will only find yourselves fighting against God.")*

There are many people in this world who are offended by those who have been called by God to speak His word. Many missionaries are being persecuted for their audacity to speak up for Jesus. And others are just simply ridiculed for their stand

On the other hand, there are men and women who are doing many activities, including preaching and teaching claiming that they have been called by God, but they are really doing them on their own volition. I emphatically believe that they will fail in the end.

As I was studying about this Scripture, I realized that we must know who to listen to and who not to. The ability to discern the difference comes through the enlightenment of the Holy Spirit. There are many wolves in sheep's clothing out there and we certainly want to identify them as such. Many people have been led to destruction because they have been enticed by the lies of evil men, who claim that they are led by God.

I don't believe we should ignore what others are saying about Jesus and His word. We need to know whether they are telling the truth or telling lies. Gamaliel suggested just ignoring what men say—but I do not believe his statement came from God. We cannot and must not ignore what others say. We need to check it out in God's Word. II Timothy 2:15 admonishes ("Study to show yourself approved unto God, a workman that needs not to be ashamed, rightly dividing the word of truth.")

# November 15

# PEACE AND PATIENCE

*(2 Corinthians 6:4-5 Rather, as servants of God we commend ourselves in every way: in great endurance; in troubles, hardships and distresses; in beatings, imprisonments and riots; in hard work, sleepless nights and hunger; in purity, understanding, patience and kindness; in the Holy Spirit.)*

According to Webster, Patience means: Bearing pains or trials calmly or without complaint; manifesting forbearance under provocation or strain; not hasty or impetuous; steadfast despite opposition, difficulty, or adversity; able or willing to bear.

Paul had many trials in his life but he certainly had learned to be steadfast in them. Not because of his ability to be content through the trials, but because of His faith and trust in God. The trials we go through show what kind of faith we have. I believe that God allows those trials in our life so that we will learn to be steadfast in our faith in Him.

Some people, when faced with trials, become angry at God and think that He should not be allowing those things to happen. But what kind of faith would we have if we never had to face conflict of any kind? Trails and hardships grow us up as we face them with patience and steadfastness in our faith and trust. (James *1:2 Consider it pure joy, my brothers, whenever you face trials of many kinds, because you know that the testing of your faith develops perseverance. Perseverance must finish its work so that you may be mature and complete, not lacking anything.)* God will never give us anything that we can't bear, if we put our trust in Him.

So when we go through the trials that God allows; let's demonstrate our patience, and be steadfast in our love and faith in The One who will take us through the fires with growth that we would never have experienced otherwise.

# November 16

# THE HOLY TRINITY

*(Genesis 1:1, 2, 26a In the beginning God created the heavens and the earth. Now the earth was formless and empty, darkness was over the surface of the deep, and the Spirit of God was hovering over the waters. Then God said, "Let us make man in our image, in our likeness…")*

There is absolutely no way our human finite minds can thoroughly explain the triune God. But I know for certain that it is a fact. God, the Father: Jesus, the Son: and the Holy Sprit is one. They are the Holy Trinity—the three in one. God was the creator of this universe. Jesus (God's Son) was the Savior of the world. The Holy Spirit came to reside in the hearts of those who believe when Jesus ascended in to Heaven after His resurrection. Yet they are one God. They are emphatically referred to in the above Scripture as one God. Again in *(Isaiah 6:8 Then I heard the voice of the Lord saying, "Who shall I send? And who will go for us?)* It is revealed again in *(John 14:11 Believe me when I say that I am in the Father and the Father is in me.)* Scripture tells us that the Holy Spirit is the third part of this amazing triune God. *(John 14:16 And I will ask the Father and he will give you another Counselor to be with you forever.)*

Last night I laid in bed thinking about the magnificent truth of who God is. He is God, Jesus, and the Holy Spirit—yet He is One. How can that be you ask? — Because He is Holy. It is by faith that we believe. God's Word reveals to us who God is, if we take the time to read and study it. There are many, many Scriptures revealing who God is. Spend some time looking up what the bible says about the Holy Trinity. It will bless your heart. One cannot read the wonderful attributes of God, Jesus and The Holy Spirit without being in awe of His Holiness, and inseparable character.

## November 17

# GROWING THROUGH TRIALS

*(1 Peter 4:12 (Dear friends do not be surprised at the painful trial you are suffering, as though something strange were happening to you.)*

Sometimes I think that Christians feel like they should never go through trials. But we are never promised that we won't have storms in our life. As a matter of fact, God's word says we will have trials. But it is through the trials that we grow as we seek the Lord for wisdom and rely on Him for strength. There will never be obstacles in our life that we cannot overcome through our faith and trust in God.

*(1 Peter 1:3-6 Praise be to the God and Father of our Lord Jesus Christ! In his great mercy he has given us new birth into a living hope through the resurrection of Jesus Christ from the dead, and into an inheritance that can never perish, spoil or fade—kept in heaven for you, who through faith are shielded by God's power until the coming of the salvation that is ready to be revealed in the last time. In this you greatly rejoice, though now for a little while you may have had to suffer grief in all kinds of trials. These have come so that your faith—of greater worth than gold, which perishes even though refined by fire—may be proved genuine and may result in praise glory and honor when Jesus Christ is revealed.)* As we read this Scripture, we can see that we are protected through each trial. Through faith we are shielded by God's power. So we can rejoice in all things with the knowledge that God is with us and nothing can destroy us. He will be with us to the end of this age. And we shall live with Him in Heaven.

So let's rejoice even in the storms of life as we boast in the Lord of His deliverance through each one. He will not only deliver us out of our sufferings but He will make our faith stronger through them. Let us exalt the Lord together.

# November 18

# LOVELY THOUGHTS

*(Philippians 4:8 Finally, brothers, whatever is true, whatever is noble, whatever is right, whatever is pure, whatever is lovely, whatever is admirable—if anything is excellent or praiseworthy—think about such things.)*

There are times when we are tempted to think on the negative things in our life. And where, may I ask, does that get us? It takes us right down to the pit of worry, depression, anger, frustration, helplessness, etc. It takes away our joy and peace. That is exactly where the evil one wants us to be. Are you ok with that? I'm not and yet I find myself in that pit more than I care to say. I am still learning that I have to turn all those ugly thoughts over to God. He is the only one who can give us peace. Satan is a liar and would like for us to remain in the miry pit. But praise the Lord; He is the one who restores our spirit when we call on His name.

I'll tell you a secret—I had been worrying endlessly about something I had been praying about. I asked God to take away the daily worry. He did and I had not agonized over it for a long time. One day, not long ago, the thought came to me that I had not been worrying about it. I immediately felt guilty. I felt like I had been neglecting my duty to worry. Now how crazy is that? That was not a thought that God put in my mind—NO, NO, NO, for I had turned it over to God. I had still been praying about it, but had peace in the thought that God was in control and that He would fight my battle.

God's word tells us to think on things that are right, pure, lovely, admirable, excellent and praiseworthy. If we replaced all of the ugly things that Satan brings to our mind with the lovely thoughts that The Holy Spirit invokes, we would not find ourselves in the pit of unhappiness. We gain peace and happiness even through the trials of life by letting God penetrate our Spirit with all lovely thoughts.

# November 19

# MAKING RIGHT CHOICES

*(2 Chronicles 21:20 Jehoram was thirty-two years old when he became king, and he reigned in Jerusalem eight years. He passed away, to no one's regret, and was buried in the City of David, but not in the tombs of the kings.)*

Wow! How sad: Jehoram was an evil man; he had caused the people of Jerusalem to prostitute themselves and had led Judah astray. How would you like to leave a legacy like Jehoram? His life is an example of making poor choices. He could have chosen to walk in the ways of his father Jehoshaphat, but he chose to walk in the ways of the kings of Israel and suffered the consequences of his sin. He died a terrible, painful death. And it is recorded that no one regretted his death. He was not even allowed to be buried in the tombs of the kings.

There are those today who are in power who ignore God. They are determined to lead people astray. They seemingly have no regard for the word of God. They want to govern the way that they want to. I think the evil one has such control of their lives that they cannot see the fallacy of their destructive leadership. Unfortunately people fall for their evil ways and follow them with blinded eyes. But just like Jehoram, they will not get by with their evil. They will one day pay the price for their evil leadership.

We are told to pray for those who govern over us. *(Romans 13:1 "Let every soul be subject to the governing authorities, for there is not authority except from God, and the authorities that exist are appointed by God.")* I don't know why God allows evil men to be in authority—but He does, and there is a reason. Could it be because we have fallen so far down in our own pit of sin that He is giving us exactly what we ask for?

When we go our own way without consulting God, we are bound to get into trouble. We have our own choices to make. We can choose evil or we can choose to walk in the ways of God. We can see by the life of Jehoram which he chose. And we can see what happened to him. It should be a wake-up call to all of us to seek God's wisdom not only in how we live, but to seek his wisdom in appointing our leaders. Our future depends on it. God must be in control or we will fall.

## November 20

# PRAISE THE LORD

*(Psalms 42:11 Why are you downcast, O my soul? Why so disturbed within me? Put your hope in God, for I will yet praise him, my Savior and my God.)*

Do we praise God for all things, in all times, and in every situation in our life? It should be easy for us to praise God when all things are going well in our life, and yet even then we sometimes fail to give Him honor and praise and glory. When we are sitting in church and everything in our life is going smoothly, we might remember to praise God. But what about the times when things are rough and the discouragement sets in? Do we praise God then?

If we know the Lord as our personal Savior, we can and should praise Him in every circumstance. He is able to lift us up and put joy and peace in our hearts, even when the evil one is trying to take it away from us. Did you know that the easiest way to defeat Satan is by praising the name of Jesus? Especially when he least expects it. God is our God of all peace—even in the midst of storms. God alone is worthy to be praised. And He should be praised every day in every way. He is our Redeemer, the One who saved us. He is our Sustainer, the one who holds us fast. He is our peace. He is our joy. He is our strength. We can trust Him in every situation and know that He will deliver us out of the storms of life.

# November 21

# THANKSGIVING AND PRAISE

*(Psalms 7:17 I will give thanks to the Lord because of his righteousness and will sing praise to the name of the Lord Most High.)*

As we enter the Thanksgiving season, I believe all of us would greatly benefit from considering all that we have to be thankful for. As I was reading the above Scripture this morning it suddenly dawned on me that all thankfulness should be directed to God. He is the one who gives us every blessing that we have. Read carefully the words of this verse. To whom does the psalmist say he gives thanks? He gives thanks to the Lord. Why does he give Him thanks? He gives Him thanks because of His righteousness. And how does he thank Him? He sings praises to Him.

God is the only one worthy of praise. Webster's dictionary gives the following words as synonyms of righteousness: all right, decent, ethical, honest, honorable, just, moral, nice, right, good, right-minded, straight, true, upright, virtuous. These words can't begin to tell all of the attributes of God. I know people who these words would describe. They are righteous people, but only because they are right with the Lord. No one is righteous except for the righteousness that comes from God. We can give thanks for everyone that God has put in to our lives but we should give praise only to the Lord: Simply because He is the Lord Most High.

Thanksgiving is a time to reflect on all of our blessings. We can and should thank people for things that they have done for us, we can love them, and honor them: But I believe that praise should go directly to our God for all the things that he provides, and all the people that He has given us to love, and for those who love us. So let's give Him glory and thanks for all things, but most of all let's praise Him because He is The Lord Most High.

God's Word tells us that He will never leave us, nor forsake us. When we keep that in mind, we can yet thank Him when our souls are downcast. I have found during those times of despair and threatened peace; when I thank God, He lifts my spirits and gives me peace.

# November 22

# UNTOUCHED BY TROUBLE

*(Proverbs 19:23 The fear of the LORD leads to life; then one rests content, untouched by trouble.)*

I don't know many people who don't have some kind of trouble in their lives, do you? It seems as though most of us face problems because we live in a world where evil seems to prevail. The enemy tries to attack us in any way he can to destroy our faith, hope and peace. But if we are God's children, he protects us from the hurt that so often threatens to destroy our peace. We may go through hurt, discouragement, and pain, but we can have peace in our hearts.

Have you ever witnessed someone who has more troubles than you can imagine: Yet they seem to keep their Spirits high? They never seem to bow down under those attacks from the evil one. Their joy is always there for the world to see. You can rest assured that those people know Jesus. He is the one who sustains their peace and joy.

Are you going through a time of trials and discouragement? You don't have to go through it alone—God will walk with you through every battle, if you let Him. He is there to guide you, protect you, encourage you, and give you peace. We serve a God who understands all of our troubles and our hurts. When we know Him as our personal Savior, we are untouched by the trouble that surrounds us. We can maintain the joy of His salvation. *(Isaiah 26:3 You will keep in perfect peace him whose mind is steadfast, because he trusts in you.)*

## November 23

# THE WANDERING SHEEP

*(Matthew 18:12-14 "What do you think? If a man owns a hundred sheep, and one of them wanders away, will he not leave the ninety-nine on the hills and go to look for the one that wandered off? And if he finds it, truly I tell you, he is happier about that one sheep than about the ninety-nine that did not wander off. In the same way your Father in heaven is not willing that any of these little ones should perish.)*

A friend and I were discussing today how panicked mothers become when they think one of their children is missing. Has that ever happened to you? It has to me, more than once. I was thinking about one particular time when our son was about three years old. He and I were outside on the back patio when our telephone rang, I hurried in to answer it and told my little one to stay where he was and I would be right back. Now the phone was just inside the door, and the conversation was just long enough to say hello and can I call you back. When I went back outside, Kyle was nowhere to be seen. I was absolutely frantic. I started yelling his name at the top of my lungs, which was to no avail. I ran to the front of the house and looked in both directions. I looked everywhere, and the more I looked, the more frightened I became. I was just about ready to call the police when a man walked up to me with my son in tow. It seemed as though my son had become curious about a new house that was being built behind ours, and he went to investigate. The laborer heard me calling Kyle's name and he brought him home. I was never so happy to see someone in my entire life. My son had been found and he was safe.

I can certainly identify with the parable of the lost sheep. Not only do I recall the time when Kyle was lost, but also a time when I was. I wandered like a lost sheep without a shepherd: But God kept calling my name, I eventually heard His voice and came home to Him and He opened His arms of love where I found safety. God is our Shepherd and He watches over all of us. Perhaps you have been wandering away from the right path. Listen for the Shepherd's call, turn around and follow Him.

# November 24

# WHAT GREATER SIN

*(2 Chronicles 33:9-13 Manasseh led Judah and the people of Jerusalem astray, so that they did more evil than the nations the LORD had destroyed before the Israelites. The LORD spoke to Manasseh and his people, but they paid no attention. So the LORD brought against them the army commanders of the king of Assyria, who took Manasseh prisoner, put a hook in his nose, bound him with bronze shackles and took him to Babylon. In his distress he sought the favor of the LORD his God and humbled himself greatly before the God of his ancestors. And when he prayed to him, the LORD was moved by his entreaty and listened to his plea; so he brought him back to Jerusalem and to his kingdom. Then Manasseh knew that the LORD is God.)*

If you will read the entire chapter of 2 Chronicles 33 you will see the despicable things that Manasseh did in the first part of his reign. He worshipped idols and he sacrificed his sons on pagan alters among many other horrendous acts. Everything he did dishonored God. God punished him. But in spite of everything, when Manasseh cried out to God, God had mercy on him and restored his position.

Wouldn't you say that is a loving, forgiving, and gracious God? Do you feel that you have committed a sin beyond God's grace and forgiveness? I can't think of greater sins than those of Manasseh's. I'm sure you can't top his actions. God forgives everyone, no matter what it is or who it is. God's mercy is so great that he overlooks every sin when we humble ourselves and come to him and ask for forgiveness. He will then create a new person in you. There is no greater love than the love of Jesus. He asks for nothing except to believe and receive Him. If you have not done that, don't wait—today could be the last day of your life. Ask yourself, "If I died today where would I spend eternity?" If the answer is anything other than Heaven, please call on Jesus, lay your sins at The Cross and allow Him to come into your heart.

# November 25

# GLORY TO GOD

*(John 5:41 "I do not accept glory from human beings, but I know you. I know that you do not have the love of God in your hearts. I have come in my Father's name, and you do not accept me; but if someone else comes in his own name, you will accept him. How can you believe since you accept glory from one another but do not seek the glory that comes from the only God?)*

I wonder how many people set in churches hanging on the words of the minister but will not accept Jesus as their personal Savior. I believe that there are many. I once attended a church where a very popular minister preached. But one was hard pressed to hear the plan of salvation. My husband and I made the decision to leave before we starved to death from the hunger of God's word. Yet many others loved this minister and his way of speaking.

I often wonder why those men in the pulpit who do not preach clearly the message of salvation, are so highly admired. Many of those listening to them think they are wonderful. And there are some who do preach the word but others do not respond to the truth and yet seem to love the man teaching it. It is a mystery to me.

It is nice to love our ministers, but we must ask our self this question—why do we love and honor them? Is it because they preach the truth of God's word, or just because he has charisma? Unfortunately many have the wrong answer to that question. A lot of people are swayed by those charismatic ministers who use their glib tongue and entice others to follow their path instead of the one that God has laid out for them.

We can listen to sermons and read God's word every day, but the truth of the matter is, if we don't accept Jesus as our personal Savior, we are lost.

# November 26

# PRAY FOR YOUR ENEMIES

*(Matthew 5:43-44 "You have heard that it was said, 'Love your neighbor and hate your enemy.' But I tell you: Love your enemies and pray for those who persecute you, that you may be sons of your Father in heaven.")*

It is so easy to pray for those who are always good to you. But how do you feel about those who abuse you, either by deeds or by their tongue? Do you find it easy to pray for them? Or do you justify not praying for them by bringing to mind constantly how they have hurt you? Well the above scripture tells us to pray for those who persecute you, that you may be sons of your Father in heaven.

Life isn't always easy and sometimes people hurt you beyond words. Yet we must not let that stand in our way of praying for them. Someone once said that you can not always be angry with a person if you are praying for them. This I know is true. I have been through that. When you pray for someone that has harmed you, you start thinking of them in a different light. You realize that Christ died for them just as much as he did for you. It does no good to hold a grudge against anyone. The only one who is hurt by that mentality is the one who holds the grudge.

If someone has harmed you in any way; let it go and pray that God will show them the wrong they have done. Love them in spite of what they have done to you. God can change any willing heart. I doubt that anyone can say that they have never hurt another, but we would want them to forgive us, wouldn't we? Jesus showed us how to pray. He prayed for all who hurt Him, even when He was hanging on the cross.

# November 27

# WOMEN AND THE WORD

*(2 Kings 22:11-14 When the king heard the words of the Book of the Law, he tore his robes. He gave these orders to Hilkiah the priest, Ahikam son of Shaphan, Akbor son of Micaiah, Shaphan the secretary and Asaiah the king's attendant: "Go and inquire of the LORD for me and for the people and for all Judah about what is written in this book that has been found. Great is the LORD's anger that burns against us because those who have gone before us have not obeyed the words of this book; they have not acted in accordance with all that is written there concerning us." Hilkiah the priest, Ahikam, Akbor, Shaphan and Asaiah went to speak to the prophet Huldah, who was the wife of Shallum son of Tikvah, the son of Harhas, keeper of the wardrobe. She lived in Jerusalem, in the New Quarter.)*

Wow! Just look at this-These prominent men went to speak to Huldah to seek her prophetic wisdom. There are not many times that a woman is sought after by men for wisdom and prophecy. They must have known that she was a woman of God. They must have had total confidence in her wisdom and prophecy. She is the one who sent King Josiah the message from God of the forthcoming days by way of these men.

Being a woman, I find that pretty amazing don't you? I don't know about the rest of you women, but sometimes I think people don't have confidence in our ability to proclaim God's word. Some think that if it doesn't come from the male species, it surely isn't worthy of attention. Forgive me, you men who do not fall in that category. For I know that there are some who do not have that mentality. The men in the scripture above knew who they were dealing with and were not intimidated by Huldah. They sought her out because they knew that God used her to prophecy. Thank God for using women according to His will. And thank God for men who recognize them.

If you are a woman and feel intimidated because you think you are not capable of hearing from God, take heart in this passage of scripture. God has plans for you, just as much as He has for men. He is not a respecter of men only; He is a great respecter of women. He can use us when we are listening to Him. We may not be prophets, but whatever He has called us to do, He will empower us to do. He does not think less of us because we are females. He created each of us in His image, so why would we think He would not use us to bring a message to the world? Take heart all of you women, God not only will use you, He wants to use you.

# November 28

# PREPARED FOR BATTLE

*(1 Chronicles 5:19-20 They waged war against the Hagrites, Jetur, Na-phish, and Nodab. They were helped in fighting them, and God handed the Hagrites and all their allies over to them, because they cried out to him.)*

I wonder how many reading this are in some kind of battle right now. I would make a guess that there are more than a few who are. I don't know about you, but in my life it seems as though there are battles to fight almost daily in one form or another. It really is no mystery as to why; since we are warned that the evil one in this world prowls around in the hopes that he will win the battle that he rages against God's people.

But I have news for you—Our God is bigger than the one who tries to destroy us. The people referred to in the scripture above were trained for battle. (Ref. 1 Chronicles 5:18)

We too, should arm ourselves with the armor we are told to wear in Ephesians 6:14-17. And pray that God will help us. That is precisely what these men did and God answered their prayers. They prepared and they prayed for God to help them. God will always help us fight our battles, when we are prepared for them and when we cry out for His help.

The evil one will tell us so many lies, and try to make us believe that we are powerless. But when we realize that we have power through Christ and through His Holy Spirit, we do not have to be afraid, we can be assured of His help when we turn to Him for our success in defeating the enemy.

# November 29

# A GIFT YOU CANNOT PURCHASE

*(Acts 8:18-20 When Simon saw that the Spirit was given at the laying on of the apostles hands he offered them money and said "Give me also this ability so that everyone on whom I lay my hands may receive the Holy Spirit." Peter answered: "May your money perish with you, because you thought you could buy the gift of God with money!)*

Simon was impressed with what Peter and John were doing. He actually thought that he could purchase the power to do the same thing. It makes me wonder how many people today think they can buy the gift that God has freely given to those who love Him and are obedient to His call on their life. And it brings me to the question of why they would want to. It seems to me that Simon saw an opportunity to either buy his way to fame, money, or both. He certainly did not understand who Jesus was or he would never have tried to buy their gift.

There is no amount of money that can buy the gift of salvation or the gifts that come with it. Without salvation it is impossible to be in ministry effectively. If one does not know Christ, he will never be called into ministry of any kind. I believe there are many ministers who are in the pulpit as a profession and not because they are called. In fact I believe many of them do not even know Jesus as their personal Savior. They are making money by using the name of Jesus inappropriately for their own financial benefit and/or fame. Simon was *told ("You have no part or share in this ministry, because your heart is not right before God. Repent of this wickedness and pray to the Lord. Perhaps he will forgive you for having such a thought in your heart. For I see that you are full of bitterness and captive to sin." Acts 8:22-23)*

# November 30

# A JOYFUL REUNION

*(Isaiah 52:8-9 Listen! Your watchmen lift up their voices; together they shout for joy. When the LORD returns to Zion, they will see it with their own eyes. Burst into songs of joy together, you ruins of Jerusalem, for the LORD has comforted his people, he has redeemed Jerusalem.)*

One day I was watching a surprise reunion of a father coming home from war to his family. What an amazing, touching reunion that was. When the children saw their father they were overwhelmed with joy and they ran to meet him. The father stooped down and embraced them as they cried with joy and excitement of their father's return.

It is a wonderful picture of when the Lord comes back for His children one day. I wonder how many people will run to Him with joy and excitement. The answer to that is all of those who know Him as their personal Savior. I don't know about you, but I am waiting and anticipating His return. I can only imagine the tremendous joy that I will have when I see Him face to face. Oh what a happy day that will be.

Nobody knows the day or the hour that Jesus will come for His loved ones. But we do know that it is going to happen one day. Are you waiting with the anticipation of seeing Jesus return? Will you cry out with the joy of it all, or will you cower with fear? Think about it—those who have given their heart to Jesus will be elated when they see Him, but those who do not know him will shake with fear. If you do not know Jesus as your personal Savior—please don't put it off. It could be any day. You surely want to meet Him with joy and gladness.

# December 1

# A LETTER OF ENCOURAGEMENT

*(Titus 1:1-4 Paul, a servant of God and an apostle of Jesus Christ for the faith of God's elect and the knowledge of the truth that leads to godliness—a faith and knowledge resting on the hope of eternal life, which God, who does not lie, promised before the beginning of time, and at his appointed season he brought his word to light through the preaching entrusted to me by the command of God our Savior, To Titus my true son in our common faith: Grace and peace from God the Father and Christ Jesus our Savior.)*

Until recently I would have read this scripture without a lot of thought about the excitement Titus must have felt when receiving this letter from Paul. However, I realize today what a thrill it surely was when Titus opened that letter.

I received a personal note from Beth Moore written in her own writing. Someone had sent her the first book I wrote which mentioned her name on the dedication page. She not only wrote that she had been touched by the fact that I had referred to 5 points that she had written which have been very influential in my life; she also conveyed the humility she felt in being of service to me, and she encouraged me to continue in my work for the Lord.

You cannot imagine how excited I was to think that this woman who is so busy about the work of the Lord would take the time to write a note to an unknown sister. It was a wonderful Christmas gift from God coming on a day that I truly needed encouragement. It caused me to start thinking of other people who I greatly admire for the work that they are involved in for the Lord: Those who take the time to write with encouragement to strive to be all that God says I can be.

Paul loved writing letters to his brothers and sisters in Christ to encourage them in their faith and their work for the Lord. We could all take a lesson from Paul. We all need encouragement at times. It is one of the most blessed gifts we receive. How long has it been since you have called someone or written them a letter to encourage them?

# December 2

# BLESSINGS IN SONG

*(Isaiah 49:13 Shout for joy, O heavens; rejoice, O earth; burst into song, O mountains! For the Lord comforts his people and will have compassion on his afflicted ones.)*

Because I was facing a very busy schedule, I decided that I would do my Christmas decorating the week before Thanksgiving, which is very unusual for me. I worked hard for two days doing things that are more physically demanding than my normal routine. By Sunday I was still not done and so I decided that I would go to church and come home and do some more decorating. By that afternoon, I was so tired that I decided I would not attend choir practice and church that night:

Just as I was settled in that decision, I started rethinking what I was about to do. I wondered if God would be pleased that I chose to decorate for the most precious time of year, and then be so worn out that I could not go to church and worship Him. I did not have to wonder for long; I knew in my heart that it was a wrong decision. I got up from the chair that I thought sure I was settled into for the night, and got ready to go.

I was extremely tired when I walked into the choir room. We were practicing for our Christmas Cantata and by the time we were finished, I was so energized, I felt like I could sing forever.

When we went in to the sanctuary for the pastor's message to us— he said that what he had planned to give, had been interrupted by God's Spirit and that we, the congregation, would be bringing the message by way of popcorn testimonies. That is one thing that I love about the church I attend: The Holy Spirit is free to have His way. I do so love testimonies about what God has done and is doing in the hearts and lives of the people around me. They are so encouraging, inspiring and uplifting.

If I had decided to stay home, I would have missed the blessings that God had for me that night. God's Holy Spirit was definitely at work. Yes it is true that God has compassion on His afflicted ones— even if we have brought it on ourselves. What an amazing God we serve. His love is more than what our finite minds can comprehend.

# December 3

# LOVE AND MERCY

*(1 Chronicles 17:13 I will be his father, and he shall be my son: and I will not take my mercy away from him, as I took it from him that was before thee.}* KJV

Most of the time I read a particular version of the bible; and I have always felt comfortable doing so; but as I was reading the Scripture above this past week, I was taken aback at the word love pertaining to this particular portion of Scripture. I immediately thought—wait a minute; I do not believe that God ever takes His love from us. I went directly to the KJV to see what it said and sure enough instead of love, the word mercy was used.

Some people think that these 2 words are synonymous, but they are not. There is a very big difference in the words love and mercy. In Webster's dictionary this is how they are defined—

Love—a: A strong affection for another arising out of kinship or personal ties; maternal love for a child. b: an assurance of affection

Mercy—a: compassion or forbearance shown especially to an offender or to one subject to one's power a: a blessing that is an act of divine favor or compassion

God's mercy is unmerited grace. And His love endures forever. Do you love your children unconditionally? Of course you do. And you would never take your love from them.

Do you approve of everything they do? Of course you don't. But when they continue to do things that they know are wrong, after you have pleaded your case for so long, you finally withdraw your mercy for them.

God sometimes withholds His blessings, but He never withholds His love. We might have severed our relationship with Him, but never His love.

I think we must read these different translations and check them out. We could get the wrong idea if we don't understand totally the meaning of each word used. There are many words that are changed to make easier reading, but we should be on guard for those words that change the complexity of the message.

# December 4

# SALVE FOR THE EYES

*(Revelation 3:17-18 You say, 'I am rich; I have acquired wealth and do not need a thing.' But you do not realize that you are wretched, pitiful, poor, blind and naked. I counsel you to buy from me gold refined in the fire, so you can become rich; and white clothes to wear, so you can cover your shameful nakedness; and salve to put on your eyes, so you can see.)*

There are many people who sit around on their own laurels—proud because they have achieved great wealth: Thinking that they have all that they will ever need. But in reality they are destitute. They are blinded by their own accomplishments. They do not see that the things they have are temporal. They are described as wretched, pitiful, poor, blind and naked.

In contrast there are people who are poor by the world's standards, but they are rich in the sight of God. They are the people who know what they need and have attained it through Christ. They do not have many material things; but they are happy people because they have the knowledge that their future is secure. They have put their faith in God and not in money. They are the ones who have sought the gold refined by fire, they are rich in spiritual things; they are clothed in righteousness, and their eyes are wide open so that they see the truth. They have invested in their future that will provide them eternal life.

I see the things that are happening in the world today. The standards of this world are all wrong. They are being blatantly promoted as we can see every time we turn our TV's on, and every time we open a magazine. People are oh so blinded, and the sad part is, they don't know it. They are not even concerned about it. They look only to those material things that they think will bring them happiness and security. They do not realize that they cannot take their worldly wealth with them when they die.

I pray that those who cannot see the truth will use the salve that will allow their eyes to be opened so that they will see that the riches of Christ are ever lasting while the riches of this world are temporary.

# December 5

# WAITING PATIENTLY

*(Isaiah 30:18 Yet the LORD longs to be gracious to you; therefore he will rise up to show you compassion. For the LORD is a God of justice. Blessed are all who wait for him!)*

I don't know about those of you who will read this devotional, but as for me I have always been a very impatient person. I am one of those people who want things done promptly. But I have learned that things do not always happen on my time schedule.

Do you wonder sometimes if God will ever answer your prayer? Have you ever become so impatient that you have taken things into your own hands in order to speed up the process? I am sorry to say that I have done that before, and I have always regretted it.

We can see what has happened in God's word when people went ahead of God and took things into their own hands. Look what happened in the case of Abraham and Sarah when they did not have the child that they had longed for. We all know the results of their decision.

When Saul became restless waiting for Samuel to come and give him Godly advice—he took things into his own hands and consulted a medium for guidance; so the Lord put him to death and turned the kingdom over to David. (Reference 1 Chronicles 10:13-14)

There are many other cases where we read about those who did not wait patiently for the Lord. Why then do we not heed the warning that is given us through the mistakes that others have made before us?

God is a God who hears and answers our prayers; in His time. God's timing is perfect; there is a reason why God does not promptly answer every prayer. We may not know the reason, but we do know our God and we know all about His love, His mercy and His kindness. When we consider that—let's remember that we will be blessed if we wait on Him.

# December 6

# TURN AWAY FROM SIN

*(Proverbs 1:10 My son, if sinners entice you, do not give in to them.)*

There is a saying that 'misery loves company'. I believe that is true in the case of sinners. How many times have those who are deep in the pit of sin enticed others to join them? I have heard many stories from those who have become victims of peer pressure: And that does not always mean teen peer pressure—anyone, regardless of age or stature can be led astray by others.

The evil one loves to use his people to entice others to sin. He is in the business of trying to destroy lives; and what better way than to use so called friends?

Sadly sometimes parents are the cause of their children's downfall. The saddest stories I hear are those whose parents have introduced their children to drugs. How in the world can this be? I cannot imagine encouraging one's own child to become involved in anything that would be destructive to them.

The fact of the matter is, sin is contagious. If anyone is trying to entice you into a lifestyle of sin—run away from them as quickly as you can: Whether it is a friend, relative, or a complete stranger. Don't let anyone talk you in to anything that you know to be sin.

Once one is pulled into sin, it is difficult to get out of it. Keep that in mind if you are ever tempted to go along with someone else's encouragement to sin. God will give you the strength to turn away from the temptation that others put in your way. *(1 Corinthians 10:13 No temptation has seized you except what is common to man. And God is faithful; he will not let you be tempted beyond what you can bear. But when you are tempted he will also provide a way out so that you can stand up under it.)*

# December 7

# CELEBRATE THE BIRTH

*(Luke 2 13-14 Suddenly a great company of the heavenly host appeared with the angel, praising God and saying, "Glory to God in the highest, and on earth peace to men on whom his favor rests.")*

Christmas is not about presents, decorations, attending parties, or even special dinners and programs. And Christmas is not about a date—it is all about a person. As a matter of fact, we don't really know the exact time that Christ was born.

For the believer, Christmas is all about who Jesus is and why He came. Even believers can get caught up in the activities of the season—so much so that we neglect dwelling on the One whose birthday we celebrate.

Many people, who do not even believe there is a God, want to celebrate the date. If they want to have a holiday season just to have some fun with parties, gifts and games—why don't they choose another time to do that? Why must they try to take away the holiness of the celebration of Christ's birth?

And most stores in this day and age don't want to acknowledge that it is the time of year to celebrate Christ's birthday. They instead have called it the holiday season because they want to cash in on it:

I believe it is just like most other things that have happened in our country—they want to kick God out to try and diminish the power that just speaking His name invokes.

I have news for all of those unbelievers—God does exist; He did send His Son to earth as a baby—He died on the cross for the sins of many, for all those who accept Him as their personal Savior. No matter how much the world tries to diminish what Christmas is all about, it will never take away from the truth of who He is and why He came.

One day all of those who have tried to deny His existence will know that they have missed the mark. They will one day understand what celebrating the birth of Jesus was all about—but it will be too late for them to enter in to His kingdom.

Do you know who Jesus is? Don't wait so long to acknowledge Him as your personal Savior that you will be lost forever. Come now and celebrate Jesus—our Lord of Lords, and our King of Kings.

# December 8

# I KNOW I CAN

*(Philippians 4:13 I can do everything through Him who gives me strength.)*

Are there times in your life when you are asked to take on a task that you just know you will not be able to accomplish? Are there times when you think you have no strength to meet the day's challenges? Are there times when you think you just cannot go on? I can certainly identify with any and all of these questions. But I have learned that I can do all things through Christ because He gives me the strength and determination to do whatever I have to do.

I admit that there are times when I become discouraged and fall back in to the place where I think I just cannot do a particular thing, but He sends me encouragers in those times to remind me of the strength that I have in the Lord.

Remember the children's story of the little engine who thought he could never make it to the top of the hill. But as he was encouraged by another, he began to say "I think I can, I think I can". At times we are all just like the little engine, thinking that we will never make the grade, but the Scripture above says we can do all things through Christ. He is our strength and our encourager to go on. Even in times that we do not feel qualified, we must remember that nothing is impossible when we put our faith and trust in God.

If you are one of those people who think you just can't go on—think again. Remember who you are in Christ. And remember that He is your strength. And go out and do what you are called to do. You will no longer say I can't do it—you will be saying I know I can because Christ lives within my heart and I can do all things through Him.

# December 9

# MOCKERY OF MARRIAGE

*("When a young woman still living in her father's household makes a vow to the LORD or obligates herself by a pledge and her father hears about her vow or pledge but says nothing to her, then all her vows and every pledge by which she obligated herself will stand.)*

The last couple of weeks the news programs have been announcing that a couple who are constantly being watched by adoring audiences are getting a divorce after seventy-two days of marriage. It was only that long ago that the news and magazines were covering their very costly nuptials. It is obvious that it was not a marriage made in Heaven. What a fiasco. It was not a marriage where vows were taken sincerely—it was a mockery of marriage.

It makes me ill to think that the world watches these type of people with such enthusiasm—simply because of the fact that they have made money and flaunt everything that money can buy: Even using a marriage ceremony to make more money. I don't know about you, but I have no interest in people like that. And I simply detest the fact that our young people see and read about such disgusting actions. What do they learn from watching these people who adults think are so grand? They learn nothing, except sinful ways.

Our children should be taught that marriage is not to be taken lightly. According to Webster's dictionary a vow means: a solemn promise or assertion; specifically: one by which a person is bound to an act, service, or condition. That means forever. And God's Word is very specific about it.

Children should also be taught that when they are thinking about marriage, to pray about the person that they will marry; and pray that God would direct their path to the right one. Marriage should not be taken lightly; but seriously and with wisdom that comes only through seeking God's will.

# December 10

# THE RIGHT INFLUENCE

*(2 Chronicles 24:1 Joash did what was right in the eyes of the Lord all the years of Jehoiada the priest.)*

If you are familiar with the life of king Joash, you know that his reign began at the ripe old age of seven and it lasted for forty years. Jehoiada, was his priest and mentor; and as long as he lived Joash listened to him. Jehoiada was a godly man and was the driving influence in the king's life.

When Jehoiada died, the officials of Judah came and paid homage to the king: And Joash began to listen to them: They abandoned the temple of the Lord, the God of their fathers, and worshiped Asherah poles and idols. Because of their guilt, God's anger came upon Judah and Jerusalem. Although the Lord sent prophets to the people to bring them back to Him, and though they testified against them, they would not listen. (Ref. 2 Chronicles 24:18-19)

How can anyone sit under the influence of a Godly man like Jehoiada for as long as Joash did and then the minute he is gone, he gives over to the influence of those who do not seek the Lord's wisdom? He not only forgot the things that Jehoiada had taught him; he ultimately killed his son. *(2 Chronicles 24:27 King Joash did not remember the kindness Zechariah's father Jehoiada had shown him but killed his son, who said as he lay dying, "May the Lord see this and call you to account.)* The end of Joash's story was not a good one because of the decisions that he made as a result of listening to the wrong people.

What a lesson to be learned from this story of Joash. It is vitally important that we seek out the Godly men and women in our lives, who will give us the right advice: Those who live their lives according to the Word of God. If we are following the advice of any other people, you can rest assured that it will not turn out good.

What kind of people do you listen to for guidance? Is it those who seek God's wisdom and His will? Or do you follow those who are influential because of their position in life? Are you tossed back and forth by other's advice? It is vitally important that we be in God's word ourselves to determine whether or not the advice that others give us checks out correctly.

We, as Christians have the potential to be a powerful Godly influence in the lives of others. In order to be a Godly influence we must be diligent in our obedience to God and His Word. Others may be watching and there might come a time that they will ask us for wisdom and advice—we must be ready to give an answer through God's word.

# December 11

# WHAT'S IN THE NAME?

*(Exodus 3:13-15 Moses said to God, "Suppose I go to the Israelites and say to them, 'The God of your fathers has sent me to you,' and they ask me, 'What is his name?' Then what shall I tell them?" God said to Moses, "I AM WHO I AM. This is what you are to say to the Israelites: 'I AM has sent me to you.'" God also said to Moses, "Say to the Israelites, 'The LORD, the God of your fathers—the God of Abraham, the God of Isaac and the God of Jacob—has sent me to you.' "This is my name forever, the name you shall call me from generation to generation.)*

Our minister spoke about I Am one morning not long ago, and that same evening, someone else spoke of Emanuel, meaning 'God is with us'. It inspired me to go back and study all of the names used in the bible to describe who God was, is, and forever will be.

I am once again blown away by the revelation of what the names of God means to me and to you. If you will just take the time to list every name used to describe Him, you would see that God is all we need in our life. His name is the answer for all of our problems, mysteries, and frustrations. He and He alone can bring us to the place that we need to be to gain peace and instruction on how to live our lives victoriously.

I wish there was time to list all of the attributes of God revealed to us through the different names that describe who He is, but the list is so long, it would take way too much time to do that. No wonder God said to Moses, "Just tell them I AM WHO I AM".

But notice also in the Scripture above God goes on to say—*"The LORD, the God of your fathers—the God of Abraham, the God of Isaac and the God of Jacob—has sent me to you.' "This is my name forever, the name you shall call me from generation to generation"*. The Lord is not only Lord of Abraham, Isaac and Jacob—He is our Lord also.

I encourage you to look up all of the names revealing God's character. I guarantee you to be blessed and encouraged just listing those names and what they mean. I think you will have a new appreciation of God's power and His grace. It should illuminate the truth that we serve the one and only true God—the only One worthy to be praised.

# December 12

# FAITH LIKE A CHILD

*(Matthew 11:25-26 At that time Jesus said, "I praise you, Father, Lord of heaven and earth, because you have hidden these things from the wise and learned, and revealed them to little children. Yes, Father, for this is what you were pleased to do.)*

There is an artist who began using her talents at the age of six. She says that her paintings were inspirations from God. I am sure that there are skeptics who do not understand such things. But when you look at her paintings and when you listen to her testimony, I can't imagine not being moved and impressed by such a divine talent.

I do not believe there is any way that a child of six could imagine the images that inspire her, unless it is directly from God's Spirit. Jesus says that He praises the Father because He hid these things from the wise and the learned and revealed them to little children. It pleased the Father to do these things.

This little girl was raised by a mother who was an atheist. But because of her little girl's talent she became a believer. Wow! What an amazing story about the grace of God. It took a little child to teach the mother that God is real—that He does exist—and that His Spirit lives in the hearts of those who believe in Him.

At the age of twelve, she has taught herself to play the piano and is now writing her own music. This is one talented little girl. She gives all of the glory to God. She realizes that it is because of His Holy Spirit that she is able to do these marvelous things.

God will use the ones who accept His unbelievable grace. He does not call those who are wise in their own ways—but rather those whose talent comes directly from the Holy Spirit. If only we could see the truth through the eyes of a child who trusts in God and listens to His call on their life. They believe without question—because they trust in what the Spirit reveals to them.

# December 13

# BYPASS THE OBSTACLES

*(Luke 5:18-20 Some men came carrying a paralyzed man on a mat and tried to take him into the house to lay him before Jesus. When they could not find a way to do this because of the crowd, they went up on the roof and lowered him on his mat through the tiles into the middle of the crowd, right in front of Jesus. When Jesus saw their faith, he said, "Friend, your sins are forgiven.")*

The men in the Scripture above did not let the crowd discourage them from bringing their paralyzed friend to Jesus. They did not see it as an obstacle at all; they just sought out a way to get him there.

Do you ever find that obstacles get in your way when you are trying to lead someone to Jesus? I have, and it is most frustrating. You know the evil one is going to put anything and anyone in the way of those trying to bring another to the Lord. But we cannot allow those obstacles to deter us from what God wants us to do. We need to search out a way to lead them to Jesus.

The man in the Scripture above was paralyzed and unable to help himself. But because of his friends, he was placed right in front of Jesus. I am convinced that he wanted help to get there. There are many people around us, who need help to find their way to Jesus. Some of them may not be ready to receive that help, but there are many others who are. We should be ready to help them in any way we can.

The crowds and noises of the world are so loud sometimes that it becomes an obstacle for us in leading others to the Lord. There most likely will be obstacles because the evil one does not want us leading someone to Christ—but never fear them—God will make a way for you.

Go out of your way if you have to because you know that God will honor your persistence and determination. *(Luke 5:20 When Jesus saw their faith, he said, "Friend, your sins are forgiven")* What Jesus did for the paralytic, He will do for you also.

# December 14

# ASK GOD

*(James 1:5 If any of you lacks wisdom, he should ask God who gives generously to all without finding fault, and it will be given to him.)*

We all go through many trials, and if you are like me, you don't know how to handle most of them. I have been going through one that has lasted for some time and I have been perplexed as to what to do about the situation. But His word says He will give me wisdom when I seek for it. I have committed it to the Lord and His answer to me is to wait on Him. As of now the situation has not been resolved but I have found peace that I did not have before I let go of the situation and let God take control.

We can take anything at all to God and He will not find fault with us. He will gently guide us and walk with us through the trials. We not only have the privilege of taking everything to Him, but that is precisely what He wants us to do. There are some things that we do not have any control over. But we know that God is willing to handle every situation when we ask Him to. He will not invade our lives without us seeking His will. He will graciously give us wisdom to wait on Him when we allow Him to take control. His word tells us that when we ask, we must believe and not doubt that He will answer our prayer. (Ref. Mark 11:23)

Are you going through a trial that you don't know how to handle? Don't fret anymore about it. Take it to God and ask for Him to take care of it. I can guarantee you that you will find peace knowing that God will answer in due time. And do not let the evil one continually try to rob you of your faith and confidence in God. Satan is a liar when he says that things will never change.

God's word tells us that we should consider it pure joy when we go through trials because the testing of our faith develops perseverance and perseverance must finish its work so that we may be mature and complete, not lacking anything. (Ref. James 1:-4)

# December 15

# WAIT WITH HOPE & ASSURANCE

*(Psalms 119:27-28 Let me understand the teaching of your precepts; then I will meditate on your wonders. My soul is weary with sorrow; strengthen me according to your word.)*

I was visiting with a friend last week who is going through some very difficult times. She is hurt, confused, and discouraged about her situation. She does not know which way to turn. I wish I could give her the wisdom and advice that she is looking for. Unfortunately, I have no right to advise her on what to do. That is something that only God can do. I did encourage her to seek God's wisdom and His peace through the storm that is raging in her life.

As I finished my prayers this morning, I was led to the passage of Scripture above. When we seek God's word and meditate on it, He will strengthen us. His word not only encourages us, He gives us peace in the midst of despair. *(John 16:33 "These things I have spoken to you, that in Me you may have peace. In the world you will have tribulation; but be of good cheer, I have overcome the world.")*

There are times when we want to jump ahead of the Lord, and when we do, we often make mistakes that we regret. I believe it is a prudent thing to wait and see what the Lord will do. *(Psalm 27:14 Wait on the Lord; be of good courage, and He shall strengthen your heart; wait, I say, on the Lord!)*

It is a fact that we do not know what to do in some situations, especially when it involves someone else—but we know that God has the answer for all things—we know that we can depend on Him—we know that He will never forsake us. Even though we walk through storms, He is with us. With that knowledge, we can rest on His promises that He will see us through. Our hope is in Him and we can be assured that He hears our prayers for comfort and peace.

# December 16

# STAND FIRM

*(2 Chronicles 20:17 You will not have to fight this battle. Take up your positions; stand firm and see the deliverance the Lord will give you, O Judah and Jerusalem. Do not be afraid; do not be discouraged. Go out to face them tomorrow, and the Lord will be with you.)*

Just about every day this past week, I have heard stories from people who are facing raging battles in their life. Is it any wonder why this seems to happen when this Holy time of year draws near?

Christmas is the season when Christians focus on the birth of Christ: So the evil one works overtime to try and take our eyes off of this blessed time. But we don't have to let the one who is trying to destroy our peace win the battles. God will fight our battle for us, when and if we allow Him to. His word tells us to take up our position and stand firm, and don't be afraid.

If you are being attacked in any way, God's word tells you to put on the full armor of God so that you can take your stand against the devil's schemes. (Ref. Ephesians6:11). The enemy is out to destroy us but when we stand firm with our armor in place—God will deliver us. I encourage you to read Ephesians 6:11-17.

Do not be discouraged—face your giant because the Lord is on your side. Celebrate the birth of the King in peace, knowing that through Him you have won the battle.

# December 17

# AN INESCAPABLE PRESENCE

*(Psalms 139:8-10 If I go up to the heavens, you are there; if I make my bed in the depths, you are there, If I rise on the wings of the dawn, if I settle on the far side of the sea, even there your hand will guide me, your right hand will hold me fast..)*

Are there times in your life that you feel like you are totally alone? Do you sometimes ask yourself if there is anyone who really under-stands you—is there anyone who even cares? I think if we are honest, we can all say that at some time or another we have felt just that way: But we are never alone when we are children of God.

Christ walks with us wherever we go. He is beside us, in front of us, and behind us. He knows everything about our lives. He knows the hurt and the pain that we suffer. He knows the ups and downs of our mental, physical, and spiritual situations. There is nothing He does not know. He is not a God who doesn't care about what is going on in our lives; to the contrary; He cares about everything that we are going through.

God is with us every minute of every day; He walks with us through the rain and the sunshine. He delivers us out of the darkness that threatens to overtake us. He gives us strength when we are weak. He turns sorrow into joy. He puts a song in our heart when we need it. He gives us peace when we are afraid. He encourages us to go on when we feel like giving up.

If you are going through a time of loneliness for any reason—remember this psalm; claim it for your own; hide it in your heart; pray it all day long. He will meet your need because He stands right beside you, holding your hand.

# December 18

# BE NOT FAINT

*(Isaiah 40:30-31 Even youths grow tired and weary, and young men stumble and fall; but those who hope in the Lord will renew their strength;. They will soar on wings like eagles; they will run and not grow weary, they will walk and not be faint.)*

We were discussing in our Sunday school class one day how many of God's people were being physically attacked by Satan. There is no wonder why; he would like to disable us so that we could not carry out God's plan for our life. But his tactics will not win, unless we allow him to keep us down. God is bigger than the one who is in the world trying to devour us. And He is able to keep us strong to endure the obstacles that Satan puts in our way.

Everyone who knows me is aware of the fact that I write. And they also know that in January I will embark on a new ministry of speaking with a group of other Christian women. I have been suffering from tendonitis in my foot and in my right hand, which makes it difficult for me to use that hand and to stand for any length of time. I am certain that Satan is enjoying my discomfort, but He will never defeat me. God will give me the strength to go on, even in the pain. I am praying that God will take away the pain, but if He decides not to, I know that He will sustain me. Sometimes I get so tired, I think I can't go on, but God renews my strength, and I am able to pursue what is most important in my life—to do the things that He has called me to do.

Paul suffered from a proverbial thorn in his side; we don't know what it was but we do know that it did not keep him down. He persevered through his weakness.

Are you one of those people who are suffering through some kind of pain? The pain may be physical, mental, or emotional; but keep in mind that you do not have to let it defeat you. God will give you strength and you will soar on wings like eagles—you will run and not grow weary. What a wonderful Scripture God has given us here. He gives us confidence in the fact that just because we might have a few problems, He does not desert us—our hope is in Him.

No matter what you are going through; just keep on keeping on because God will give you the strength to do what He has called you to do. There is eternal hope when we put our trust and faith in God.

# December 19

# WHERE IS JESUS?

*(After Jesus was born in Bethlehem in Judea, during the time of King Herod, Magi from the east came to Jerusalem and asked, "Where is the one who has been born king of the Jews? We saw his star in the east and have come to worship him.")*

As we move in to the season of Christmas, it seems as if our entire life becomes absorbed with the hustle and bustle of preparations. We are either shopping, attending parties, Christmas programs, decorating, or entertaining. There just doesn't seem to be enough time to do all of the things that we want to do. In fact, we are so busy that we many times ignore the reason for the season.

There was excitement in the air when Jesus was born: But it was a different kind of excitement. Many had been awaiting the birth of Jesus for a long time. Some were very excited and couldn't wait to meet this baby Jesus. Others were frightened of His birth, and even started plotting to get rid of Him.

Where do you stand today? Do you understand who Jesus really is? Do you know where to find Him? Do you know why He was born and why we celebrate His birth with such fervor; or do you just simply enjoy the excitement of the season?

Jesus is the reason for the season. He was born to die for your sins and mine. If we accept that fact and understand the magnitude of His birth, we will surely understand that we need to know where he is. Does He live in your heart? If not, invite Him in so that you will know for sure where He resides; so that you will be able to answer the question, 'where is Jesus'?

He lives in my heart and I pray that He lives in yours also. If not invite Him in today, so that you can truly understand just why we celebrate Jesus—THE KING OF KINGS AND THE LORD OF LORDS, OUR SAVIOR!

# December 20

# BELIEVING GOD

*(Luke 1:19-20 The angel answered, I am Gabriel. I stand in the presence of God, and I have been sent to speak to you and to tell you this good news. And now you will be silent and not able to speak until the day this happens, because you did not believe my words, which will come true at their proper time.)*

Gabriel appeared to Zechariah (John the Baptist's Father) and told him that Elizabeth would bear him a son and that he should give him the name John. He told him all the other things pertaining to his birth: But Zechariah doubted the words that God had spoken through Gabriel. And as a result Zechariah could not speak at all until this prophesy was fulfilled.

I wonder how many times we don't believe what God is telling us. If we don't believe God's word, we certainly can't praise Him? I think we miss out on a lot of opportunities to sing God's praises just because of lack of faith. When God speaks to our heart we must listen, or like Zechariah our mouths will be shut.

Now read what happened. (*Luke 1:59-64 On the eighth day they came to circumcise the child, and they were going to name him after his father Zechariah but his mother spoke up and said, "No He is to be called John." They said to her, "There is no one among your relatives who has that name." Then they made signs to his father, to find out what he would like to name the child. He asked for a writing tablet, and to everyone's astonishment he wrote, "His name is John." Immediately his mouth was opened and his tongue was loosed, and he began to speak praising God.)*

Zechariah had nine months to think about his mistake in doubting God's word: During the months when Zechariah could not speak, he saw the Word of God become reality. How he must have sorrowed over the fact that he had not believed from the beginning. God is a gracious God, he forgave Zechariah and the minute Zechariah did what God instructed him to do his voice was restored. God is the same today. When we truly believe and receive God's word, He will open our mouths to speak of His grace.

# December 21

# YES, LORD

*(Luke 1:30-31, 38 But the angel said to her, "Do not be afraid, Mary, you have found favor with God. You will be with child and give birth to a son, and you are to give him the name Jesus. "I am the Lord's servant, "Mary answered. "May it be to me as you have said." Then the angel left her.)*

Mary—what a woman! Can you even imagine the thoughts that went through her mind when Gabriel came to her and told her that she had been chosen by God to carry His child? She was engaged to be married to a man that she loved, and now her entire life would be changed. Do you think in the few minutes that Gabriel revealed God's plan to use her to be the mother of God's son, that she fully comprehended what it all meant? She must have known the ridicule that would be hers when people found out about it. She was a young girl facing something that she never in her wildest dreams, could have imagined. Yet she was able to say. "May it be to me as you have said."

Did you hear one argument out of Mary, during this encounter that she had with Gabriel? I didn't. It seems to me that she understood that God was her Lord and that whatever He asked of her, she was willing to do: Yes, in spite of all the things that she would suffer from others. She pondered it all in her heart in a few minutes notice, and still was able to allow God to do whatever His will was for her life. I don't believe that God revealed everything to her; but she trusted Him and said "Yes, Lord, I want to be your vessel." Now that is a picture of total submission to our Lord.

Do you think that you could respond like Mary did during her encounter with God's messenger? We will never know the answer to that because we will never face that particular situation. But how quickly do we say, "Yes, Lord, do with me whatever you will." Do we argue with God, or do we just simply allow Him to use us whenever and wherever He pleases.

## December 22

# BLESSED INCONVENIECE

*(Luke 2:6-7 While they were there, the time came for the baby to be born, and she gave birth to her firstborn, a son. She wrapped him in cloths and placed him in a manger, because there was no room for them in the inn.)*

My husband came home from a trip the other day to discover that our hot water heater was spewing water everywhere. Being Sunday, we did not have access to the help we needed, so we were without water the rest of that day and part of the next. Have you ever had to live without hot water? It is pretty inconvenient isn't it? As I was basking in the glory of a bathtub filled with hot water, I started thinking about all those who not only have to live without the convenience of hot water, but without a roof over their heads.

I thought about the night our Savior was born. There was no room for Him anywhere; so Mary and Joseph prepared a bed in a barn for this Holy one to be born. Can you even imagine such an inconvenient place to have a baby? It would be bad enough to have to find shelter in a barn, even without the added concern of preparing to deliver a baby. Just think about it, they had no shelter other than a barn, they had no bedding other than hay, and they had nothing to wrap their baby in other than cloths that were probably no more than rags. They had no prepared baby crib to place him in; so they placed him in a manger.

This was God's only Son; the Savior of the world that we are talking about. God could have planned for him to be born in a palace with every convenience imaginable; but He chose for Him to be born in the simplest way possible. He could have come in to this world as the kind of king that the world expected. But instead God chose for him to be born as a common, ordinary man. Yet He was no ordinary man—He is King of Kings—He is Lord of Lords.

When we think that we are inconvenienced in any way, let's remember Jesus and His humble birth.

# December 23

# HALLELUJAH

*(Luke 2:13-14 Suddenly a great company of the heavenly host appeared with the angel, praising God and saying, "Glory to God in the highest, and on earth peace to men on who his favor rests.")*

Talk about a Hallelujah chorus! Those shepherds standing there taking all of this in must have been completely in awe of all that was going on around them. Just imagine being in a field watching over a flock of sheep in the quiet of the night when suddenly an angel appears bringing the news of a baby being born who is Christ the Lord. I can imagine that they were still trying to digest all of what they had just been told, when suddenly this multitude of heavenly host appeared praising God. What an exciting time that must have been for those lowly shepherds.

They didn't waste any time getting their gear together and taking off in pursuit of finding that baby who they were told would be found in a lowly manger wrapped in swaddling clothes. And notice after they had seen Him, they then quickly spread the word. And Scripture tells us that all who heard it were amazed at what the shepherds said.

Wow! What an exciting thing to meet the Savior of the world. Can you just imagine the love they felt as they looked in the face of this Christ child? It is just as exciting today when we meet the Savior. Have you experienced it? If not open your heart and ask Jesus to reveal Himself to you so that you also can experience the same peace, joy and love that the shepherds did on the night that Christ was born. He can be born in your heart today. If you have experienced the birth of Jesus in your heart, are you spreading the news?

# December 24

# THE TREASURED GIFT

*(John 1:11-12 He came to that which was his own, but his own did not receive him. Yet all who received him, to those who believed in his name, he gave the right to become children of God.)*

Can you remember a time when you received a treasured gift, one that you asked for but maybe doubted that you would get? I do. I remember the year that I asked for a watch for Christmas. I was raised in a family that did not have a lot financially, and somehow even at my age (probably 10 or around there), I seemed to understand that. But oh I wanted that watch so badly. I could not wait for that Blessed day, that awesome time of the year for children—Christmas. That time of year when everyone seemed to be in such high spirits: Or most everyone. Our family had a tradition that the youngest one always got to open their gifts first and then according to age the others followed. I was the youngest in my family so I was very eager to open mine. I opened them (if memory serves me correctly, there were two). Mother almost always made a garment of some kind for me. I frankly do not remember what they were; the only thing I remember was I didn't get that watch I had wanted. I tried to act as happy as I could but down deep I was terribly disappointed. The other members of my family opened their gifts and we were finished, ready to move on to other things, or so I thought. Daddy suddenly said, "Look Mother, I found another gift under the tree". He picked it up and said, "Well this is for Dumpsy" (yes that was my nickname). He handed it to me and I opened it up and, you guessed it, there was to me the most beautiful watch I had ever seen. I was so happy and eagerly accepted it from my father.

As I got older I learned that if you want something you must ask for it and be willing to receive it. I heard a speaker say once that a gift is not ours until we accept it. Do you realize that every one of us has been offered the most wonderful gift in the world?—the gift of eternal life. God sent His Son to earth to die on the cross for our sins, so that we could have that eternal life.

Sadly many have not received His gift because they have not believed in Him. We may get every gift that the world has to offer, but they will not last, they are not eternal. The only gift that is eternal is Jesus: The gift that goes on throughout eternity. If you don't know Jesus as your personal Savior—Believe in Him and receive Him today. Your Christmas will never be the same. He is the reason for the season. Do you really celebrate the reason, or just the earthly gifts?

## December 25

# THE SEED—JESUS—THE SAVIOR

*(Galatians 3:19 What, then, was the purpose of the law? It was added because of transgressions until the Seed to whom the promise referred had come).*

This Scripture should give us the answer to why we celebrate the birth of Jesus, The Seed. And it should make us shout for joy for why He came. If you have read the Old Testament, you know how often sacrifices were made for the sins of the people. All of those sacrifices were temporary and had to be repeated over and over again.

When Jesus came, He fulfilled the law. He was God's Son sent to earth as a baby—the baby who was The Seed that is talked about here: The Seed that was foretold in the Old Testament about 700 years before the birth of Jesus. *(Isaiah 9:6 For to us a child is born, to us a son is given, and the government will be on his shoulders. And he will be called Wonderful Counselor, Mighty God, Everlasting Father, Prince of Peace.)*

The Seed, Jesus, was born for the purpose of taking away the sins of the world. They were laid on Him at the Cross. If He had not been born, we would still have to make temporary sacrifices for our sins. But He was born to die for us. What a Savior!

His birth is something to celebrate with enthusiasm: With the full knowledge of who He is and why He came, why wouldn't we be happy to celebrate the birth of the King of Kings, and Lord of Lords?

Do you celebrate the birth of your Savior? Or do you enter into the festivities of a holiday? There is a huge difference between a holiday and Christmas. If you don't know the difference; if you don't celebrate Christ's birthday in every sense of the word—you do not understand the meaning of Christmas. You do not know who Jesus really is and why He was born.

Receive the gift of Jesus and experience a VERY MERRY CHRISTMAS!

# December 26

# SIMEON'S EXAMPLE

*(Luke 2:28-32 Simeon took him in his arms and praised God, saying: "Sovereign Lord, as you have promised, you may now dismiss your servant in peace. For my eyes have seen your salvation, which you have prepared in the sight of all nations: a light for revelation to the Gentiles, and the glory of your people Israel.")*

Simeon was an old man who had been told by the Holy Spirit that he would not die before he had seen the Lord's Christ. He did not go to worship the baby Jesus and then go away and forget Him. He was aware of His Holiness and what His birth meant to all people.

As I was taking down my Christmas decorations today, I could not help but wonder how many people would put away everything that reminds us of the birth of Jesus and then forget that He even exists until the festivities begin again next year.

There are many who celebrate the birth of Jesus but they don't really understand who He is and why He came. And yet they will go to great lengths to celebrate the holiday. Even Christians sometimes forget to worship Him every day of the year. We go to church and sing the beautiful Christmas Carols that talk about worshipping the King: But do we remember Him the rest of the year?

Jesus who came to this earth to die for our sins deserves better than an occasional mention of His Name. He is worthy to be praised every day. I don't think He is happy that we use His birthday to celebrate and have fun, and then when the season is over, forget that He is the Savior of the world, do you?

Don't you think that He would be happy if we were all like Simeon: Ready to die because he had seen Jesus? Don't put away that nativity scene and then forget Jesus for an entire year. He wants us to worship Him daily because we know who He really is and we have met Him personally. He wants to hear us say that since we have met Him, we are ready to die.

# December 27

# WAITING FOR HOPE

*(Titus 2:11-14 For the grace of God has appeared that offers salvation to all people. It teaches us to say "No" to ungodliness and worldly passions, and to live self-controlled, upright and godly lives in this present age, while we wait for the blessed hope—the appearing of the glory of our great God and Savior, Jesus Christ, who gave himself for us to redeem us from all wickedness and to purify for himself a people that are his very own, eager to do what is good.)*

Are you a procrastinator? Sometimes I am. I always dread the seasonal changing of my closets. When it comes time to change them from summer clothes to winter and vice versa, I sometimes wait beyond the time of need. The weather changes suddenly and I find that I have procrastinated too long: So I hurry to get the job done that I should have already accomplished. Can you identify?

We can get by with putting off certain things. But when it comes to putting off the offer of salvation, we cannot afford to procrastinate. It's not a matter of life and death if we put off preparing our closets for the season; but it sure is if we put off clothing ourselves in righteousness. We do not have any idea when Christ will return for His bride, so we must make sure that we are ready to meet Him.

Are you one of those who have been procrastinating to make the choice of salvation? Putting it off until another day may just be one day too late. Instead of waiting to make that decision; I implore you; don't delay. Make that change and choice today and then you can look forward to that blessed hope—the hope of glory.

# December 28

# RESPONSIBLE ACCOUNTABILITY

*(1 Corinthians 5:11-13 But now I am writing to you that you must not associate with anyone who claims to be a brother or sister but is sexually immoral or greedy, an idolater or slanderer, a drunkard or swindler. Do not even eat with such people. What business is it of mine to judge those outside the church? Are you not to judge those inside? God will judge those outside. "Expel the wicked person from among you.")*

How many of us have a tendency to judge those who are not Christians? I would guess that most of us are guilty of that. But how often do we hold our Christian family accountable for the sins that they commit? The above Scripture is very plain about what we should do.

If our churches were filled with more people who are living the life that God has called us to, the Holy Spirit would bring a revival like we have never seen before. But because of the sin that so often goes on in our congregations and because it is not addressed and confronted, I do not believe that we will see that kind of revival, do you?

We are not only accountable to God; we are accountable to one another. If we see someone in our midst who is casting a shadow on our Christian name, we should bring them to account. Those kinds of people are destructive to the church. *(Joshua 7:12 That is why the Israelites cannot stand against their enemies; they turn their backs and run because they have been made liable to destruction. I will not be with you anymore unless you destroy whatever among you is devoted to destruction.)*

We should never hide the sins of others in our own Christian family. The two Scriptures above tell us how we should handle these kinds of situations; and what will happen if we fail to do so. God will judge the unsaved but it is our responsibility to hold our Christian family accountable for the things that they do that dishonors God.

It is definitely something that we do not like to think about; but consider this; there are many congregations that are destroyed by the sin that goes on within their own walls that is not dealt with.

# December 29

# A COMPROMISING WALK

*(Matthew 6:22-23 "The eye is the lamp of the body. If your eyes are good, your whole body will be full of light. But if your eyes are bad, your whole body will be full of darkness. If then the light within you is darkness, how great is that darkness.)*

One of the saddest things in the world is when Christians begin to compromise their Christian ideals. The wrong choices they begin to make are subtle. They begin to be sidetracked by the things of the world.

Such a thing happened to a woman that I know. She was a wife and a mother. She was active in her church and had fellowship with her Christian sisters. But little by little her life began to change. She started hanging out with the wrong crowd. She began to spend less and less time with her Christian friends and more time with those who were worldly. She began to compromise everything that God's word says. She justified her behavior with the fact that she was not having her needs met. She was tired of the boring life that she had convinced herself she had. She wanted something more. Her actions eventually led to adultery and the breakup of her marriage and her family. I believe she would tell you today that it was the biggest mistake of her life.

Eli E. Stanley Jones was a wonderful missionary and evangelist. His wisdom and knowledge of God was amazing, and he shared it with the world. When I read the following statement, I thought to myself that it describes so many people who compromise the word of God. The statement he made was this—"If you don't make up your mind, your unmade mind will unmake you."

That's what happens to people who begin to compromise their Christianity. They begin to spend time on the things that draw them away from their relationship with the Lord. They have no time for God's word or His people. They convince themselves that they don't have to do the things that Christians normally do, they can do their own thing. They convince themselves that since they are a Christian they are free to make their own choices. And that is true; God does not make us robots. But the word of Jesus in the above Scripture says it all: They are no longer living in the light of Jesus; their eyes have been blinded. Scripture tells us that we cannot serve two masters.

Many people destroy their life because they put everything else ahead of their relationship with the Lord. They have traded truth for lies, and light for darkness. They have a way of justifying their actions, but in the end they will reap their sins of compromise.

## December 30

# WITNESSING IN THE FACE OF ADVERSITY

*(1 Corinthians 1:30 It is because of him that you are in Christ Jesus, who has become for us wisdom from God—that is, our righteousness, holiness and redemption.)*

Have you ever surrendered yourself in obedience to do something that God has called you to do, and then been attacked by the evil one with the thoughts that you are not worthy, you are a sinner, you are not capable, and on and on with all the negative thoughts that can possibly come to your mind. I have many times fought the lies that Satan tries to tell me.

We are all sinners who have been saved only by God's grace. He has brought us out of the chains that had us in bondage. Why then do we allow Satan to nag at us about our past sins and our inabilities? It is because he would love to enslave us once again. He wants us to believe that we are good for nothing.

We are able to do all things through Christ who strengthens us— yet we seem to forget that at times. When we surrendered our life to the Lord, He not only set us free—He made us righteous. He gives wisdom to those who seek it. He has made us holy people through His redemption. We should never forget who we are in Christ.

As I was listening to a minister this morning his words were: "The devil wants to stop us from reaching our world. He might whisper, "Well, God would never use you! You are just a sinner! You are a failure!" So the next time the devil reminds you of your past, just remind him of his future. He will get his due and will face judgment from God—and he knows it."

Our power comes through Christ. He not only calls us to carry out His plan for us, He equips us for every job that He gives us. The main purpose for each of our lives, no matter what job He calls us to do, is to be His witnesses. Don't you know that it frightens Satan? No wonder he tries to defeat us. But he will never defeat us because God delivers us out of his hands.

# December 31

# A NEW BEGINNING

*(Lamentations 3:19-23 I remember my affliction and my wandering, the bitterness and the gall. I well remember them, and my soul is downcast within me. Yet this I call to mind and therefore I have hope: Because of the Lord's great love we are not consumed, for his compassions never fail, they are new every morning; great is your faithfulness.)*

Wow! I can hardly believe that this is the last day of the year. I don't know about you, but it seems to me that the older I get the faster time flies. As I look back on this past year, I am astounded at all that has transpired in my life; some good things and some bad. Have you had a year like that? Most of us have been high on the mountain and down in the valley over the course of the past year. As we reflect on the past 12 months will we dwell on the bad or the good? No matter what has happened, because of God's great love, we are not consumed. The Scripture tells us that His compassion is new every morning. What a comfort that is. Let's not dwell on the past but look forward to the future.

Tomorrow is not only a new day; it is a new year and a new beginning. Let's enter into the New Year with joy and an eagerness to be all that God wants us to be. Let's leave our past hurts and failures behind and remember only those things that are good and worthy of our thoughts. We cannot look forward to the future if we are carrying around baggage from the past. *(Philippians 4:8 Finally, brothers, whatever is true, whatever is noble, whatever is right, whatever is pure, whatever is lovely, whatever is admirable—if anything is excellent or praiseworthy—think about such things.)*

# EPILOGUE

*A* watchman is someone who looks out for others. His job is not only to warn people of impending danger, but he is also to bring good news to the people. I pray that through this book I have been a watchman for you and that you have been blessed by the pages within.

In a world of uncertainty, we all have a need for a Savior. God's Word opens up to clearly proclaim the message of hope to those who want to listen. Without Jesus Christ as our Savior, there is no hope. But in Christ we have the hope of Glory. We have nothing to fear in this world, for we are assured of a secure future.

Have you found that hope? If not I pray that you might take the opportunity right now to invite Jesus into your heart. I have provided a prayer for you to follow or you may want to use your own words. It doesn't matter how you say it as long as you pray sincerely from your heart to invite Jesus in.

*Dear Jesus,*
*I believe that you are the Son of God and that you are the Savior of all who accept you. I am a sinner and I ask that you come into my heart and cleanse me from all sin. I desire to know you as my personal Savior. Forgive me for all of my transgressions and lead me to a full understanding of you and your will for my life,*
*In Jesus Name I pray,*
*Amen*

CPSIA information can be obtained at www.ICGtesting.com
Printed in the USA
LVOW11s0156181213

365679LV00002B/3/P